Findhorn Community Fables

KAY KAY

Third Edition
First edition published in 2001

Book designed and published by Tim Kay
University of Life

www.unioflife.net

You Make the Difference logo © Tim Kay
Each contribution is © of that author.
Author photo by Lina&Linda AB
Stockholm, Sweden

F

This book is dedicated with love and appreciation
to the three founders of the Findhorn Community:
Eileen and Peter Caddy and Dorothy Maclean

CONTENTS

F

ACKNOWLEDGMENTS

I am grateful to all of the contributors to this and to the two previous editions of this book (1. Growing People and 2. Growing People, Growing Community).

Some of these pieces were already written for the community magazines One Earth and the Network News – no longer in existence - and I'm grateful to Eva Ward, Betsy Van der Lee and Michael Hawkins for their permission to publish these items.

Many more have come from current and former Community members, visitors and guests. I have received stories, letters, poems and lyrics from people all over the world. They have arrived by post, fax and email. They have come on disks—some I easy to read and some not—on post cards (large cards and small writing), I even had a story, mercifully short, left on my answering machine!

I am grateful for the parts played by those people who shared in the experiences about which I have written for this edition.

The stories brought forward from the first edition benefitted from the editorial support, the eagle eye and clear mind of Solasan (Mandy) Wilkinson. Recent ones have been edited by Tim Kay.

The design and appearance of the book, that was created by Sally Kendall for the first edition has influenced the appearance of this book. Tim Kay has converted the manuscript into paperback and e-book with his usual care and commitment to excellence.

Peter Lloyd, who published Growing People in paperback, has generously encouraged and supported the creation of this current book.

I greatly value the commitment to personal and planetary transformation by those past, present and future people involved with this Community. I am especially grateful to my friends and colleagues within the Community and for the mutual respect, affection and support that we have shared.

KAY KAY
February 2013

CHAPTER ONE

ARRIVING

Why do people come to this Community? Where do they come from? What circumstances bring them here? What are they seeking? How do they become integrated into this place? What do they discover here? The answers are as varied and as interesting as the people themselves.

In The Beginning

Charles, the alcoholic head chef we had brought along with other members of staff when we were transferred from the Cluny Hill Hotel to the Trossachs Hotel, regarded me shrewdly. As manager, I had assembled some of our key staff and told them to forget about Cluny Hill: it was our task to bring in to the Trossachs the same qualities of light and love that we had achieved there. "The evil is in the very bricks of this place," said Charles, "and you will not get it out."

Charles had never been wrong in his prophetic utterances, drunk or sober, but this time I did not believe him. Time seemed to prove him correct, however. One after the other of the staff I had brought with me went downhill, physically, morally and spiritually. They took to drink, drugs, theft and promiscuity. No matter how hard we tried, we did not seem able to do anything about it.

As the season drew to a close I knew that it wouldn't be fair to ask the staff to come back for another one. I wrote to Mrs. Bruce, the hotel chain's general manager, asking if we could go back to Cluny Hill. I explained that it was rather like putting a man and a woman together and telling the man to love the woman; but "love bloweth where it listeth" and the man can try with all his might without any success. This was true of my relationship with the Trossachs Hotel. I wanted to go back to my first love Cluny Hill Hotel.

Mrs. Bruce did not reply. Week after week we kept asking her by letter to visit the Trossachs, as there were several matters requiring discussion (for example I had invited Naomi, the sensitive I'd met in the Philippines, to come over and join us for the winter) but Mrs. Bruce remained silent.

On the morning of the last day before the hotel closed for the season, Eileen received a strange piece of guidance. *I want you to keep very, very positive about tomorrow, over everything. If you are in constant touch with Me you can change quickly in midstream without it throwing you out and you must be ready to do this. You must be ready to change your course at a minute's notice ... it is vitally important.*

The next day, 11th October 1962, Mrs Bruce arrived with an army of stocktakers to go over the books. Most likely she was looking for something amiss, but she found everything in order. She then called Eileen and me into my office and handed us our notice and a cheque for a month's wages: we had four hours to pack up and go. It was a complete and utter shock. Weren't we to be returning to Cluny Hill in the spring?

"No", said Mrs. Bruce.

She offered no further explanation for our curt dismissal other than "a change in company policy." We could, however, stay at one of the company's 21 hotels in Scotland for three nights until we sorted ourselves out.

I phoned my parents in Devonshire, where they had a huge six-bedroom house that could easily accommodate us until I got another job and a place to live, but they didn't want us and were extremely unhelpful. We realized that God must have something else in store for us. It was also clear that Dorothy Maclean was to come with us. We packed up as quickly as we could, throwing out a lot of things because we had no room in the car, and went to pick up our three boys from school (they were very bewildered, but children take changes better than adults). We had no idea where we were going or what we were going to do.

Then I remembered that we had a caravan on a public site in Findhorn. I had wanted to bring it to Cluny Hill when we were working there, but Eileen's guidance had been to leave it at Findhorn and rent it out–it would always be a home if we needed it. So we decided to drive to the Stotfield Hotel at Lossiemouth, about ten miles east along the coast from Findhorn, and take Mrs. Bruce up on her offer of free accommodation.

On our way, I pulled the car over and asked Eileen to get guidance on our bewildering situation. We were told that we had many lessons to learn and that the tests at the Trossachs were important for our future. We were to send love to Mrs. Bruce, because she had an important part to play in God's plan.

"Send love to that bitch?" I exploded. "I have worked day and night, week after week, month after month, year after year without a single day off, and this is how she treats us. How on earth can such a woman have a part in God's plan?" We did our best to follow the instruction, however, and sent her love.

After two days at the Stotfield Hotel we moved to our caravan at the Findhorn Sands Caravan Park, overlooking the Moray Firth—a bleak site in the sand dunes, exposed to freezing winds that blew out of the north east. We knew that our stay was to be a short one: like many hotels, the caravan park closed for the winter. There was no room for Dorothy in the caravan, so she found a very small hut attached to the Culbin Sands Hotel nearby; it had a bed but no heating, and she lived there throughout the following winter.

We had very little money. Hotel managers are poorly paid, as accommodation and meals are provided as part of the salary; I had also poured my own money into various projects at Cluny Hill Hotel, such as the landscaping, and therefore had no savings. Dorothy and I had to draw Unemployment Benefit and later National Assistance, which shocked Eileen. How much lower could we sink? She was horrified that I had to stand in the queue at the local Labour Exchange for my unemployment money, along with many members of our former staff—where once I had been one of the biggest employers in the district! Yet Eileen's guidance insisted that we would return to Cluny Hill. This was exciting: we thought that Mrs Bruce would change her mind and send us back. So when the end of October came and we had to find another site for the caravan, we thought it would only be for a short time. We determined to find a secluded place to sit out the winter and I turned for assistance to the Sanitation Inspector, an acquaintance of mine in nearby Elgin who was responsible for caravan sites throughout the county of Morayshire. When I did find a private site, however, still in Findhorn, he would only give permission for us to stay there until Christmas.

The one place we knew we could never stomach was the Findhorn Bay Caravan Park. For years we had passed it on our way to the beach at Findhorn, and I had often made remarks like, 'Fancy living in a dump like that, cheek-by-jowl with all the other caravans.' 'Never' is a dangerous word in anybody's vocabulary, and particularly if one is living according to the direction of spirit. After weeks of fruitless searching, we were told that there was a vacant site down by a hollow in the Findhorn Bay Caravan Park—and what a dump it was, beside an old garage with broken windows, and surrounded by old tin cans, broken bottles, blackberry bushes and gorse. At least it was away from the other caravans on the site. Eileen had clear guidance that it was the place for us; we still thought it would be only a matter of weeks before we returned to Cluny Hill or found other employment. So on a snowy day, 17 November 1962, the owner of the park towed our 30-foot caravan onto the site where it still sits today. The pipes were frozen. Nobody wanted to know us. We had less than ten pounds a week income. The only clue came from Eileen's guidance: *Step fearlessly into the new, knowing I am with you, and all is very, very well.*

Years later I happened to be in Edinburgh and decided to visit Mrs. Bruce, whose address I'd found. I phoned to see if she was in, and when she answered I rapidly put down the receiver. I took a taxi to her flat and was surprised to hear her say, "Come in, the door's open." She was expecting her son, but when she saw me she said, "Of course I remember you, Mr. Caddy, do come in." She offered me a cup of tea.

As she had friends gathered, I followed her into the kitchen. I said, "Mrs. Bruce, I've long wanted to tell you that without the part you played, the Findhorn Community would never have been created."

"Oh! Tell me more," she said, astonished.

"Well," I replied, "You prevented me from getting a job as you would not provide me with a reference. I was very upset with you at the time, but if you hadn't blocked me I would have found another job and the community would never have been founded."

Mrs. Bruce smiled sweetly and said, "Well, we all have to follow our guidance, don't we?"

I was astonished and delighted and soon left for my train, having parted with Mrs. Bruce on the best of terms.

PETER CADDY

*An extract from Peter Caddy's autobiography, 'In Perfect Timing'
edited by Jeremy Slocombe and published by The Findhorn Press
www.findhornpress.com
Peter left the community in 1979 although he returned to visit from time to time. He died in a motor accident in Germany in 1994 just as he was finishing this autobiography.*

Following Commitment

Dear Kay,

I've written so much about my time in Findhorn that I don't know what to say now. For me there were no unusual circumstances for arriving there (we just needed a place to live), nor any healing aspect (that just sort of grew later). After all, we were simply coming to an ugly caravan park for lack of any other roof.

But what happened there was because we three chose to follow our commitment to what we called God's will. We had been doing that for ten years before coming to Findhorn, and choosing to start the day with inner attunement was almost a habit by then. Its guidance asked us to stay at Findhorn at the time our world fell apart when Cluny Hill Hotel opened without us. We did not know why we should stay there, but had learned to abide by our inner guidance because it had proved utterly reliable through the years, quite apart from knowing it was right to be obedient to it.

This may sound very goody-goody. Nevertheless the reality of attunement to God met every situation. Basically all the thousands of messages I had had through the years were to put love first in one's life, and I am still finding that is utterly appropriate. There we were, basically three disunited people working together, and staying together, because from our inner attunements we knew it was right, for some unknown reason. We did not get along; we were very different personalities who often clashed, and it was not an easy life living on National Assistance, with no friends, starting a garden in sand because we didn't have enough money for decent food.

Yet every day, and as often as I wished, I could choose to enter into the beautiful energies of my inner divinity, and be embraced, uplifted and changed by them. At first I had resisted making that choice, for instance not wanting to get up early to meditate. I had had to practice a lot, and eventually realized that that time of inner attunement was the highlight of my day, the time when I was truly happy and fulfilled. In the Inner Presence I was whole, loved, loving and delightful. God was delightful, far more than I was! Oh, I might get ticked off, but always in an acceptable or humorous way. Working in the garden or the office, clashing with Peter, would be what might be seen of my life at Findhorn, but my private inner life always empowered me. And I needed that. We all do.

Peter was a completely focused and positive person, trained to be positive, seeing only the positive, and in his view making no mistakes. That is wonderful, and that type of energy is very necessary for getting projects going. But I am a balancer and could see the positive and negative in situations. When I voiced another perspective, a view opposite to his, Peter considered I was attacking him, being negative, not supporting him, etc. I reacted to his views resentfully. Unfortunately I only realized this dynamic long after I left Findhorn. At the time I felt he treated me unfairly, found that the then small community agreed with me that he did, and I wallowed in my resentment for a while. But I didn't feel good with my reactions, and eventually followed my guidance and chose to see the aspects of Peter that I could love. When I did that, he treated me differently. So I learned that I

11

had a part in creating his treatment of me. The community gives us the opportunity to see and accept what we react to or don't like about ourselves and to choose to be loving. It is amazing how harmonious things can be when love is there. And we all know love in some form.

Often I would wake up in the morning feeling heavy and fed up with the dull routines of my life. Then I would turn within and receive words of comfort and encouragement. Whatever came in those times of inward seeking would always help, uplift and make me feel joyous, changing me in both subtle and evident ways.

Of course Peter, in his commitment to do God's will, often bullied me or Eileen into turning within for guidance, especially when we didn't want to and were busy with something else. That was annoying at the time, but now I am grateful for his insistence. Whatever it is that causes us to choose to turn within is turning us to the ultimate, to our union with the universe, the goal of humanity.

It was during a meditation that the Presence told me I had a job to communicate with nature, which led to my contact with the devas and angels. I had always loved nature, but finding it had an intelligence that we can communicate and cooperate with was another wonderful revelation. And a very necessary view in this day and age when we humans are despoiling the planet and vitally need to change our outlook and our treatment of nature. Also, all the beautiful energies of nature are within us humans, and we enlarge ourselves and become more aware when we resonate to any aspect of it. Our greater awareness is greatly needed.

So, for me the reality of Findhorn continues to stand for those wonderful moments of inner attunement. That is what built it, that is what will continue it, that is what matters most for all of us.

With love,

DOROTHY MACLEAN

I received this letter from Dorothy from her home in Canada, from where she had been travelling the world teaching, running workshops and sharing her insight and wisdom. 10 years after writing this, and to everyone's delight, Dorothy Maclean, the remaining founder, returned to live in the community. 2012 was the year of her 90th birthday as well as the Community's 50th.

Time To Meet

In late '60s and early '70s I was frequently lecturing around the United

States, and on one of several occasions, at Ojai, California. At one end of the secluded valley that cradles the town is a hill upon which sits a major branch of the Theosophical Society. At the very other end of the valley up on a ridge, was (and is) a 'newcomer': Group for Creative Meditation, an off-shoot of the Lucis Trust and Arcane School.

The mentor of this body was Roberto Assagioli, founder of Psychosynthesis, a new and holistic psychology. Roberto also provided teachings to GCM, or 'Meditation Mount' as it was known, that were in advance of both the Theosophical Society and the Arcane School. Not being exclusive, I had lectured at both ends of Ojai Valley. At Meditation Mount, I came across something entirely new: a tape recording of a young man in his teens, giving forth teachings beyond anything heard at either end of the valley. I was stunned. His name was (and of course still is) David Spangler.

I wanted urgently to meet up with this young spokesman of the future, and it came about in a most pleasant way. We met at the United Nations upon some kind of arrangement, I showed him around, and we talked. I remember David saying, as he sank into one of the overstuffed armchairs in the Delegates' Lounge (to which I had legitimate access), "Feels like Home!" He didn't elaborate. I also had the pleasure of introducing David to my close friend and teacher Erling Thunberg, of Sweden, founder of 'International Center for Integrative Studies', and 'The Door', a drop-in centre for dropping-out youth in New York City.

As I have heard the story from Peter, David had said that Peter ought to see me when next in New York. And as you well know, Peter followed through on potentially useful suggestions! Already aware of Peter's weak point, I took him to lunch in the UN Delegates' Dining Room. We had a grand coming together. And I said to Peter, "Well, now that I have met you here, and received the scoop, I won't have to go to Findhorn!" Immediately I knew I was absolutely WRONG!

Within a very short time I and my eldest son were airborne for Scotland and Findhorn. Interestingly, we flew directly to Findhorn! It came about in this wise: It seems that the proper airport, 25 miles away at Inverness, was undergoing repairs, so we were flown to the RAF base, at Kinloss, which is next door to the Community. We had only to carry our bags up the road a hundred yards or so, and walk in the gate!

It was evening. The small gang of the time was gathered in the small kitchen-and-dining room facility, and Peter was holding forth in grand and what I learned was typical style. Peter immediately made the most of our impromptu entrance with a grand and flowery welcome, and seated me in the only empty chair—his. I do not hesitate to say that it was 'hot' from two sources: Peter and God!

I learned then that there were no 'ifs, ands or buts'—there was only manifestation, and that was it! Nothing else had a look-in.

Thus began a long love affair with Findhorn, including giving many workshops there. As Findhorn began graduating people back into the world, it was discovered that after being in Findhorn for a few years, many were having trouble readjusting to life 'outside'. For Findhorn was a new world, an experience of what was, and still is to come, both in human behaviour and understanding in the world at large. The workshops were geared to helping with this 're-entry problem'.

It has been a pleasure to have a thread of my life woven into the Findhorn Fabric!

DONALD KEYS

ℱ

Waking Up . . . To Love

I arrived at Findhorn in September of 1977. I had been the pastor of a six-hundred-member United Methodist Church in Yuma, Arizona. When I assumed the pastorate of this congregation in 1975 it had been described as a 'dying, downtown congregation'. Perhaps the powers-that-be had assumed that I would close the place down with youthful gusto (I was thirty-three years old at the time). Instead the congregation, which had dwindled to about eighty active participants, began to flourish. The sanctuary began to fill on Sunday morning, and we were forced to begin a second service in order to accommodate those who came to worship on Sunday morning.

In the midst of that phenomenal growth I felt 'called' to join the Findhorn Community (this was after participating in a two-week guest programme in the summer of 1976. So, in the Autumn of 1977 we (a family of four) pulled up roots, sold everything and moved to that 'place' often characteristically described as a 'windswept peninsula in Northern Scotland'.

I did not realise, upon arrival, that Findhorn, as described by Peter Caddy, is a 'grave-yard for egos'. Nor did I realize that my ego needed burying. The surprise was to come.

My assumption, also upon arrival, was that I would assume some position of leadership within the Community. After all, I was a celebrated young theologian (my assessment), and my name was David to be directly associated with that genitor of 'Limitless Love and Truth', David Spangler. Surely I would be on the Core Group.

Not so. My place was in the basement of The Hall, in the Maintenance Department, which was not only the darkest, dankest place in The

Community it was likewise the most anonymous. Now I could be neither seen nor heard. What a terrible shock.

The situation did not get better. I grew increasingly depressed and started to surmise that the New Age wasn't quite as glamorous as I had anticipated, and that, perchance, I had made a radical mistake in committing myself to three years of this subterranean hell.

In January of 1978 the temperature dropped to a record low for an extended period of time. Most of the pipes in the caravans froze, including Siri's caravan in Pine Ridge. The call to Maintenance went out and I trekked off to resolve the situation, along with Dr. Arnold Meyerowitz, a successful chiropractor from Santa Barbara who had obviously also not heard the ego death knell of Findhorn. I crawled under Siri's caravan with a pail of warm water, some cotton wraps and a small hammer. Because of the urgency of the crisis I first addressed the challenge of frozen waste pipes. I carefully wrapped the PVC pipe with warm towels, and gently tapped the pipe with my hand. Nothing. So I wrapped more towels around the pipe and tapped again … gently with my hand. Nothing. In an effort to increase the possibility of dislodging the frozen waste I turned to my trusty hammer, tapping ever so lightly on the PVC pipe. There was a slight cracking sound, followed by the disintegration of the entire waste pipe, which I had positioned directly above me. The result 'human waste', completely covering every inch of my body!

At that moment Arnold, who was kind enough to hand me warm towels, and who was likewise unaware of this 'disintegrating' situation, bent over and uttered these timeless words: "David, I love you." Now I would be the first to acknowledge that I was in no mood to be loved at that particular moment. And I would also acknowledge that Arnold's message did not immediately sink in. What had sunk in was a stench that was so repulsive that I could not inhale. What had sunk in was the concrete commitment that I was getting the hell out of this g-d---ed community on the first train to Inverness.

It took about an hour for Arnold's message to enter my soul. But it did. And I realized that I was not only loved by Arnold, but I was also loved by Peter and Eileen, and those members of the community that longed and prayed for me to move beyond my infernal self-centredness into the Light of a new day and a New Age. I realised that I was loved by God, you know, the same God that created 70 billion galaxies, and that all this was a Divine set-up, if I might so describe it, for me to WAKE UP.

I did wake up the next morning with what I might minimally describe as a change of attitude. I saw the basement of The Hall in a new Light: the Light of God. I saw my colleagues in Maintenance in a new Light: the Light of God. I even saw myself in a new Light: the Light of God. And, wonder of wonders, I began to love working in the Maintenance Department.

Cleaning a Don Burner, re-wiring The Park, fixing toilets, all these 'dirty' jobs became my opportunity to serve God.

I would actually whistle while I worked. Maybe that was the giveaway. For as I was walking toward Pine Ridge one gloriously rainy day, who should approach me but Peter Caddy and Francois Duquesne. I realized as they approached that they were eyeing me in such a way as to indicate they had something to say. I greeted them both. Then with not so much as a trivial effort at chit-chat Peter looked me square in the eye and said: "It's time for you to be on the Core Group."

To misquote my favorite Saint: 'It is in giving that we receive. It is in pardoning that we are pardoned. And it is only in serving that we can truly serve.' I hope I never forget.

DAVID WILKINSON

⌾

Journey to Findhorn

As I dream back over the years before I came here to live my mind settles on the morning of August the 17th, 1987, two years before I had even heard about Findhorn. I had read of an event called the Harmonic Convergence and the author of the article, Jose Arguelles, spoke of an emerging new consciousness. To support the opportunity that it represented for humanity he was calling for as many people as possible, world-wide, to meditate at noon GMT for one hour, which in Calgary, where I was then living, happened to be at 5 o'clock in the morning. The world of the 'New Age' was very new to me then, but I was excited by it. That morning was a watershed for me, a first conscious act of alignment to something beyond myself. I didn't call that something God, or Spirit, at the time. Nonetheless it was an invitation to the mystery that I now define with those words. It also meant I was aligning myself to a movement for change, for the creation of a better world.

Things unfolded from then much more dramatically and more quickly than I could have imagined. Events that shattered me, cracked me open to accept change in my own life, and that prepared me for the letting go that would allow me, seven years later, to move my life to Findhorn.

At the time I was working as a geologist in the oil and gas industry. The company I worked for had just been taken over, and adjustments to the changes that this involved were creating extra stress. My wife and I were both working, and we had been trying to have children without success for several years. I was drinking heavily, as I had since I was a teenager, and I was still using other drugs occasionally.

The previous year problems in our marriage had led us to seek marriage guidance counselling, triggered in part by my drinking. Then a friend introduced us to a group called Omega, which organized group therapy weekends, and we decided to try it out, as the counselling didn't seem to be getting us anywhere.

I think it was the sympathetic listening I experienced, both from the marriage guidance counsellor and from the people who ran Omega, that started the first changes in me. The message I got from them was, "You're absolutely fine just as you are. We're interested in you, we believe in you, and you have the potential to change your life". It met a very deep need in me, a need that until then I had been trying to satisfy with drink. It dawned on me that life might not be quite as I had come to believe it was. I began to notice my stress level at work, my boredom, my unhappiness, all of which I had taken for granted, and thought were symptoms of a failure on my part to cope as well as I should have been able to.

Immediately after the first Omega weekend I wrote this:

'My life has been a long dark tunnel through which I was running to reach the unknown goal at its end. Now I'm standing in an open meadow, no longer needing those comforting and confining walls, able to go in whatever direction I choose, because I have released myself.' This seemed to flow out of me quite spontaneously, and it expressed something deeply true for me. It amazed me. I hadn't written anything except technical reports for years. My dreams too became incredibly intense, and at the same time I found that I had new friends who were not only interested in these dreams, but could help me work with them. Friends that also inhabited this other world of new hope that I seemed to have stepped into. It was through these friends that I heard about a retreat in Mexico during the following spring and I decided to go.

The retreat centre was called Chac Mool, and the setting was beautiful. We slept in thatched cabanas clustered among palm trees along the beach, and looked out over the blue waters of the Gulf of Mexico. Nearby were the ruins and pyramids of the Mayans. Every night there was the incredible star-filled sky, seeming to hang just above our heads, and a fluorescent line of waves breaking along the beach.

On our ninth day there I had what I can only call an experience of grace, a rebirth. It began as I was talking to one of our group, Loria, and we touched on a memory of childhood that brought tears. Quite spontaneously energy started moving, first in my hands, then moving up my arms, and eventually taking over my whole body. It would be impossible to adequately describe all that happened then. I can say that at one point I felt bathed in a beautiful warm light that moved up from my feet to completely cover me. At times it seemed to meet blocks in my body that became very painful, but under Loria's guidance, with gentle massage and working with the breath, one by one they were cleared. I experienced a love so all-encompassing that I felt I understood how Christ was able to endure the crucifixion and still love those who were crucifying him. I found myself saying yes to whatever pain I might be asked to bare for the sake of that love, realizing as I did so that I had just said yes to life in a way that I never had before.

Throughout the experience I had the sense of a loving presence standing in front of me. And what really blew me away was that I could give this being no other name than Jesus. It blew me away because, from the time I was a teenager, I had wanted nothing to do with Christianity. The experience was so real and so powerful I simply knew that there was a whole dimension to life that I had previously been blind to, that I could no longer live the way I had been living. My priorities were completely changed. It gave me an experience of the reality of Spirit. And it called for and received my total surrender.

A few weeks after coming back from the retreat my mother called from the UK. She had been diagnosed as having kidney cancer. My father, who had nearly died from a brain tumour twelve years earlier, and had been an invalid since then, needing twenty-four-hour care, had had to be moved into a nursing home. Without my mother to motivate him he deteriorated rapidly, and died six weeks later, on the morning of July 17th.

My mother's cancer continued to develop, and had spread to her spine. Exactly a month later, on August 17th, she also died. It was a year to the day after I had got up that morning to meditate, though I didn't think too much of it at the time.

I had lived a long way from my parents for most of the previous fifteen years, needing the distance, but their death was still a profound shock for me. What I remember most strongly about that time was the relief I felt every time I broke down and cried, because I realized that I had loved them. It wasn't something I had acknowledged for most of my life, and without the changes I had gone through in the previous months it may have stayed hidden.

Their death brought my wife and I closer together for a while. At the same time it brought clarity, and that clarity for me was that we were growing apart. It also strongly confronted me with my own mortality and the fact that one day I too would lie dying. I knew that if I carried on with my life as it was I would feel incomplete, that there was something more.

In June the following year I asked Michelle for a separation. There was grief, but a strong sense that this was the right thing to do. I have much to be thankful for in the grace with which she released me, and for what our marriage had been.

It was only a matter of time before I left the oil industry too, though just then I had no idea what I would do next, and I carried on a strange kind of half-life in my job, struggling to give it my focus, still having loyalty to the people I worked with, even if not for the company, and watching my relationships shift and new ones form as I changed.

Then one morning a letter was placed on my desk. It said that there was to be a rationalization of staff following the merger, and that to ease this process for employees, a voluntary severance package had been prepared, starting with exploration. They were hoping to shed seventy five percent of the workforce. I went straight to my manager, signed the proffered form, and walked out of the office for the last time at 5pm that day. The date was August 17th. I was reeling. The coincidence of it happening on the same day as my mother's death, and before that the Harmonic Convergence, left me with the eerie feeling that when I got up that morning two years previously it was more than a random event. It took on a huge significance, and was too strong for me to miss the sense of synchronicity. This threw me even more into the New Age and Alternative movements.

I was now on my own, in this open meadow of a life. What direction would I now choose? I loved Canada, and living in Calgary. A good friend had offered me a room after the separation from my wife. It had a view of the river, and was out of downtown, away from old haunts and painful memories. It became a kind of retreat house for me. I found a teacher and therapist, Hal Boulter, and worked with him for six months. It was a period of intense inner work, integrating all that had happened, and dealing with the grief and the shock, not only of losing my parents, but now my marriage and my career of fifteen years. It was mostly through him, and a group in Calgary that called themselves the Emissaries of Divine Light, that I learned about spiritual community. I felt that somehow this would be part of my next steps. I signed up for a semester of evening classes in creative writing, did my work with Hal, and waited.

In October I had a phone call from my sister in England. She had not been able to find a buyer for our parent's house, and it was beginning to look pretty derelict. In a collapsing house market we were chasing a price that seemed to be in free fall. It occurred to me that I could return to the UK for a while, and look after the house until it was sold. That would give me a clean break from Calgary, and might help me to get some clarity about what to do next. The house was in Haddenham, the village where my grandparents had lived, and where I had spent most weekends as a child. We had lived thirteen miles away, in Cambridge, where I had been born. I still had relatives in the village, and other family nearby, so it would give me a chance to reconnect with them, and with my roots.

The down side of the idea was leaving the many close friends I had in Calgary. They were a great support to me in the changes I was making; though some of them challenged those changes too. But I told myself it would only be for a few months.

When I told Hal of my plans he said I should check out a place called Findhorn. This was my first introduction, and I knew at once that I would go there.

That November I flew back to see the house for myself. It really was a mess. The large garden was completely overrun. The house itself looked very sad, with damp showing on many of the walls, and wallpaper peeling off in many of the rooms. Though my parents hadn't lived there that long, having moved back to the village only five years before they died, it was still full of their presence. On the positive side it had a fully equipped kitchen, and a functioning heating system. Although sorting it all out seemed like rather a daunting task, I could also see that I would be quite cosy there, and it gave me a purpose. At least money wouldn't be a problem for some time.

So in the spring of 1990 I returned to the UK for an unspecified time. Being a dual citizen I had no visa problems and could come and go as I pleased. I booked an Experience Week at Findhorn, along with two follow up weeks, for that summer. Then I got stuck into work at the house, first restoring the garden, and then, little by little, tackling the house. I also joined the village art group, and began to make new friends.

In July I drove up to Scotland. Arriving at Cluny Hill College I felt immediately at home, and that feeling was strengthened as the days passed and I got to know people. The community felt very much akin to what I had left in Calgary, though the context was very different. I might well have stayed on after those first three weeks, but I still had the house to sort out, and I still planned to return to Canada. More importantly, I had met someone on the Experience Week who lived in London, and that gave me another reason to stay south.

When the house did finally sell, I moved neither to Findhorn nor back to Canada, but down to London to deepen my new relationship, and to begin exploring how I might live in the UK. Thinking to apply my geological expertise in a more positive way I found work in conservation that took me down to the New Forest, in Hampshire. But I continued to visit Findhorn once or twice every year, because somewhere in me there was still an unfulfilled need for spiritual community.

After three years I found I could not commit fully to this new relationship, and it came to a very painful end. I realized too that my heart wasn't in the conservation work I was doing. On my own again I began to think seriously about Findhorn for a longer-term stay.

In 1994 I signed up for a week planting trees with the Findhorn based charity Trees for Life. My thought was that experiencing what had been a life-changing inspiration for Alan Watson, the founder of Trees for Life might help me find my own inspiration. As it turned out Alan himself was co-focalising that week. It was as profound an experience for me as my first visit to the Foundation, and led me deeper into a link with nature. That week I heard the music of waterfalls, and breathed with the trees. I cried with a lonely old pine for the death of its offspring and the dwindling forest. I felt the new upsurge of hope in the depth of its loss because of the work being done there now. My gratitude to Alan for creating this initiative for the regeneration of wilderness was, and still is, huge.

Following on from those two work weeks I returned to the Glen on my own, on a kind of vision quest, and I decided to walk round Loch Affric. About four hours into the walk, feeling full of the trees and the mountains, I heard a clear question in my mind, "Will you be my artist?" It seemed to come out of all that was around me, a sense of all-pervading presence. I felt a surge of enthusiasm, and shouted "Yes!" at the top of my lungs and just about fell over laughing at myself, but also laughing with the joy of it. I had thought of my writing, the art classes in the village, as hobbies. Suddenly, I saw that they could be my primary focus, and part of my spiritual path too. I was not, I realized, and never had been, a scientist at heart, though I was good enough at it. A few weeks later I was enrolled in a new workshop at the Foundation called 'The Essence of Arts in Community', which was to start that autumn.

Back in the New Forest I received a phone call from Calgary, from a former manager. I had often said that if ever I returned to the oil industry it would be to work for this particular man. His integrity, his putting people first within the aggressive business world of oil exploration, and his own enthusiasm, his leading by example, were qualities I really admired. He had just moved to a new company as vice president, and was putting together an exploration team. Was I interested? I thanked him but said no. I was going to embark on a new direction as an artist. When I put the phone down I realized that I had finally said no to ever going back, no to the financial security that that career had offered me. The path I now chose was one in which I had no expertise. It was purely a heart response. It meant stepping into the unknown, following my heart, and trusting.

I returned to Canada for a few weeks to tie up loose ends there, and in August drove up to Findhorn in my Nissan Micra with everything I owned piled in the back. I felt light, and freer than I had done for years. This time when I arrived at Cluny I had my whole life with me. There were no strings pulling me away. I certainly still had my doubts. Whenever they arose I had only to take myself back to the place I had found when my parents died, imagining my own death. How would I feel about a decision to stay in the oil industry, keeping to my expertise, denying my heart? The doubts are still with me. But they are fading with time. And they are changing. Now they are about my ability as a writer, as an artist. Not about whether this path I have chosen is the right one. They are about my relationship to Spirit, when my life seems so mundane at times, lacking the magical highs of those early days of opening. They are perhaps more questions than doubts. I often need to remind myself that we each have a unique path, and that I have not failed because my life does not look like somebody else's.

After completing the Essence of Arts programme I decided to enter the student year at the Foundation, and it was while working in the Park garden that I met Kathy, now my wife. Our journey together has not been a straightforward one. We have left Findhorn twice, ready to settle elsewhere if that was what Spirit wanted, but both times were led straight back. We lost a son, Ben, in stillbirth, and experienced the blessing that this place can be in times of deep loss and crisis. We still struggle to stay open to his death as transformative, as a rebirth in our own lives. It has certainly deepened us— and all of our relationships. We live now in the village, in our own home, putting down roots. I am part of the open community, while Kathy is working at the Foundation. We work in our own ways toward a shared goal, a life with Spirit. I am still exploring my creativity, through writing mostly. I still live very much with the unknown, and constantly need to surrender to it as my ego gets desperate for certainty.

It's now twelve years since that morning of the Harmonic Convergence; eleven years since my experience in Mexico and the death of my parents. I am clearer than I have ever been about saying yes to God, to co-creating a better world, of the importance of surrender. More certain than ever that I need to follow my heart and ask for guidance constantly.

As I complete this first draft, strangely, it is again August 17th. Apparently something they call the Grand Cross is occurring, and I can't help wondering whether my dance with that date is truly over.

MICHAEL WHITE

Moving Closer

In the early seventies, having moved to London from my beloved wild Atlantic West Wales, I went on a Wrekin Trust course about Sacred Architecture where I met and was inspired by Sir George Trevelyan, Theo Gimbel, and others. By some collective transport arrangements a group from the Findhorn Foundation, another person and myself ended up arriving, after dark, at a magnificent house on the outskirts of Birmingham. The walls were awash with faded murals of flying figures, trailing clouds and plant forms in warm, muted greens across the door arches, all in a vaguely Bloomsbury style.

Stories were shared late into the night. When we finally slept it was in an attic space on a long communal bed of seven mattresses pushed together to accommodate ten people. There was an extraordinary unreality about the whole night but the joy and openheartedness had left its imprint on me. The next Wrekin Trust course I attended was led by two women from the Foundation. On return to work a student I was asked to tutor announced his project to design a community centre for a by now growing Foundation.

All the while came the invitations, "Come to Findhorn", "you'd love it", "It's everything you're interested in", "we need people to work", "come and look me up." And inside, my implicit "No Way, I'm not like you". 'You' I saw as all joyful, playful, full of light and sharing, affluent and confident, embracing openness. Inside myself I felt dark, dark, dark. I dare not look into your eyes for fear of what you might see there.

I am not like you. I am one of the others, the hurt, the troubled, the ones who behave badly. My origins, my family is working class. I am full of outrage at the world's cruelties.

My way is revolution not tenderness.

Time passed. And after a long journey I became a Buddhist and a regular visitor to Samye Ling Tibetan Centre in the Scottish Borders where I met many others with one foot or more in the shadow side and gradually transforming themselves. I was living by now in rural Aberdeenshire among rolling greens and honey-gold barley fields, beneath the rose pink and apple green Northern Lights. Here I practised meditation and yoga, art therapy and my own art work with regular visits to Samye Ling, Greenham Common Peace Camp and a social scene in Edinburgh.

More time passed.

When a close friend moved to the West Coast and then to Findhorn my visits up here resumed. Still I had experiences like sitting in the café in my biker's black surrounded by talk of crystal healings, life lived by guidance received and followed—often, it seemed, to travel internationally at a moment's notice—the 'sacrifices' made to be here, the city job released, the house in the south sold... While carefree faces with northern European accents beamed out of the brochure. Where were the visibly downbeat ones, the dispossessed and despairing? The black and brown faces, the Scots?

I saw my own simple, subsistence-level life so rich in time and wonder and creativity but lacking anything like the finance and material signs of success, or the confidence in my external or innate sunny goodness still to make attending a course here possible.

Bitterness and old pains were lurking. After much work I'd come to know I had a 'higher self' of sorts, roughly translating 'Buddha nature', but it didn't seem to be easily accessible. Feeling precious to me and vulnerable it had become yet another closely guarded secret. The fight was continuing it seemed; Findhorn Community as the angels and forces of light, myself as shady-spirited underdog. I learned the value of envy as a guide to what one's dream and aspiration is and I kept visiting though not the Park but the bay and Back Shore.

Every day I walked the same route like a pilgrim entranced as indeed I was by Culbin's bright streak of sand, the dark forest and white gulls. I walked out as far as I could every low tide and stood, I fancied, at the meeting point of two seas, lay on the sand singing to the seals. Much artwork arose out of these excursions. Much thinking.

When I received another invitation to come and live here I paced the beach, uncertain. I asked what I should do, stopped walking and, glancing down, saw at my feet a perfect globe of white stone and heard in my mind's ear a firm "not yet".

But I moved nearer and visited more. Dharma teachers and other friends from Samye Ling visited too and something began to connect, like mother and father, some inner and outer exchange and a corresponding shift in my perceptions. From then on change was fast. Struggling to live a life based in meditation and according to ecological principles in relative rural isolation was proving tiring and I began to look for a 'sangha' that would also be an enriching place for my partner and son.

Eventually a moment arrived. We offered our beautiful if rugged farmhouse for rent and within a day it was taken. We had one month to find a place near Findhorn to live and meanwhile moved into a neighbour's caravan. The week our stay there was due to end we found number eighty-four in the centre of Findhorn village to rent. It's been like that, what we need arriving at the eleventh hour, ever since we moved here, three years and eight house moves later.

With a view of the bakery's grey stone wall and tin roof I began to write, every day, 'seriously' as they say, including a story I'd been told twenty years earlier by Theo Gimbel at that first Wrekin Trust weekend. It became a poem that won the 'Northwords '99' annual competition and brought my first ever payment for poetry. Called, 'Journey with the names of God', the responses when I read it at a writer's gathering varied; for some it was the story of a/my life, for others the story of a people, or a metaphor for all journeys of transformation.

Some days I feel called to the Park and I've learned to follow this and turn up. The 'chance' meetings often prove to be profound, to touch on some deep, mutual chord of the moment. Healing is passed from smile to smile, hand to hand. The Universal Hall might be the twinkling eye of a slow hurricane, drawing in all she needs, radiating out all that is needed beyond, into the landscape, distant peoples' hearts, the world.

For the best part of a year I spent a great deal of time in the Hall; sitting, meditating, playing music, at some kind of prayer in some kind of temple, a new being forming in this motherly womb, not to mention the big community celebrations and a bit of cleaning.

When I sat meditating in the Universal Hall Sanctuary in December '98 and asked, if it were for the highest and best for all, might my dream of participating in something theatrical for the Hall be realised I didn't expect what followed. Five minutes later, I walked into the café upstairs where Richard Penny asked me to read the part of the empress in his play 'The Present'. This was not what I'd had in mind at all but there was no doubt that this was a reply to my prayer. Richard co-wrote the play with George Ripley, based on George's idea and to honour his long-held dream to see the ideas it represented played out in the Hall he'd had so much part in creating around millennium time. This was the clearest opportunity I could imagine to give something of myself back in gratitude to this wonderful Hall and its creators: To honour those who'd designed and worked on building the Hall who had so often been in my meditations in an abstract way, as people not known to me personally. A circle completed, one of many such 'harmonic convergences' that the 'field' around Findhorn and the Community seems to nurture.

Meanwhile the apple tree planted by my Tibetan teacher continues to grow in the Park's original garden. Samye Ling has adopted and adapted some Findhorn ways and the 'Living Machine' reedbed sewage system, was built in the Park coincidentally with a growing awareness of the need for the community to acknowledge and process more of its 'shadow' aspects. Both places remain welcoming to people of all faiths. For years I felt held between these two 'poles', as it were, these two powerful Scottish centres which, between them seemed to stand for all that I hold most precious in life and span the far-reaching polarities this can encompass. For many years it felt there could be no more 'right' place for me to live than on the road between these two. Now both are somehow more united in my mind and conversing harmoniously, exchanging practices from permaculture to meditation I can relax into living here. I guess I may have been one infinitesimal thread in a process I will never comprehend.

The big gatherings in the Hall are what concentrate my awareness of the wonder of this place. Our 'Process' sessions where old and new conflicts are enacted and transformed, our rituals resonant with chanting from Taizé to Sufi, our turning circles-within-circles of dancers making the music of the spheres manifest. Beneath a galaxy of rainbow lights in the dark wood of the honeycombed roof, the eye out onto sunlight or night sky, the ringing, humming, vibrantly expanding silences as three hundred or so of us practice 'inner listening', attuning to spirit and one another in community. We might be in a vast bell, a cathedral, a star, a great lens magnifying— as 'my soul doth magnify'—beaming out to all corners of the earth and beyond. A perfect place to practice and to radiate the effects of that practice.

Arriving back at my home in the village after the fire ritual concluding the Forgiveness Conference I discovered that my son had built his own small fire on a rock on the kitchen table. Together as a family we continued (more safely) outside and it was as if the ritual was continuing, radiating out from the four fires in the dunes and the two hundred pilgrims who were connecting home and friends and distant family to the heart of the conference and the spirit of forgiveness.

It is often easy and seductive to see oneself as the centre of the universe but there is a positive and true meaning to this too. If we are all one small centre of 'God' then we can all add to the sum of goodness in the world.

Great teachers pass through here, and keen students celebrating and working alongside committed community members, day visitors and local residents—all with 'the world at heart', to use Richard Penny's favourite slogan, creating a resonant field effect, a field of devotion, purification and accumulation (of merit, good karma) and 'guru yoga'—the aligning and merging of one's awareness with the 'teacher', as the great old Buddhist texts describe. This is my way of thinking about 'the Findhorn effect' that so many others have described in other ways, and a very, very good reason for being here.

Thank you Eileen, Dorothy and Peter.

BEVERLEY A'COURT

From Bush to Bay – Out of Africa

Ten years ago all I knew about Findhorn was that it was a spiritual community and that they had grown forty-pound cabbages in their early years. That was all, but as I travelled around Europe I remembered this little place in the north of Scotland and I decided to 'pop in' for a couple of days. That was several years ago and I've been here ever since! As I set foot in the Caravan Park I knew my travelling time was over. I would be staying here.

For many years I had been living outdoors in nature in South Africa; sleeping under the stars, cooking on the fire, carrying water from the spring, living with the rhythm of nature and the song of the birds. I supported myself through my creativity, making flutes, drums, and other instruments and items out of all kinds of natural material that I could find in my environment. Gradually I began to play the drums as the heartbeat of Mother Earth played through me. (Playing the drums also helped me earn my living.)

So after months in the Bush, walking and sleeping out around Europe I came to look at this far-away Highland community. Imagine, I arrived in high summer and it felt like I was in the middle of New York City! So many people overwhelmed me and the size and complexity of The Findhorn Foundation Community: the Houses, electricity, computers, cars, offices, Visitors Centre, programmes. Help! I guess I'd expected a type of idyllic Asterix village! Yet here I was with a deep inner knowing that I was meant to be here but not yet understanding why, and I struggled for quite a while with my resistance against settling into the full stream of the Community and leaving my free life behind. And Programmes! Ugh! I couldn't understand this! Why should I do a visitor's programme? I didn't want to be a visitor, I wanted to live here and be part of the Community, not just visit.

All this I didn't understand and everyone I asked about my way of being here told me to do the 'Experience Week'. Well, I finally surrendered and signed up for the next Experience Week and went to registration on Saturday morning, my guts full of resistance.

During this week I slowly started to understand. I absorbed a little taste of the magic of Findhorn, of its incredible beauty and richness and I started to see the value of the programmes. I started to open to what the Findhorn Foundation has to offer and to adapt to the life-style here (with some resistance of course!)

I've worked in Cullerne Garden ever since I came here, keeping in touch with nature and being outdoors. I remember when the autumn came and it was getting cold, it took me weeks to get my feet used to shoes again. And through the winter I spent much of my time indoors, apart from my work in the garden because of the cold—but I didn't mind as it was such a gift for me to be here. I've since discovered that the reality of being here is that every day there's a lesson to learn or a challenge I have to take in order to grow. But every evening when I go to bed I can say "thank you" for another beautiful day. I guess these things happen everywhere on the planet, but this place makes me conscious about how God works in our daily lives.

To backtrack, in March '96 I started the student year programme, hungering to be in the full steam of the Community. Well, during the first three weeks of the programme I experienced resistance, especially as we were together as a group virtually all the time. Meetings and discussions, group sessions, talks, Transformation Game etc. Every day was a big challenge for me to be with the group and I was reluctant to open up. Some nights I'd take my sleeping bag on to the lawn and breathe easily and sleep deeply under the expansive northern night sky.

This is what I am learning here. To open up more to others and myself. I am learning about honesty and communication, about 'being' and

27

self-acceptance, about living in community, and of course deepening my connection with the Essence, Spirit, God, All That Is.

For more than a year now I've been going to the six-thirty morning meditation and the whole day feels different when it is started with an hour of silence. I am learning to find more balance in my life, getting less entangled in 'outside' activities and giving more attention to the inner, spending time in quiet.

Again to backtrack, in March '96, with the first sunshine I couldn't hold myself back from being outdoors anymore and I took my backpack and moved straight into Cullerne Garden. First I stayed in the barn for two weeks and then I discovered a little garden shed that I then made my home, calling it 'little Africa'. My heart was jumping and it felt so good being in touch with Mother Earth and the elements again; being back in touch with that part of my spirit. I could now enjoy the sunrises and the sunsets from the garden, absorbing the total peace of that place and having daily swims in the pond and lighting little fires in the evenings. And to my delight I was totally supported by the Cullerne Garden focaliser, Christopher, and others in the group who, recognising what I needed to do for my spirit, encouraged me.

All the love I feel for Mother Earth, for God and Nature, my passion for life and all the beauty it has to offer, I express through drumming. It is the tool I am using to express that part of me. I often feel I can't really say with words what I want to say but when I take my drum and play, my heart and my soul are speaking and people start dancing. I also know that my days here in Findhorn are numbered. For me being here is the breath in between; it is a place of learning that prepares me for a new step in my life.

I feel there is a place, a life ahead that will join within me all the things I am learning here about living in community and my simple down-to-earth lifestyle which is a big part of my spiritual path that I carry in my heart.

I don't know when it will be time to go or to where, but I do know that I will not forget this Community and the life lessons that I am learning here.

JOBINA PINKENBURG
Network News

Fanning the First Spark

A spark was growing inside me. I had begun to pester the few people I knew who had visited the Findhorn Foundation Community for information. When I asked too many questions they told me to go and see for myself, reminding me that living near Perth, only 120miles away, I was near enough for a day visit.

So, one sunny morning in November 1997 I arrived at Findhorn for the first time. So what happened that day? Well, I fell in love with the Nature Sanctuary, the barrel houses, the sandy beach embedded with multi-coloured pebbles, the organic stonework of the Universal Hall, and far too many books in the Phoenix shop. As a full moon guided me over the moors on my journey home, I determined to come back for longer.

Within a month I was following the driveway up to Cluny Hill College for an Experience Week. The wooded hill seemed to hold the overgrown grey building in an embrace. Those pines would be my second home.

My first impression was that everyone seemed to be speaking with an accent (except me!). In fact, among twenty course members and two focalisers, twelve countries were represented, with only six individuals living in Britain. We were given a guided tour of the college, which seemed to be a cross between a hotel and a boarding school that had been taken over by grown-up children.

Experience Week is difficult to describe objectively. My lasting memories include meditating on glassy waves in the river at Randolph's Leap, pulling up couch grass with painfully cold fingers in Cullerne Gardens, building physical trust through games, and listening with childlike rapture to a story about wolves after a Five Rhythms dance session.

I learnt most through our lengthy group sharing sessions. These were often exhausting, with so many voices to listen to and with traumatic issues frequently rising to the surface. Somehow the love and non-judgemental approach of the group provided a safe space for individuals to confront their shadows. Through empathy with all these different people my consciousness expanded much more than would have been possible through my own experience alone. To start with, the week seemed to stretch ahead into infinity, but all too soon we were in the throes of the final day.

The intensity built as we worked our last morning and prepared for completion. I skipped lunch to walk along the shore and seek inspiration. It came to me in the form of a seal, through which I was able to tell the rest of the group my own story. In the final evening a party atmosphere prevailed with a special dinner at Cluny then on to The Park for the Winter Gathering, the annual entertainment to which the locals are invited. It was a delightful climax to join the Community in this vibrant celebration. On Saturday it was hard to leave. I needed to drink my fill of the atmosphere and people before facing the outside world.

I deeply regret not setting some time aside to reflect on the week immediately afterwards. Instead I was straight into a round of Christmas parties and family visiting. The calm, strong composure with which I had left Findhorn soon cracked and I found myself being very irritable with my mother. Where had the sense of oneness and deep understanding I had enjoyed gone?

Sadly, I realise that I am still near the start of my journey and have much travelling ahead. Despite attempting to develop a regular spiritual practice, I often feel out of touch with myself and anything beyond. But at times when I stretch out my mind to the Friends and Stewards of Findhorn Network, I begin again to feel a web of connection to the universe. I can forgive and have patience with myself, and therefore with others. When I left the Foundation in December, I sensed that I had to establish a new role in the wider world. I am now doing so, applying myself to freelance writing.

As I struggle for some calm in my current turbulence, I reach out into the light above Findhorn. And I make myself a promise before long I will return for another lesson in life.

FELICITY MARTIN
Network News

F

Love is the Key

"Without love, life is impossible. We have to learn the art of loving. We need to support each other to build communities where love is tangible. The well-being of the world depends on the way we live our daily lives, on the way we take care of the world, and on the way we love."

These beautiful words by Thich Nhat Hahn sum up for me the essence and core of the Findhorn Community. The Community has been in my consciousness since the end of the seventies. I have only over the past couple of years, however, come to know the Foundation as a Steward and a regular visitor. Findhorn is where my soul feels most at home. I feel nourished by the love, which is expressed in so many different and often very creative ways. As friendships deepen my relationship with the community becomes an ever more meaningful and important part of my life. I have also at last found a place where spirituality is not categorized or defined in any one particular way—people from many different backgrounds of faith or none at all are welcome, and there is great richness in the extraordinary diversity of each individual's spiritual path. At the heart of it all there is simplicity and ordinariness - if we want to know God, look within and take time to be quiet. In Eileen Caddy's words—"it is in the inner peace and stillness that things begin to happen."

When I first heard of the Findhorn Community I was living in London, qualifying as a medical student, searching for some kind of truth and believing deeply in the need for social change. I was interested in eastern spiritual traditions, but was not on a spiritual path. I was trying to find my identity and purpose as an activist, challenging the status quo and the many injustices that I could see in the world.

At that time in my life I was exploring thresholds of consciousness— I tried marihuana, and LSD. I wished I could have been part of the flower-power hippie explosion of love and joy, but more serious concerns dominated. I put my career first and after graduating from St Thomas' Hospital I started working as a junior doctor. At the end of my first 6-month job I had to look for a new post and happened to notice one advertised by a hospital in Inverness. It lit a spark because Findhorn was a place which I had wanted to visit. Like many others I had been fascinated by the story of Eileen and Peter Caddy's arrival in the caravan park and their work with the nature spirits ... and of course I wanted to see the giant cabbages for myself. Findhorn was not far from Inverness, so trusting my intuition I applied for this job, packed everything into a Volkswagen car and headed for the far north. It's difficult for me to remember quite what I was looking for at that time, but London had overwhelmed and consumed me. I was at a very low ebb in my life and my soul was thirsting for something new.

When I arrived in Inverness and saw the snow covered mountains in the distance my spirits soared. I felt cleansed from all that had been dark and difficult for me during my years in London. I visited the Park at Findhorn, not being sure what I would find. The community centre was warm and welcoming and friendly people served beautiful food. I went looking for the very large cabbages and found them, but no fairies appeared to me! An elderly woman who gave me a foot massage invited me into her caravan for a cup of tea. The door was opened, but like a fruit that is not yet ripe, I had further to go on my life journey before I would be able to see with my inner eyes and recognize the extraordinary power of the place. However the magic did touch me, although I wasn't aware of it as such at the time, and it was not in a way which I could ever have imagined or expected. Divine forces seized hold of my life and I was swept into a big adventure, which began, on Inverness railway station.

I was browsing at the station news-stand and I picked up a book called 'A Sense of Freedom'. This book was written by a prisoner called Jimmy Boyle—it was an extraordinary account of his life in the Gorbals slums of Glasgow, his descent into street fighting and crime which resulted eventually in him serving a life sentence, of his years in solitary confinement in the Inverness cages and his transformation in the Special Unit in

Barlinnie Prison. This was the man who was to become my future husband! The Spirit does indeed move in mysterious ways.

How we met and married is a story in itself—the experience of falling in love in such exceptional circumstances with a man who had survived all that Jimmy had been through in his life, left me feeling that we had been brought together for a purpose which went beyond the two of us. It was wonderful to find such depths of trust and love. Two years after we married Jimmy was eventually released from prison and we decided to establish a centre together in Edinburgh, which we called the Gateway Exchange. We brought together people from different walks of life, many of whom had backgrounds of prison, drug abuse or mental health problems and created a community where the emphasis was on what each individual had to share— their qualities, uniqueness, creative talents and if they could make a good bowl of soup, or help put up a fire escape, they were definitely welcome!

It was moving and sometimes sad to see how difficult it is for those who exist on the fringes of society to find warmth, acceptance and a role or place in life. I became aware that despite our many successes, the barriers within were sometimes more difficult to shift, and more impenetrable than the outer ones. I knew at this point that I needed to look deeper for ways to help, heal and understand those who had been seriously damaged by their life experiences. So many of them existed in inner prisons, with their uniqueness and potential submerged. Yet I knew, because I had seen so much evidence of it, that the human spirit is incredibly resilient and universal. The light is within us all.

By this time I had become a mother, an experience which I will always treasure and which opened me to love in a new and wonderful way. Our two children became a nourishing and important part of our lives. As they grew we felt a need to let go of the centre which had been such a rich learning experience and given us so much as well as helping others. We handed it over and it became the first HIV/AIDS support centre in Scotland. I stepped back into my own career, entering the world of counselling and embarking on a Diploma course in the Person Centred Approach. This is based on a relationship between client and therapist which offers unconditional acceptance, understanding and genuine caring, and allows an individual to naturally unfold and get in touch with their own capacity for healing and growth. In order to help others I had to peel back the layers in myself. As I did so I glimpsed depths which had eluded me before. I began to discover who I was beneath the surface of my life. It was a time of deep inner change as I reconnected with my core.

At a certain point in my training, unexpectedly and out of the blue, I had an experience which cannot be described in words but which suddenly and beautifully opened me to Spirit. This was the beginning of my spiritual path. I learned to meditate, to quieten my active mind and to listen in the stillness to whatever moved me from within—sometimes this would be words, sometimes images, sometimes just a feeling of warmth and of closeness to God. This brought me strength and comfort, but I entered a stormy passage as everything in my life started to change. I faced innumerable tests and challenges. I know that breaking down is what needs to happen in order for the new to emerge, but going through and sticking with this deep inner process has been extremely testing—not only for me, but also for others close to me, particularly my husband and children.

My search for ways of making sense of what had happened led me into the world of transpersonal approaches to therapy. One day a brochure arrived in the post for a new psychosynthesis course starting in Scotland. As I read it, the sky lit up above me with a special radiance and I found myself overwhelmed with emotion. The course was to take place at Newbold House which was close to Findhorn ... and so twenty years after my first visit I was coming back to revisit this community—which, although it is world famous, has not had a particularly high profile in Scotland.

On my first visit to the Foundation I began my exploration at the Universal Hall. Walking into the Visitor's Centre I came across the pictures of Findhorn in the early days and noticed a photograph of Sir George Trevelyan. He was my Father's second cousin and I had of course heard of him through the years. I had hoped to meet him at some point, but by the time I was open and ready for this, he had died. Learning of his death was a source of great sadness to me at the time. However, I remembered thinking that if there was truth in his beliefs that the spirit continues on after death, then perhaps the fact that we couldn't meet physically wouldn't matter so much—he might contact me from the other side! This felt a far-fetched thought at the time, but when I stood looking at his photograph I knew that in some kind of way his spirit had led me here.

I had a strong intuitive feeling of wanting to meet those who had known him and in meditation Eileen Caddy's name came to me. I wrote to her and was astonished to get an immediate answer in which she suggested meeting me after the early morning sanctuary. After the meditation she invited me in for breakfast and a chat. This was the first of several wonderful breakfasts and the flowering of a friendship, which we are both grateful for. Her clarity and honesty have touched me, and also her willingness to share her own personal struggles, which make her as human as the rest of us! She gives me toast and honey and eats the crust while sharing her deep faith in God. She embodies the love which she speaks of and lives this out in a very practical way in the community. Her prayer is for the highest and the best in all situations and for unity, harmony, love and oneness in the community.

Findhorn has a very special place in my life now and I am a regular visitor. My work as a counsellor and psychotherapist, and my family keep me in Edinburgh. I feel fortunate to do the work which I do—I see myself as a companion to people who are committed to their own healing and the often challenging journey of self-discovery, healing and growth. I see this as spiritual work as it frees and releases a person into a deeper trust of his or her own being. It has been an honour and a privilege to facilitate workshops at Newbold House where we have been working with people who are willing to look consciously at death and dying. This has put me in touch with the work of Alanna, which offers support and respite care to those who are terminally ill. This work, which is young in its development at the moment, is one way of offering a valuable service and skills to the wider community.

Many doors have opened for me since I've journeyed back 'home' to Findhorn. It is difficult for me to say in a few words how the community has influenced my life, but there is no doubt that it has. It has opened another dimension for me—almost as if I was living in some kind of bubble before and now I find myself with more expanded and spacious horizons. I have discovered a spiritual community, still resilient after 37 years, addressing the challenges of growth, while safeguarding its roots. I was especially pleased to meet someone who taught T'ai chi to prisoners in the same physical area of Inverness Prison where my husband was once confined in the brutal and notorious cages. This is a miracle! It is in places like this that the spiritual gifts of healing, creativity and love are so badly needed.

The thread, which unites my life with the groundbreaking history of Findhorn, is that the key to open the door to inner growth and freedom is simple, and lies within. We find it in the stillness and in those moments when the heart softens into the warmth, love and inner knowing of the divine flame within. May we all embrace and know our true nature.

I'll end by sharing some words of Peter Caddy that encourages the turning of this inner key:

"There is a world within,
a world of thought and feeling and power,
of light and life and beauty and,
although invisible,
its forces are mighty."

(Reprinted from Peter Caddy's autobiography, 'In Perfect Timing', published by the Findhorn Press).

SARAH BOYLE

F

Intriguing Possibilities

I thoroughly enjoyed my experience week in 1990 although it had not created an awakening in me as it had for some others in my group. I'd already been meditating for several years by then and had been working on my self-development through a number of organisations and so group sharing and loving support were not new to me. Even so, it was a nourishing time and learning about how the Findhorn Foundation worked was interesting.

Towards the end of the week my car was discovered to be leaking what was thought to be oil. It would not start and so I had to arrange for it to be towed to the nearest garage. I was obliged to stay on and so I participated in the week long Departmental Guest Programme.

Towards the end of that week the mechanics had still not discovered what was wrong with the car. As there were no further Foundation workshops that I wanted to do and there was no accommodation for visitors in the Park at that time I was directed across the road to Minton House, a retreat centre that also offered bed and breakfast.

That was where I discovered the Community who were living around the Foundation. Several dozen people, who were in a loose form of association with the Foundation, were living in houses that they had bought or rented in and around Findhorn Village. These people worked locally or ran their own businesses and most of them offered occasional or regular voluntary service to the Foundation whose work they wanted to support.

I had some interesting conversations with these very special people who came from all walks of life and from several places on this planet. I visited some of them in their homes in the attractive Findhorn village. With others I walked along the shore of the glistening Findhorn Bay and watched the little boats bobbing at anchor or scudding over the water, or I strolled with them down the long, beautiful, almost empty beach on the other side of the peninsula.

These enjoyable conversations were very stimulating and opened up some intriguing possibilities in my mind. At the time I was re-evaluating my life and considering the options for my next steps. The main purpose for my visit had been to get a taste of community life Findhorn style.

Whilst I had enjoyed the Foundation workshops I had recognised that the lifestyle in that institution was not one that would suit me and I doubted that the good folks in the Foundation would find this very independent person really suitable for them. However, the idea of having my own home and living my own life whilst being around others who were also working with the ethos of bringing spiritual and high human values into everyday life really appealed to me.

Around an hour after having that realisation the mechanic phoned to say that the car was now working fine and I could drive home. The thought came to me that perhaps I was already there!

I moved to Findhorn a few months later and remained for 18 years. My first project was to create the Friends of Findhorn. This global network was intended to support people around the planet to have a tangible connection with this community and to one another. This was achieved through a quarterly newsletter, The Network News and a regularly updated Directory of the Friends.

I voluntarily co-ordinated this network for 3 1/2 years until it was eventually adopted by the Foundation. It was renamed The Stewards and became part of the Fundraising Department. It eventually became the web-based Global Network connecting thousands of like-minded people.

KAY KAY

Long Way To The Light

I'm sitting in my bedroom
overlooking Findhorn Bay
Cluny Hill in the distance
summer on the way
Blue skies and sailing boats
like a picture in a book

Living one step at a time
putting one foot in front of the other
  it sure feels right
Healing on my mind
been a long way
been a long way to the Light

I'd made it to Manhattan
built myself a nest
I meant to get right back to doing
exactly what I do best;
Plugging in an electric guitar,
leading a band
Well, if you want to give God a laugh
  —tell him your plans!

Summer in the city
wilting in the heat
buzzing up and down to Bearsville
and back to Hudson Street
I learned meditation
and how to visualise –
just breathing, being still
    never felt more alive!

    I spent fall in transit
circling the moon
like a cat on a hot tin roof
like a fiddle without a tune
I found what I was searching for
in Mrs Caddy's book
I had to go there straightaway,
have myself a look

    I flew back to Scotland
anticipation in my bones
the old country welcoming me
like a prodigal coming home
I knelt and kissed the tarmac
in the wild atlantic rain
felt the fiery gaelic blood
    rising in my veins

Living one step at a time
putting one foot in front of the other
    it sure feels right
Healing on my mind
been a long way
been a long way to the Light

    I spent the night in Glasgow
flew to Inverness
I found the Place and at the first
I was not impressed
nobody said hello
the faces left me cold
back then how was I to know
all that would unfold?

I entered the Sanctuary
—heard the voice of a girl
sending out a circle of Light
clear across the world
I shuddered in the Power
like a seedling in a storm
I've been travelling to this place
  Since the moment I was born

  Flew back to New York City
singing the big city blues
the sand of Findhorn Bay
still clinging to my shoes
I tried to restart my life
but the life I knew was gone
I had to let go of everything
but that's another song...

Living one step at a time
putting one foot in front of the other
  it sure feels right
Healing on my mind
been a long way
been a long way to the Light

  So I'm sitting in my bedroom
overlooking Findhorn Bay
Cluny Hill in the distance
summer on the way
I'm watching the sailing boats
bobbing to and fro
—time to hit the road
  the only way I know...

Living one step at a time
putting one foot in front of the other
  it sure feels right
Healing on my mind
been a long way
been a long way to the Light

MIKE SCOTT
Words taken from the album, 'Bring'em all in.'
By kind permission Sony/ATV Music Publishing

F

CHAPTER TWO

BEING THERE

This collection of pieces is intended to give a cross section of the wide variety of activities, philosophies, interests and events that go into making the rich dish of life around Findhorn.

F

Every Leaf is
an Expression of the Divine

The Findhorn Garden is now well over thirty years old and the lives of many have been enriched by their experience of being in this nature-filled environment. Years of caring for and loving the plants, shrubs and trees can be felt in the garden; all it takes is to slow down a little and breathe in the stillness, listen to the light wind blowing in the trees, take in the sunlight filtering through the maturing trees and bushes and let the different scents of pine and delicate spring and summer flowers fill you with their subtle fragrance.

The garden is a stream down which hundreds of guests have travelled, exploring the original impulse that brought the Findhorn Community into being: the connection between spirit, nature and ourselves. The magic of the garden still draws many to come and visit this community. It is here in the garden that the work of balancing nature with humankind takes place most directly. People come looking for contact with their own inner nature and find it in the simple beauty that is reflected back to them as they work.

Expanding our understanding of the interconnectedness and oneness of all life—which embraces both the visible and invisible realms—becomes possible, sometimes for the first time, through our daily communion with nature.

As a garden group, we consciously invite the nature spirits, devas and Pan to work with us each day. By doing this we acknowledge the unseen angelic energies working with each species and welcome them to co-create beautiful, vibrant gardens with us. In slightly different terms, this can be translated as working together with nature, listening and looking to see what seems to enhance the natural flow and form of life, rather than imposing a disconnected idea of what needs to happen.

As the vision of an ecological village begins to take form in our community, landscaping that reflects love and stewardship is becoming an integral part of the work of the gardeners. As we begin to shape the Village Green, the open spaces in the Bag End cluster of houses and the Field of Dreams, the natural contours and existing ecosystem are supported by choices that, where possible, include indigenous trees and shrubs. Wildlife too is considered in the designs.

As part of the ecological village, we built a new and more ecological greenhouse in which each seed is given maximum opportunity to grow with love, warmth and ideal conditions. The greenhouse is part of our new garden centre, which is more visible, more efficient and more available to our visitors as an inspirational and educational resource.

As the gardens become more mature, so the garden group also grows and changes. Marijke, who has worked and focalised in the Park Garden at different times over the last ten years, notices a deepening in the personal interactions of the members of the group: "We are more honest and profound in our sharings, and our love for each other and the garden is heartfelt. This radiates out to enhance the beauty surrounding us. We often sing together at our daily attunements, bringing a real sense of joy into the work we do, and we increasingly carry the awareness that the land is sacred. We often feel honoured and filled with gratitude to have the opportunity to work with so many people in this beautiful place—the gifts they bring are many."

The garden continues to be an integral part of the community and the principles that everything we do is service to God, and that work is love in action, are central to our calling to be here. Throughout the year we take flowers and greenery into the indoor spaces, connecting the inner and the outer. We harvest vegetables from the garden and take them to the kitchen to be prepared and served to the community, bringing us all closer to the natural cycles of planting and harvesting. The community as a whole also recognizes the importance of the natural cycles and it honours these times with celebrations at solstice and equinox, and with full moon meditations.

The vision we hold is that all those who come here may be inspired by the beauty and sacredness of all life forms, that this awareness enhances not only our own thoughts and actions but also those of the people we meet. And that by being conscious custodians of the earth here this awareness will radiate out to the rest of the planet and affect decision-making in the minds and hearts of all people, helping to protect our beautiful planet so that it may be a healthy place for our children and our children's children.

GILL EMSLIE
One Earth

F

Who Can Cook?

It was 1977. During my seven week orientation programme at Cluny I had elected for some unknown reason to do my work shifts in the kitchen, where I was so overwhelmed by the size of everything that I spent the first weeks scrubbing carrots and peeling eggs. This did become rather boring so one day when a pastry was called for to cover an onion pie I volunteered to do it as I knew I could make a really good pastry.

However...I made my pastries with white flour and butter, mixing them to a fine crumble. Now I was presented with brown flour and oil, and vast quantities of them to boot. I added oil to the flour little by little, stirring bravely with a huge wooden spoon, and as time passed the focaliser kept coming to peer over my shoulder anxiously asking if it was nearly ready yet. Eventually as the deadline approached, in desperation I climbed on a stool, poured water into this hateful stuff and used both hands to mix it. Then I slapped it frantically into the trays and it all went into the ovens.

My distress was not over. I felt certain that it would turn out to be inedible and 150 people were about to go hungry and all because of me. I went to my room at the end of the shift not wanting to have to observe everyone's disgust.

Ah well, all things come to an end and so did orientation. On my last shift in the kitchen it was again onion pie on the menu. Who would volunteer to do the pastry? A little chorus said "Katherine must do it! She made such wonderful pastry last time!" I wished that someone had thought to tell me that earlier!

KATHERINE INGLIS

Home is Where the
God of Creativity Dwells

"For the human being, defined by Thomas Aquinas as a being with brains and hands, enjoys nothing more than to be creatively, usefully, productively engaged with both his hands and his brains.
EF Schumacher, Small is Beautiful

I only read those words for the first time a short while ago, but it's as if the truth in them has been bubbling to the surface of my life for years. I had somehow bought into the belief that, to be successful, I had to go to university and then find work that relied mainly, if not entirely, on my intellect, and that to train, say, as a carpenter or a plumber was somehow to tread a lesser path. So to university I went. I did well enough, and even enjoyed it most of the time. But in the jobs that followed I never felt fulfilled. Something was missing.

What I had known since I was a child was that, more than anything I loved using my hands to make things. But I never received enough encouragement or had a strong enough sense of myself to take my creative urge seriously. Not, that is, until I came to Findhorn.

On my first visit, in 1990, the houses and the building programme which inspired me, was in full swing. And this, more than any other single thing, is what drew me back in 1995. After stints in the Park kitchen and Park Maintenance during my student programme the chance arose for me to work on the new Eco-house at Bag End with David Caddy, who has built many houses at Findhorn and in the USA, and so I jumped at the opportunity.

After the time I spent on the building crew I wonder if there is anything more satisfying than building a house and I honestly doubt it. Partly, I think it must be that in building we are responding to an ancient, deep-seated instinct to provide ourselves with shelter—one of our most basic needs. I believe that to deny ourselves this pleasure, this connection with our fundamental selves through the skillful use of our hands is to leave a vital part of ourselves undeveloped, unexpressed.

It would be difficult for me to exaggerate the deep satisfaction I get from the simple act of cutting a length of timber, of mixing and spreading mortar, of cutting and laying terra cotta roof tiles in tidy rows, of nailing a floor of tongue-and-groove pine, of setting out and cutting scarf-joints from freshly milled, salmon-pink Douglas Fir beams. The list is endless. Here dwells the god, not of large gestures, but of manual dexterity, imagination, even sensual pleasures.

Neatly dovetailed with these joys are the frustrations and challenges: the bowed or twisted board, the four-metre floor joist cut two centimeters too short, the missed nail and the hammered thumb, steps taken out of order. Sometimes it seems that for every nail holding up a board, there are two bent ones lying under the scaffolding. Perhaps as much as half of a builder's skill goes into artfully correcting mistakes.

Clearly, my hands could not do this work alone. The scope for planning, making decisions about details not shown in the architect's drawings, efficiency, reduction of waste; not to mention geometry and trigonometry, is enormous. Truly, this is work for hands and brains. Physical agility, good balance, and a certain degree of physical strength come in very handy as well.

I couldn't have asked for a better crew to work with either. Harmony is a word that springs to mind. Scots, English, Canadian, Norwegian, although from varied backgrounds, and not all experienced builders, I think it's safe to say we all enjoy the work, and put a lot of ourselves into it. And I'm happy to report that there has been virtually none of the macho posturing and hair-curling humour that is rife on many building sites.

I appreciate as well that this is not just another house going up, but is another attempt to expand our cluster of energy efficient and environmentally-friendly houses. But if I have a wish about house building—here and everywhere—it is that we find ways to liberate it from the complex, time consuming, and expensive affair it has become. I don't believe any family should have to work for 15 to 20 years, and pay two to three times the house's actual value (due to interest charges) to provide themselves with this basic need.

There is a scene in the film Witness that says it all for me. Scores of neighbours, friends and relatives have come together in a traditional Amish community to raise a barn. It's a gigantic post-and-beam structure that no single farmer would dream of trying to build. And yet there it was. No money was changing hands and food was brought by all. It was potluck on a grand scale. Next year it would be someone else's turn. Can you imagine helping out in that way, not just once, but as part of your way of life? Can you imagine receiving that much help?

Ultimately that is what I would like to see house building return to. It was that way for millennia, all over the world, and still is over most of it. People helping each other, not for profit; but simply because that's what needs to be done.

MICHAEL SHARPE
Network News

Update: Michael's vision of building has not quite happened the way he envisaged (not yet!). The closest we came to this was in the completion stage of one house on the

Field of Dreams. See Chapter 12

ℱ

Away with Words
Just Follow Your Trust

'Truth lies at the bottom of a well', an ancient philosopher pronounced. I don't believe it! I've been there in the dark many times in the six years that I was a Trustee of the Findhorn Foundation. Surely the Trustees hold the record for the longest meetings, the most paperwork and the best camaraderie. Since I resigned I feel simultaneously sad and relieved. Relieved at not having to read the constant flow of minutes, or feeling frustrated when sitting in all day meetings and having little chance to participate in the many groups and activities going on all around me; and sad that I shall not be with my fellow Trustees at their meetings.

Especially when so many things are on the move—the Reinvention proposals for re-organisation, the continuing development of the Eco-village, the Foundation's accreditation by the UN as an NGO, the development of the College, the production of a strategic plan defining sustainability.

But that's not all! The Trustees, encouraged by the experience of other groups in the Foundation, have resolved to set up a system of regular group supervision for themselves. Also it is agreed to invite individuals to become Special Advisors to the Trustees; not to meet as an Advisory Board, but to be available to the Trustees on an ad hoc basis. The first of these is Lawry Gold, whose initiative, skill and involvement in accredited education in the United States and in the Foundation will be a valuable resource. Because of their experience and insights, it was also agreed that former focalisers of the Foundation would be included as special advisors and Judy Buhler McAllister and Craig Gibsone are two such welcome friends, with long term experience of overall and detailed running of the Foundation.

A philosopher, (it wasn't Roger Doudna, but it could have been), said: 'What is right but what we prove to be right? What is truth but what we believe to be truth?' Now is the time to prove and test the truth of those beliefs and re-inventions which have been distilled from the many hours of discussions and the many sheets of written words. So now I say—'Away with words—just follow your trust!'

So what is your trust? Disraeli said: 'The Youth of a Nation are the Trustees of Posterity.' And to complete the following sentence, what do you say: 'The Trustees/co-workers/stewards/RP's/NFA members/ friends and supporters of the Findhorn Foundation are the Trustees of...' ?

My dictionary defines Trust as 'confident expectation, firm belief in reliability, honesty, veracity, justice, consolation, support'. From the same root as other words: true, truth, truce, tryst. Essential for the flourishing of the common weal or commonwealth—the garden of the true, the good and the beautiful. Whilst looking up the word fidelity, I came across FIDO, an acronym for Fog Investigation Dispersal Operation—a device enabling aircraft to land by dispersing fog. Yes, this I believe is an important role of the Trustees, to help the Foundation retain a clear view of itself and its destiny, to help others see clearly the Beauty and Truth of the Creative Spirit at work in hearts, minds and deeds, at play in song and laughter, dispersing the fog which isolates and separates. In trust and truth, in truce and tryst we find that 'all are but parts of one stupendous whole, whose body Nature is, and God the soul.' Upon this Foundation of Limitless Love and Truth, the Community enacts the Divine Comedy of Life.

But I wander. And why not when life is so wanderful. The Trustees were sent an e-mail by Suzanne who was working with the Reinvention group. She was pondering on having more Trust in her life, and wonders whether the Trustees as a group had a role to embody the quality of Trust more deeply in its care of the Foundation. What would this look like? How would it express itself? The Trustees are entrusted by the Charity Commissioners to ensure that the Foundation adheres to its aims and objects and is run in accordance with its legal obligations. Sometimes the Trustees ask Foundation groups to trust it in its decisions, sometimes vice versa and the Trustees are asked to trust. As we follow a move towards creating greater autonomy within groups in the Foundation, as we see the development of the Eco-village and stronger links with Findhorn village, as the NFA explores its own role so our trust is tested within and among each of us. Whom do we trust, what do we trust, how do we trust? So often as a Trustee I felt ignorant, ill-informed, confused, suspicious, impatient, tired and overwhelmed by those same feelings I have linked in to in the Foundation. But equally I have been exhilarated, humbled, inspired, refreshed and moved to laughter and tears by these qualities in my fellow Foundation co-workers.

So, join me in remembering the wisdom of our dearest Eileen, that all is very, very, well. That ancient Greek philosopher was perhaps right after all. How could I not trust him when he said: 'Truth lies at the bottom of a well.' From that I can draw refreshment.

NICK ROSE

F

Memories of a Focaliser

The journey into my focalising the Findhorn Foundation began in my kitchen while I was reading the management minutes in the Rainbow Bridge. The minutes described the ideal focaliser with, you know, wonderful qualities and the final line said, somewhat tongue in cheek, 'We realise what we're describing is a priest-king and would candidates step forward'

I had this incredible sensation in my stomach (that I've learned to pay attention to!) and I knew that although I did not fit the priest-king role, somehow I was being called. Thus the process began and in the Hall on the evening of 23rd January 1992 we had shared our views, meditated and the body of the Foundation was asked if they could support me in this role. A sea of hands surfaced and part of me went into shock. I was moved at the level of support as we were experiencing a time of discord and disharmony. So, a potent moment, given the situation, that we could have a consensus. Thus began the journey! Later I found out that I had stepped into office within minutes of the Community's Saturn return point, so my term could not be other than somewhat eventful!

At the time there was no set term of office and no one asked me, so when Craig Gibsone tuned me into the energy, I asked the Angel. I was told it would be between three and five years.

In my naiveté I thought I knew what my time of office would be about, and to a certain extent it has proved correct. I came into office with a couple of images, and being a Libran my images often come in pairs. One pair consisted of a stage coach driver and an orchestra conductor. Another pair of images behind the first ones were less clear and didn't make sense at the time.

I began to comprehend the second pair as I reached the three-year point. One was of a hospital room with a patient on a life support machine with a figure beginning to pull out the plugs, and the other image was of a midwife helping the birth process. It is only in hindsight that I understand these and what the assignment was that I was asked to undertake. Now, with all that is in process in the Foundation and the Community, they make even more sense to me.

Even though there have always been more women than men here, when I became focaliser, the Management Committee was all men except for the secretary. The board of New Findhorn Directions (the business arm of the Foundation) that I also joined then was all men too, except for the secretary. Within months the secretaries left and were replaced by men and I was then the only woman in two very potent groups of men (no pun intended!). It was challenging and it was fun! The Angels took good care of me and I worked with delightful groups of men who in their own ways welcomed the gifts that came through the feminine principle. I was encouraged to bring those aspects of my being present. Proving that things do come full circle, a few months ago I started laughing in a Management Committee meeting because the only man in the room was the secretary. Both extremes have proved themselves unhealthy and I've learned a lot about the need for both principles to be very actively present in various circles within the Community. Over time I found myself taking on the role and energetic principle that I had seen men carry in Management, becoming more structural, linear and goal oriented. So, because of where I've been privileged to sit I have been taught a lot about that other energetic stream; how it needs to be present and how it has been undervalued and not honoured in our collective body. At a personal level, it's been quite a journey!

When I am asked about my connection with the Findhorn Angel, I'm not even sure how to talk about that connection. For me it's an ongoing almost moment to moment experience. In some ways there are things I do automatically that if I stopped and analysed them I'd realise came from that connectedness; that ability to respond without having to process it through my mind *per se*. I'd say the connection is quite deep, it's not taken for granted but it has become almost "ordinary" and goes through cycles and phases. I believe the connection is always there and always present. There have been times when I couldn't experience it, when times got tough or I would lose the sense of feeling it as a tangible experience. But I never lost faith that this was still true. Over the years, there were times when it was only my faith in this as a concept that kept me going because I wasn't always able to connect with, feel it or experience it in every moment. Leadership is a lonely place.

Throughout these years I've had very powerful experiences of being awakened during the night and having a clear sense it's because I have work to do or some meditating that needs to be done. Consistently it's between two and three o'clock in the morning. It has a very unique quality. At times it felt like someone was literally tapping me on the shoulder, like there was a presence with me in the room that had shaken me awake. Initially, I must say, it was uncomfortable, but now I accept it as part of what I do. But that, plus getting two schoolchildren ready for their day, does rule out 6.30 am meditations in the sanctuary.

I have a spiritual practice, which is virtually daily. What I have not mastered is having it be daily at a consistent time. I go through cycles. There are periods when I'm not able to get to sanctuary at given times and I wrestle with that. So it would be less than honest if I didn't admit that sometimes I don't feel like I embody what I wish 'we' would embody collectively, in terms of my practice being consistent, constant and visible to others.

I am sometimes asked if I have a teacher or guru. I have God! I watch the proliferation and diversity of spiritual practices here and on one level I think it's great because it honours our trust deed, and another part of me doesn't get it! My own particular path is very simple: there is God. God exists within all things and therefore exists within me and so I cultivate my ability to listen and that, I consider, is all I'm required to do. Everything else will follow on from the listening. This, I realise, is essentially Eileen's message, which has been my path too. I haven't felt the need to adopt a particular external teacher.

What holds and sustains me is a deep and abiding sense that I am doing what is required of me by that which I listen to inside myself, that which has pushed me beyond personal limits, personal boundaries. Whether that place inside is the Angel or God, it's what guides me and experience has shown it deserves to be trusted. For me that's the essence of Findhorn that we learn to listen inside ourselves and remain true to that place. It's what I require of myself.

For me there were two outstanding highlights of my tenure. The first was the seven-week tour of America. I was profoundly touched to discover the esteem in which people hold the Findhorn Community. Its very existence, and what it aspires to, does truly offer hope and a dream of what might be, even to those who have never been here. I realized that while it's a privilege to be part of this, it's also a responsibility to be a custodian for these hopes, dreams and inspirations. It was an amazing time. In hindsight I see that because it came at the end of three years of my focalisation it became a benchmark. After that trip life changed for me and the Community and if I go back to the original images I had, I see it was then that I/we began to move into the energy of the second pair of images.

The other highlight is more personal and came while Patch Adams was making one of his visits here, encouraging us to be outrageous. Unannounced and dressed as a washerwoman I abseiled from the lantern inside the roof of the Universal Hall into a Friday night sharing. It was a huge personal edge for me and I enjoyed it immensely—truly a moment of frivolity!

It is around my children that I have the biggest regrets about those five years. They definitely paid a price for their mother occupying this job and it is the area where I am least proud of what I have managed to do. I feel that I simply did not maintain a healthy, wholesome space for them. I wasn't able to draw boundaries around my work that allowed the time the kids deserved, needed or were entitled to. So I don't think Vadawn and Aidan had enough of their mother available to them over that period and I have a deep sadness around that. At head level I can attempt to console myself but it doesn't ease the pain in my heart. I feel ashamed of not having done a better job in this area and this is my clearest commitment for life after Foundation focalisation; to make choices that allow time for a home-life with my children.

I'm incredibly hopeful with regard to the changes and restructuring that the Community is going through, and will continue to go through during the next few years. What's happening is perfect. It's painful, it's difficult, it's scary and more. Yet underneath it all I have the abiding sense that the Angels and other beings have gathered around and are saying "yes!" It's a wake-up call, it's a call back to fundamentals, and it's a call to review what we're doing, why we're doing it and how we're going about doing it. It's a call to many things and it feels like there's no stone being left unturned. It's no accident it started to happen as the Community reached 34 years of age. This is a Christed community, built on the principle of the Cosmic Christ and that archetype is very potent in this energy field. So what happens is that as we pass 33 and head for 34 everything starts to disintegrate. The first 33-year cycle is done. Now is a new beginning and we are empowered to co-create the new. It's very exciting.

The image I work with is of a caterpillar and a butterfly. I have no doubt that the butterfly will emerge, and while there is some danger, I choose instead to focus on the opportunity.

JUDY BUHLER MCALAISTER
Adapted from an article in One Earth

It Matters

It doesn't matter if you chose
The wildest sea or the stillest pond

It doesn't matter if you chose
The raging wind or a gentle breeze

It doesn't matter if you chose
The tallest mountain or the smallest stone

It doesn't matter if you chose
A furious passion or the subtlest love

It doesn't matter if you chose

A life on Earth or a life elsewhere

But it matters that you chose.

JO MULLEN
*Jo wrote this for Maia, the first person to receive
care from the Findhorn Alanna Hospice project.*

F

The Life in a Day of Hilary

Seven fifteen am, the brain wakes up to the sound of the alarm and gets the body moving. And so to one of my favourite times of the day: breakfast. Hot tea, our caravan robin outside the kitchen window enjoying the bread I have put out for him, and my Course In Miracles lesson for the day. Lesson number 303, which seems like a miracle in itself after many initial attempts to get past lesson 14.

The Course feels like an old friend now, like Eileen's guidance. So sane and sensible, always so relevant. I take my thankfulness to sanctuary and join Eileen and the Community for our morning meditation. I feel really privileged to have her in my day to day life.

Afterwards, walking through the garden to our garden group meeting place, I look around and note what work needs to be done this week and enjoy the colours, smells, sounds and history of this amazing place. Trees that Peter planted, Scottish heathers, wind chimes from Nepal, a thorn bush from Glastonbury—all coexisting here, together with people from all over the world.

Today is Monday and a first meeting with the guests who will work with us this week. So we each tell our name and country and how we are feeling, before we close our eyes and attune to the garden, to nature, and invoke the Devas and Nature Spirits to work with us and help us to know what the garden wants. Monday is compost day. Some go off to the stables in Tipsy (our tipper truck) to get manure. Some go off to the beach to get seaweed. The rest start chopping, shredding, mixing and turning the other ingredients. And watch out for Sandy's bees in the Tree Nursery—sometimes they don't like us working so near the hives.

As we work, the sharing begins in two and threes—what drew each of us here, telling of home, of life here, of jobs, of family. Getting to know each other, relaxing, settling. By the end of the morning the hands we hold for the closing attunement, to bless and release our work, are already beginning to feel more familiar.

My overwhelming feeling over lunch in the CC is gratitude. Having spent many years doing the whole range of chores—planning, shopping, cooking, cleaning, career, bringing up a family— this lunch is just wonderful. Someone planned, shopped and cooked for me while I gardened. Big luxury. And it looks and tastes good. Bliss. And I get to eat with friends, with hugs freely available if the need arises.

Then time to make some music with three keen singer friends. We all get really exhilarated by the end of the session when the voices and the piano are well warmed up and in tune. Beautiful harmonies and melodies fill the room. Wow. I hum my way back to the garden and to more new guests in the afternoon.

In general, the afternoon work tends to be more gentle—maybe a group project to weed, dead-head, prune or plant bulbs, depending on the season. Working together helps to keep the energy up, especially if the weather has turned dull, wet or windy, or if we are experiencing, Scottish style, all four seasons in one day! In the winter we work straight through to 4.30 pm and make our way home in the dark.

Today I find myself at a loss to know how to start on a patch of root-bound earth. There seems to be very little soil to nourish a great web of fine intertwined roots, with nothing on top. And, as often happens, I begin to see how the work I have chosen serves as a metaphor for what I am experiencing in other aspects of my life. In this case, it's me holding onto some old patterns of behaviour which are not nourishing me. I begin to look at the options of adding more soil and/or clearing out the old growth, and possibly introducing new plants. And what that could mean in my life.

It's 5 pm and home to a deep, hot, bubbly bath with my book and a cup of tea. More bliss—very necessary as I am on KP (kitchen cleanup) after supper this evening. Our KP focaliser helpfully reminds us that this is an opportunity to serve with love. Then she gets us psyched up with some boogie music while we work.

Winding down time for me is late evening. With my journal, a bit of TV, and then a book. Eleven pm. Wrapped around by the Community, but in my own space, in that special twilight time before sleep. Mmmm.

HILARY MILLICHAMP
Network News

Experience Week

Saturday morning, Experience Week
I'm so nervous I can hardly speak
Arrive at Cluny Hill, half past ten
Almost turned and went home again.

My focaliser showed me my room
Like she was consigning me to my doom
What am I doing here? What's going on?
Who are these people? What are they on?

Here comes my room-mate, he sure looks weird
With black hair and a big fuzzy beard.
Met the rest of the group after lunch
What a strange and motley bunch
What a strange and motley bunch

Sunday morning I'm feeling bad
Enjoyed the dancing but now I'm sad.
Things feel different, I don't know why
Feelin' lonely, wanna cry.

Monday afternoon, I've learned everybody's names
We all go down to the ballroom to play some games
Something happened I can hardly describe
Changed my feelings, changed my life.

Tuesday morning, with a Hoover in my hand
Cleaning out the dining room,
beginning to understand
Tuning in, tuning out
Startin' to see what Findhorn is all about.

Wednesday morning in the winter sunshine
Down at Cullerne garden everybody's feeling fine
In this wonderful place, as smooth as a dream
Eleven strangers have become a team

Thursday morning, at a quarter past three
I'm wide awake in the Sanctuary

Opening myself to the love and the light
Thanking God for steering me right.

So now it's Friday, almost time to go home
And back into the big wide world I must roam
But I'll take it with me, every single thing
Send it out with every song I sing.

So that's the tale of my Experience Week
It was beautiful. It was unique.
It made me friends and it opened my heart
This isn't the end, it's just the start!

MIKE SCOTT
'Experience Week Song' Words by MIKE SCOTT
With kind permission Sony/ATV Music Publishing.

F

A Tribute to a Grand Old 'Lady'

The Community Centre located in The Park is of the busiest places 'on campus'. Since the earliest years it has always been thus. If you wish to find someone for a specific reason or just need someone to talk to, head for the Community Centre, or CC as it is affectionately called. It is here that we serve meals twice a day to guests and those who live here. At lunch or supper there can be up to 250 people, and during the day different groups meet at the CC to take their tea or to have scheduled or impromptu meetings. I can't think of a time of day when there isn't at least a dozen folk milling about. It is certainly known as the 'heart' of the community.

I'll tell you a little of the history of the CC by quoting from the book, *The Faces of Findhorn.* Peter Caddy wrote:

"In the beginning of 1970 there were only ten people in the Community, so we were really surprised when Eileen received guidance one day that we were to build a Community Centre with a kitchen to serve 200 people. It didn't make sense. Why should we build a Community Centre for 200 when we were only ten in number? We had no money, but we went ahead in faith, and all the materials manifested in perfect timing. The Community Centre was completed in six weeks. That year the community grew from ten to forty-five people, and we had hundreds of visitors. We would never have been able to accommodate these people had we not manifested that building by going ahead in faith. Within a year the Community had outgrown the dining room and we had to add on an extension."

53

For the next twelve years the CC remained as it had been originally built. However, just as our need to improve our housing situation increased, so did our need to create a more 'comfortable' space in which to prepare food. Although this kitchen was designed to cook for 200 people, it was also used for washing the dishes and pots and pans afterward, it also contained a small storeroom for people to get their essentials for breakfasts. So, in 1982 the kitchen itself was remodelled and by removing a couple of interior walls it was expanded so that we have the present kitchen today.

As the demand became greater the dining area was extended to meet that need. In 1987 a major building project created a beautiful circular extension to the CC that is two-storeyed, with the upstairs being a pleasant place to sit and meet or just view the magnificent Findhorn Bay. The downstairs eating area was designed for more intimate meals, with the idea that this would be a 'quieter' dining environment.

The Community Centre is a unique place as it plays a central role in embracing a much wider community than just the Foundation and its educational programmes. Everyone living nearby, whatever their connection to the Foundation, feels that this is 'their' Centre, too. It is really a miracle that the kitchen can produce meals for so many folk and that there always seems to be 'just enough' room. It's a bit of a madhouse, though.

Imagine this scenario: The kitchen and the group that takes care of the CC begin their day at 9 am with meal preparation and 'homecare' happening respectively. At about 10:30 am different work departments and individuals arrive for their morning tea (which the CC crew have prepared for them). The Centre is vacated by these folk at about 11 am and the place is tidied up ready for lunch at 12:20. At this time, the whole of the Community descends-this could be up to 250 people! Lunch is served and eaten in about one hour. By this time, clean-up (KP) is already well underway and needs to be finished by 2 pm, when the next cooking crew comes in to prepare the evening meal to be ready by 6:00!

During meal preparation the CC crew is again cleaning the building, arranging flowers, etc. All through the day people are coming in to get their much needed 'cuppa'. The supper cleanup crew begin at about 6:30 and they usually finish by about 7:45.

On many nights at 8 pm there is some kind of meeting that the Centre is used for, or guests might use the space for informal gatherings. At about 10:30 pm the nightporter will come to lock up the building and put it to bed until the next morning. Occasionally the CC is used for a disco and then closing time is much later. I wonder, sometimes, how this wonderful old lady of a building does it.

LOREN STEWART
One Earth

Madsummer Mindness

Summer: The season of feasts and fruitful mellowness.

A sub-etheric buzz resonates in the Foundation as June shades into July. The Universe, I suppose, has its silly season too as it watches our poor deluded earthbound souls whirling dervish-like around the planetary orbit. Somewhere beyond Earth's point of perigee, just where the gravitational force of the Sun nearly drags us down for good, the Universe playfully applied the Laws of Physics. Our orbital velocity, having increased on our plunge into the heart of a towering Solar Prominence, now carries us back off into the outward journey to apogee and the whole rotating spectacle of what we call seasons.

The Sun of course gets all spotty and in a terrific huff ejects massive flares and solar winds which over-excite our depleted ozone layer and play hell with the Archers on Radio Four long-wave. The Universe laughs quietly to him-or-herself.

And you may think that the gentle zephyrs of Findhorn would be unaltered. Alas, no. Through the magical portal (known to the Armed Forces as the Kinloss Window) in the otherwise dreadful British weather, the heat-crazed solar brainstorms beam down undiminished on the tranquillity of the Foundation and totally disrupt it.

There is a pandemonic urge amongst many to escape at this time. These are the ones who truly walk in wisdom. However, those left behind to hold the fort do so with an equally pandemonic urge to act as if nothing has changed. But it has changed unutterably. The solstice is over. The wise ones have departed. Everything is left to be done and there are few of us left to do it.

In the Park new buildings spring up like new shoots in the fresh rain of Summer. Here is one way of demonstrating that someone is doing something. At odd hours of the day small groups of people in overalls cluster together and attune, sometimes with each other, sometimes with the orientation of architectural drawings or with the arcane meanderings of drains and pipework—sometimes with success.

Scotland is a sea of tourists. In the Park it is true that the tourists are more spiritual but they are no less invasive. People turn up in this well ordered haven of peace wearing the spiritual equivalent of knotted hankies on their heads. They are taking photographs outside the Phoenix Shop. (That's my son and my co-parent Zabeena and that's my psychotherapist Olaf with his complete works of Carl Jung and his Zen one-hand-clapping-machine under his arm.) They are doing T'ai Chi (or is it T'ai mai shu?) on the runways to the detriment of passing 2CVs. Driving to your caravan past the earth moving equipment and breeze blocks you are dazzled by Rap-attack Bermuda shorts, day-glo T-shirts and MC Hammer outsize baggies. Cool-dudeness stalks the sanctuaries like a spectre with shades.

Even under the cool eaves of the Helios Cafe there is no escape. It takes several minutes now to queue for a bowl of soup and a giant crusty. Outside in the sun the air vibrates with the sound of people earnestly in pursuit of Truth through the al fresco eating experience. Some of them are so keen they are trying to pass some of their Spare Truth to others. All this at lunch!

"have you ever tried Gestalt cream buns? They have a surprising way of filling the emptiness of spirit you get after a lifetime of."

"is this your first time here? Yeah? I've been coming here since 1969. Since then I have travelled to seventeen different countries in the Third World, become a Methodist-Yoga Minister and I can scratch my left ear with my right foot."

"pardon, did you say 'OM'?"

"I now practise Retro Being, a technique in which you rediscover all the things you discovered were dreadful about life. You need a blanket, a carpenter's mallet and a two-litre bottle of Don Cortez."

"what's Lemon Verbena? A drink? Is it like Ribena? No? Gi' us a Coke."

Someone is standing on my toe and asking me with a breathless, love-filled heart if this seat is free. It is not occupied but enslaved by its devotion to the human fundament, I reply. But the sense doesn't survive translation. I feel like all those other summer outcasts on the pier at Clacton-on-Sea or Cleethorpes. I have lost all charity. I am rude, hot and on the verge of spiritual disintegration.

I stare desperately across a seething landscape of heads, pigtails, ponytails, afros, smiles and embraces melting together in the humid heat. My sanity is beginning to wane. Suddenly, through the crowd I see a familiar face. It's Jim! Old Guru Jim we used to call him back in the squat in Earl's Court. My God, he hasn't changed a bit. Well, less hair, more width.

"Hi Jim.....what brings you here?"

"come every summer, what about you Brian?"

"yeah, well I'm into Instinct Gratification Therapy my therapist thinks I have a great soul if only I could find it."

"oh."

"yeah, I do a Reawakening Maleness Drum-Bashing twice a week, to y'know, get back to the essential man I didn't become."

"no"

"hey try some herb tea: its Strangulated Nettle Root and Vine Shreddings. Mmmh, it's delicious and it'll help your alopecia."

"thanks."

'this sixties-style Batik head-band is great for keeping me cool. Hey, where did you get those neat shades? Gee that sun is hot."

BRIAN HILL
From the series 'Making Light' in One Earth

Love Centered Life

One day late in August 1999, I was down by the Findhorn River where I had taken a Reiki class for our tea break/celebration. I raised my cup to toast our progress and heard the words, "Here's to love centered life" flow past my lips. Aware that I was also a songwriter, my student innocently remarked, "What a great title for a song!" Before retiring that evening, I decided to play with that phrase and see what might come of it. As soon as I connected to the first line, I realized that this song not only was for Eileen Caddy, but that I was writing it on the eve of her 82nd birthday. I had the great pleasure of presenting it to her the next day at her birthday celebration in the Community Center! I love how life is so full of wonderful surprises to share.

There's the lady in white, she lights up the night
She's leading the way to a new understanding
She is patient and kind, keeping fledglings in line
When they're arrogant, stubborn or over-demanding

In her love centered life,
following guidance whenever she
  knows it
In her love centered life, whatever her feeling, she honestly
  shows it
In her love centered life, searching for truth so she can fully
  expose it
In her love centered life, she tells me she never regrets that she
  chose it
Though the road has been long and she hasn't felt strong
She kept placing one foot square in front of the other
God has shown her the way to stay centered each day
In the love that is shared with her sisters and brothers

In her love centered life, following guidance whenever she

knows it
In her love centered life, whatever her feeling, she honestly
shows it
In her love centered life, searching for truth so she can fully
expose it
In her love centered life, she tells me she never regrets that she
chose it

For it's been quite a ride learning God is inside
And our power is there when we're ready to choose it
We can never go wrong when our spirit is strong
With the power of love and the courage to use it

In a love centered life, following guidance whenever we know it
In a love centered life, whatever our feeling, we honestly show
It
In a love centered life, searching for truth so we can fully
expose it
In a love centered life, she's shown us we'll never regret that we
chose it
Love centered life, love centered life.

NANCY JANE SMALL
Lyrics by NANCY JANE SMALL © *1999*
Taken from the CD "Spirit Through the Heart"

CHAPTER THREE

ARTS AND CELEBRATION

*This Community is richly blessed with artists of all disciplines.
There are potters, painters, dancers, designers, photographers, puppeteers,
and musicians of all kinds. Sharing these talents with one another is an
important part of Community life. As is celebrating together, whether it
is birthdays, weddings, religious festivals, equinoxes or the solstices.*

The Circle Turns and the Singer Sings

I arrived to live at the Findhorn Foundation just before the summer
solstice. This is a particularly powerful time here in the north of Scotland;
for two weeks the sun hardly seems to set and all the light and energy make
it difficult to sleep. As I sit writing this in an early August which is already
autumn, I am aware how precious that midsummer time is, before the all
too rapid turn of the season.

The year I arrived, the solstice was also full moon and the first night of
my Experience Week. The moon was exceptional—huge, golden and
hanging low on the horizon. Expectantly, we gathered at Pineridge for a
midsummer bonfire complete with chanting and dancing. Before I came to
the Findhorn Community I had been involved in organising many wild and
creative celebrations with live music. I had also begun, with others, to play
live music for sacred dance sessions—so now I was amazed and
disappointed to discover we were going to do our sacred dancing around

60

the bonfire to tape-recorded music.

There and then I vowed that at future celebrations people would dance to live music.

It did not take me long to team up with other local musicians and form what we called The Ceilidh Band. ('Ceilidh' is a Gaelic term meaning 'a gathering with music, songs and stories'.) Over the years we have come together as a group to play English and Scottish dance tunes, sacred/circle dance music and contemporary songs; and to teach dances and tell stories. We have played at weddings, concerts, celebrations and many home ceilidhs around the fireside. We have also, ironically, made two tapes of sacred dance music!

Our aim has been to encourage other people to sing, dance and play. To that end, band member Barbara Swetina organises regular singing events in the community and she also runs a children's orchestra at our local Moray Steiner School. I offer voice workshops and choirs. One summer our work came to fruition in a glorious week-long Midsummer Festival based around sacred dance, which included Taizé devotional singing, Sufi Universal Peace Dances and African songs and dances. Seven years ago, during the last sacred dance festival held here, only recorded music was played, but this time, ninety per cent of the music was live.

During the week we organised a participants' orchestra (or scratch band) under the guidance of Bill Henderson, a musician we had met at a dance camp in Wales. I was quite nervous about how this would work—or if indeed anyone would come—but in the event the band had fifteen people; Festival guests, children from the Steiner School, local community friends, and members of The Ceilidh Band. There were recorders, guitars, percussion instruments, flutes, a bassoon, fiddle, piano, accordion, bagpipes, even some Romanian pan pipes, and we played for one whole evening of dancing.

It was my dream come true: we demonstrated that in one week we could put together an orchestra with people who did not usually play in a band. And similarly, we formed a choir to sing songs for sacred dancing.

The sacred dance tradition is well established at the Findhorn Community. In 1976 Bernhard Wosien arrived here with some European circle dances, some choreographed meditation dances and a vision—to revitalise the sacred element in the folk dance tradition, which he felt had died out in parts of Europe. He wanted to get people dancing again.

His idea fell on fertile ground and the Findhorn Foundation Sacred Dance Department evolved under the guidance of community member Anna Barton. The folk dances and meditation dances that were taught here always emphasised that the Earth can be healed as we dance. The dances spread, more were brought over from Europe, and in England the term 'circle dance' was coined in an attempt to demystify the dance and make it more accessible. Dance camps sprang up, people danced in circles under the sun, under the stars, around bonfires and increasingly they danced to live music. Musicians and singers were inspired by the excitement of the dance to tackle Bulgarian bagpipe tunes, Middle European 7/8 and 11/8 rhythms and get their tongues around Armenian and Romanian lyrics.

My husband, Rory, one of these extraordinary musicians, delights in playing weird and wonderful musical instruments, always seeking an 'authentic' sound. At present he is perfecting Bulgarian tunes on the Irish bagpipes. I too love to collect and sing songs from the Balkans, Russia, Israel and Greece, feeling the essence of the cultures carried in them. I see the present interest in playing and singing the folk music of these countries as a celebration of individuality and also as one more step towards European unity. On a personal level I feel that by singing all of these songs I am bringing together and integrating many previous incarnations.

At many creative sharings here in the Universal Hall, people get up and sing their songs and play their music, and what strikes me time and time again, is that it is not the excellence of the musicianship that touches me, but the feeling that comes through with the song.

Similarly, as folk musicians we practise the art of communication —the rapport between the musicians and singers and their relationship to the audience is what inspires me. It is this connection that makes the special magic happen, not the technical excellence of the music, though that has its place and I am not saying that a band should not work to make their presentation as fine an offering as they can give.

A big inspiration for me at our recent Midsummer Festival was working with Colin Harrison and Anne Monger. Just the two of them, with guitar and two voices, often play for dance sessions, and their aim is to make dance readily available to people by showing them how easy it is to have a good dance session with simple live music. They teach dancers to sing the choruses of sacred dance songs and to imagine there are violins, saxophones, bouzoukis etc. playing with them—and it works!

Colin joined our festival band as a drummer and, for me, was the essential member of the band, the link between us and the dancers' feet. This has taught me that two of the main ingredients for good dance music are simply rhythm and enthusiasm.

Colin also likes to tell this story: An anthropologist went to visit a tribe to record them doing one of their traditional dances. Later, the anthropologist asked one of the dancers if he would dance again to the tape recording, to make sure that he had written the steps down correctly. The dancer listened to the recording, tried a few steps, and said, "It's no good! I can't dance! That machine can't see me!"

The difference between dancing to a machine and dancing with musicians is unqualifiable but very tangible.

The Midsummer Festival was a truly wonderful and inspiring event, from the sublime Adorate, the song that Thomas Aquinas sang just before he died, played on harp and lyre; to the passionate and gutsy Misirlou; or the jazz piano and clarinet version of Chekassia Kfula. Colin and Anne led us in a session of African dancing and singing which almost raised the roof off the Universal Hall. Afterwards it felt as if every cell in my body had been washed clear and filled with light.

KATE H O'CONNELL
One Earth

℉

The Seasons I am Part of...

Within the changing seasons we can see mirrored our own lives. Scottish tradition tells us that when Beira, the Hag Queen of Winter, grows weary and old she must drink by the first light of dawn from the Well of Eternal Youth. Thus is she transformed into Bride, the peerless Queen of Summer. This transformation can only take place when day and night are equal in length. Should Beira miss this opportunity, we are told, she will crumble into dust. The power of the well is only available to those who are attuned to the forces of nature and recognise the time to act.

It is the function of seasonal festivals to remind us that we are responsible for the well-being of our world. Our every action makes a difference and must be considered. Those who live close to the earth, like the Kogi Indians of Colombia, who consider themselves the 'Guardians of the Heart of the World', still remember this when they say:

We have not forgotten the old ways
How could I say that I do not know how to dance?
We have forgotten nothing!
We know how to call the rain.
If it rains too hard we know how to stop it.
We call the summer.
We know how to bless the world and make it flourish.

They do this not just for themselves but for the benefit of all people. Ochwiay Biano, a chief of the Taos Pueblo, once said to Carl Jung, "If we were to cease practicing our religion, in ten years the sun would no longer rise. Then it would be night forever."

Within the Findhorn Foundation Community we celebrate a wide diversity of seasonal festivals, ranging from the Solstices and Equinoxes to Burn's Night, the Full Moon and the Community's Birthday. Although no one group or person is responsible for all these events, a certain form and rhythm of celebration can be discerned, with different individuals and groupings being drawn to particular events.

Two of the functions that Joseph Campbell ascribed to mythology are that it must "waken and maintain in the individual a sense of wonder and participation in the mystery" as well as fulfill the sociological function of "validating and maintaining whatever moral system and manner of life customs may be peculiar to the local culture."

Over the last five years, a loose network of creative artists have been inspired to create events rooted within the Celtic tradition. These have taken place within the Universal Hall at the heart of the Findhorn Foundation, at Minton House overlooking Findhorn Bay, in Cullerne Garden amidst the growing vegetables and on the dunes and nature wilderness that stretches from the Foundation to the sea. Through song, dance, story and music, we seek to create new life in the land and within our community.

The four great Celtic fire festivals of Imbolc, Beltane, Lughnasadh and Samhain occur at the very beginning of each season. At Beltane on May 1st. we invoke the fertility of summer by leaping over the fire as high as the crops should grow. In the Maypole dance, the ribbons weave the old patterns of the Tree of Life which link us to the other world of spirit. The tree at the centre of our circle responds to the dance by becoming more alive.

Tarthang Tulku describes the importance of music in Buddhist ceremonies where "sounding the drum symbolises spreading the dharma (teaching) throughout the universe. The music is to attract the attention of the deities and give them pleasure. Finally you give your prayerful message and ask that all living beings be protected."

At the Findhorn Foundation we often close our meditations and events by radiating out the energy we have created as a blessing on the local community, our country and, finally, the world. In our seasonal festivals we often use prayers adapted from the Gaelic, which were collected together in the *Carmina Gadelica* at the turn of the century. The following was recited at the close of our Samhain evening:

*May the blessed angels keep guard around our community this
    night.
A circle, sacred, strong and steadfast
That will shield our soul-shrine from harm.
Protect us from every distress and danger,
Encompass our course over the ocean of truth.*

The festival of Samhain stands directly opposite *Beltane* and marks, on November 1st., the beginning of winter. As we enter the season of decay, it is traditional to honour our ancestors and food was always left out in the home on retiring for the night. The ancestors were considered to have knowledge of the future and in some districts of Scotland it was the practice to place a stone by the fire for each person in the household. If by morning any stone had moved, it meant that person was destined to die within the year.

Divination, as one of many ways in which we listen to the earth speak, was widely practised at *Samhain*. It was considered that at this time the veil between the worlds grows thin and knowledge of the future may be obtained. Through meditation and dreams we can access the wisdom of the earth which speaks to us in the dark nights of winter. "In the beginning of all things, wisdom and knowledge were with the animals….through them and from the stars and the sun and the moon, we shall learn." This truth, passed on to Natalie Curtis by Chief Leakots-Kesa of the Pawnee people, teaches us how to listen through the winter months. If we are lucky, animals will come to us in our dreams and speak to us. As winter comes, the Pleiades return to the night sky and their story told around a fire brings their light closer to us: the sparks ignite our inner fire and lead us deeper into the dark mystery, trusting that in darkness there is light.

At *Imbolc* on February 1st. we celebrate that light on Bridget's feast day. Bridget, whose name appears in many forms, is the guardian of the hearth fire, and her light cannot be extinguished no matter how violent or destructive a storm may become. For countless generations, her flame was kept alight within her sanctuary at Kildare in Ireland. Today it is our responsibility to tend her flame and express it through healing, creativity and right action in the world.

Bridget's feast day is a call to dedicate ourselves to creating a new spring in the world. Growth begins with the gathering together of people in community. At the Foundation the *Imbolc* celebration follows on from the Community's internal conference when we review our past year and affirm new directions for the future. The celebration of *Imbolc* allows us to stand in the presence of spirit and know in truth that what comes to us is what we need.

The festival of *Lughnasadh* on August 1st. falls at a time when many community artists are away at the Dance Camp in Wales. This meeting place brings a fertile harvest to all and indeed it has long been traditional to celebrate *Lammas* with a great fair that would bring people together from far and wide. Dance Camp Wales was created by a group of Sacred Circle Dancers who trace their lineage, as does Sacred Dance at the Foundation, back to Bernard Wosien, who described the human being as "a worshipper with wings". He goes on to explain that, "In dancing we can get the wings. Our dance should be our prayer, not only in the stepping of the *andante* but also in the joyful leaps of the *allegro vivo*. I have been greatly concerned to teach at Findhorn those dances which reveal and express this sense of worship through form and symbol"

At Midsummer, the Findhorn Foundation has a week-long Sacred Dance Festival, which draws dancers, singers and musicians from all over the world. On Midsummer night, upwards of one hundred and fifty people gather in the Universal Hall, spiraling around the musicians and massed choir. Joy and exuberance is mixed with deep meditation to create an evening of rare delight. As we leave the Hall to process to the beach where the Midsummer bonfire will be lit, the sun is still bright in the sky. It will not set until 11.30 pm. As the sun sets, we light the bonfire with prayers and blessings for the world. Then with drums, stories and chants we stay awake through the shortest night, for, as tradition tells us, those who sleep on Midsummer night, will be sleepy through the rest of the year. All night we can see the glow of the sun on the horizon as it makes its short passage beneath the waves. In the distance dawn begins to lighten the mountaintops. We can, perhaps, begin to understand the Navajo chant, which says:

The mountains I become part of it.
The herbs, the fir tree, I become part of it.
The morning mists, the clouds, the gathering waters, I become
 part of it.
The wilderness, the dew parts, the pollen,
I become part of it.

PETER VALLANCE
One Earth

Sound Progress

My whole body is singing, tears stream down my face, I have no way of expressing how it is. There is a deep, deep sense of stillness in me, all of me tingles with joy , I feel spread out, I touch the stars. It is silent but the silence is filled with echoes, with music, with harmonies, moving round and in me like waves of the sea without the water. My heart is filled with feelings with no names.

I am standing in a half light, high above the dancers in the Universal

Hall at the Findhorn Foundation, together with eight other people from the choir. There are another eight singers across the other side of the hall. We have just finished singing a piece of music made in heaven called *Seraphim*, a sixteenth century piece by Gallum. There are eight parts to this piece for two choirs, the parts interweave producing a million different harmonies. I will never forget this moment. The setting is vivid in my mind: The choirs standing in the half light, Barbara our leader dressed in blue, and on the floor below the dancers in two circles weaving between themselves, then side-stepping, moving slowly and elegantly, bending down and rising up, arms outstretched, turning in unison, in time with our voices.

It felt as if all the angels were singing and dancing with us, the music ethereal, the dancers angelic, gone the anxiety of knowing the steps or coming in at the right time, the music poured over us, liquid light. In the distance I heard the applause but I was transfixed, way off, imbued in a bubble of beauty, reluctant to return to earth. Filled with deep cleansing love and joy. Complete.

This is just one evening of our annual Sacred Song and Dance Festival here at the Foundation. We have spent the week singing, dancing and playing dance music, using music from different places and different periods of time.

I have had this experience before, last year when we sang a Russian Mass *Tibie byom*. I am filled with gratitude to be here, to actually live at Findhorn. I have been here seven years and despite the many demands, the busy life and the weekend shifts, I still love being here. What an opportunity, what a music school! We sing Sacred songs every morning in a circular sanctuary, dedicated to Nature. This is a small, delightful building, which has a turf roof, and a design of the sun and the path of the moon in its floor. Afterwards there is a daily silent meditation in the main sanctuary.

We have several talented musicians who share their skills freely with us. They teach us to sing and dance and play music from our hearts. We are often asked to sing for weddings, celebrations, festivals, conferences and as part of some workshops, so we get lots of practice at performing in a supportive uncritical environment. My confidence has increased beyond bounds.

I came here knowing I enjoyed singing but I couldn't read music, didn't understand harmonies. Now I lead groups large and small at the drop of a hat. I look back gratefully over this time and see my gentle, safe and loving progress.

CLARE CUMMINGS
Connections magazine

The Pursuit of Beauty

I remember when I was a little boy, in my family's suburban house, I was watching television. The programme was a performance of a dance: a farm, a preacher, a wedding. The ritual taking place was joyful, then solemn. It reflected the waning weekend that was that Sunday. A time out of time. It wasn't go-to-school time or come-infor dinnertime. I remember that I physically felt this performance and the feeling was from the bottom to the top. It stayed with me, this feeling of elevation. The work was *Appalachian Spring* by the pioneer modern dancer Martha Graham, and the music by Aaron Copland. It was different from the chill-up-the-spine that I would get singing my country's national anthem or seeing a big marching band, a chill which always embarrassed me but rather a quiet and eye-opening happy/sadness.

With this pleasurable and out-of-time reaction, I recognised that there were two worlds of feeling: the pedestrian and the elevated and with that it became clear to me that there were two results of human endeavour: artefact and art.

Again as a child, and again in my small world in front of a television, I watched the opera star Maria Callas in her dressing room abruptly turn toward the camera, slapping down her mascara, "People work all day", she said, "at jobs they hate. They come to the opera to hear Beauty."

And as a grown-up, busy at work, someone invited me to watch a video during lunch break. I brought my lunch and watched. It was Billie Holiday's last performances. It was entertaining but at one point she alone was lit on a black stage as she sang *Strange Fruit*, a song about lynched blacks in the south, like fruit hanging from a tree. Her last note of that song cut through me in a way I could not have anticipated. I could not move. I could not eat I could not cry. My sandwich stayed in my lap while the busy world of work went on outside. I had never known a silence like that.

I draw and paint, and have done since I drew my toys as a boy. I make pictures of souls; beautiful souls and I don't paint alone.

Some years ago, I needed to make something more than what I knew. After a number of years of self-portraits, painting friends and acquaintances and hired models, I had become bored. I shared an office with a woman who seemed like such a strange package: shaped like a football player, misanthropic and ultra-right wing politically who always left work at mysterious hours for mysterious reasons. I asked her, since she was a sculptor, conceptual albeit, if she knew any beautiful souls that she could send my way to paint. Beside the unusual package, she seemed so spiritually inclined, in fact, she had in a drunken state once confided in me that she was 'born again'. As a secular Jew, this mystified me.

The souls did start appearing. She sent me men and women from nearby and from far-off corners of Staten Island. (I lived in Brooklyn at the time). The most incredible people: a woman who had recently come out of an institution after having tried to take her life and had come back to sanity only through her newly adopted spiritual path, a man who had survived terrible beating and abuse from within his family also coming slowly back to life, an actress who lived only from day to day on the barest of means but nonetheless pursued her art happily. Many souls, beautiful souls! All so similar in their 'deaths' and so illuminated in their resurrections.

After two years of meeting such extraordinary souls and making paintings of them, they decided together to tell me that they were all alcoholics recovering in Alcoholics Anonymous, and that they had all come close to death and were all saved by God, the higher power. I, an atheist at the time, was moved by all their stories. They became my family, my family that painted the world with meaning when I had seen none. They gave me hope and a new philosophy for my life.

I began to see, in my painting, that the harder I tried the less in the way of beauty I accomplished. I couldn't understand this. I had always believed, "Try, Push, Do, Make—and I will make it". But this had stopped. I began to invite the people I was painting to see themselves as collaborators in the work of art: to ask for their comments and criticism, but more to let the conversation, whether spoken or unspoken, become the subject of the painting. I found that I needed to, to some degree, fall in love with my collaborator and let the atmosphere of love drive and carry the painting.

I first visited Findhorn from New York in 1990, not knowing anything about it but liking the name. Kathryn, my sweetheart, had brought home a book, about Findhorn, wrongly placed in the fairy tale section of the Brooklyn Public Library (She was researching for her elementary school class on art from classic fairy tales). Within minutes of seeing this book, I knew I'd be living there. During the week that I spent at Findhorn, I told no one that I was an artist. I wanted to be seen only as a man working in the garden, sharing my feelings in a group, blending into all the work that needs to be done to help the community function. But for some years, I had been itching to find an integrated way to live, where there was no need any more for the words 'Religion, culture, art, work'.

I came back again the next year and was ready to be a man and an artist.

At meal times and in the evenings I drew and painted men and women I thought I could love. (I believe that art only happens from love and that pictures made without love remain artefacts). This has caused me to define 'Art' for myself as love in concentrated form.) I awaited each sitter's coming, nervously, like anticipating the arrival of a lover. Sadly, living in community means lots of distractions and broken appointments. But the 'lover' or 'Beloved' element of my experience with each sitter kept me persevering.

Imagine being able to glance at any individual, see the glory in them, and go quickly into the deep 'river' of their soft, loving soul, in a communion rather than conversation with them! Maybe only hairdressers have access to other men and women as I do—going quickly in to know what their love and longing is all about. (Funny, I am a hairdresser as well!).

The 'soloist' in me became a stronger calling. So much so, that at the 'dirty and grungy' work of my first KP (kitchen patrol) I revolted at doing such menial, slavish work. Mopping the floor while listening to a pop singer on tape, my inner voice ejaculated, "I want to be the one on the tape, the artist! Not the one that all the drones listen to". I could see that I'd have to accept the tension that is created by personal versus community needs. It was exhausting working in the maintenance dept., scraping the paint off bungalows, taking up rotten floors in caravans and painting food sheds, all the time planning to meet people at all hours to make pictures of them. I once felt inspired to give an art class, but the Art Studio was dark and no key could be found at all.

I came back again the next year, this time with my bicycle, a big roll of canvas and boxes of paint, and settled down to live here. Boxes arrived daily that I had sent with all our things: clothes, documents and books. For the first seven weeks Kathryn and I were told, "You can't work here, since you are not from the EEC." "Since you can't work here, then you can't stay in our caravans." "Well, it's sunny out and that's so unusual, since you can't work or live here, why not just enjoy the weather?"

After a series of cries for help, and friendly focalisers who loved breaking the rules, we did live and work here. And this time I wandered up to the Art Studio and a woman was there and as she handed me the key, she asked, "Can I also give an art class here? I've never taught before." And at that point all became a green light for me. My partner Kathryn Kusa and Clive Kitson and I opened up the studio, cleared away the cobwebs and started giving classes in drawing, painting, play and inspiration. A woman turned up happy to let us draw her for a life-drawing class—staying stone still for hours. Clive donated enough art materials to set up a working studio. Kathryn gave a class in water and oil colours and people started turning up by word of mouth, from as far away as a half-hour's drive.

Before no time we were offering twelve classes a week, and open studio sessions—where people could experiment with various materials. Clive offered a class in creativity and personal growth; various people offered veil painting as designed by Rudolph Steiner, three-day classes in primal painting—a process of designing in gouache paint, washing the painting off, and painting again in successive layers—and I offered perceptive drawing and painting from the nude.

Looking for people to sit for paintings was a bit of a trial: since some would say they'd love to pose, but then would be, at the appointed time, too tired, too emotional or too forgetful. Not infrequent were my bicycling forays into the night, at five minutes before the beginning of a class, to find a willing body! I began publicising all the arts, by designing a flier distributed in a 50mile radius of the community, and asked all those who were offering classes to list their classes only if they would promise that they would run their classes professionally, with no class cancellations. I wanted all the participants to be satisfied, spread the good word on the classes and to lay the foundations for a school for the arts. We wish to contribute quality art experiences to this part of northern Scotland.

By people in the Foundation I was told time and again, sternly, "There's no place for art and artists here." "You can't be a member and be an artist—it would kill you." "No one's going to study art here—everyone's too tired." I found that I could be an artist here and that I could give art classes that are well attended and students that develop into...artists! Now the Art Sanctuary has more than 2000 participants coming to draw and paint each year.

Wanting to increase the level of sophistication in aesthetic appreciation, I began to take an active role in education. What I found the most difficult to change were negative attitudes towards art. For students or would-be students, fear of judgement of the quality of their artwork would often keep them away from drawing and painting. Carefully, I pointed out to students that the marks they drew were beautiful and didn't need to be compared with anyone else's. To facilitate a student's ability to see beauty in what they make and how they see is really my purpose as teacher.

I have worked very hard to dispel the notion that the market place is right when it comes to aesthetics. The way I teach painting is the same as the way I try to live: 'Spiritually with Joy'. I tell myself, as well as my students, "If you feel bored, stop what you're doing and start again from a different angle." "If you are having a difficult time with a picture, make one mark with your pencil and say to yourself, 'I like that.' and keep saying that with each successive stroke."

Art gives me an excuse to live by a philosophy based on pleasure first. Now, drawing and painting in the Findhorn community, I am taking collaboration with models a step further. I have no categories for my sitter, whether friend, acquaintance or work-mate. I live with my 'models' now. And if they would like an exchange of energy, I will do that, and if they really like the painting, when it's done, they can have it. If, by chance, the painting is sold, I will split the takings with my collaborator.

After the basic 'boundaries' are set up, I want them to live in a way that giving and receiving get all mixed-up. I am beginning to fill each minute of my life with poetry: the elevated rather than the pedestrian, to speak words that are communion rather than chatter (someone asked me what I meant by chatter and I responded, "It's what you say when you're not in love."), and to pray and work towards art rather than artifact; like a beautiful song that leaves me in silence.

One hears often enough around here, "Empower yourself." "Create your own Reality." And it is so; nothing has stopped me or the others who continue to teach, and create their art. I keep on saying, "Art is meditation and the pursuit of beauty is a spiritual practice." I don't scream it. It's not that important to me. I'll just keep on exhibiting the artwork of the students and myself and maybe someone will get a whiff, like walking by a bakery, and turn in their tracks and say, "Smells good, give me some of what you've got!" I'll be happy to give it.

Art is an excuse for many things for me: freedom to express anything, to let my imagination go beyond the known into realms of beauty that I can't as yet imagine, to reveal my 'devil' nature, to feel deep, loving intimacy, to let my feelings of joy overflow (generally I'm quite afraid to appear a ninnie) and maybe especially, to surpass limitations. (I grew up hearing, "Love is dangerous", "work is pain" and "life is unfair".)

For the future, I'm planning to build a new art studio, bigger and with better facilities, establish a trade of art exhibitions between intentional communities and university and professional galleries, create a school for the arts, and publish an arts and culture periodical with pictures, poetry and discussion submissions from other communities and big-city people as well. Anyone want to join the fun?

RANDY KLINGER

Update: The Moray Arts Centre

Randy manifested the Moray Arts Centre in 2004. It is a large, beautiful, light filled timber construction. Built on two floors there are several studios and workshop spaces as well as ample gallery hanging space. Facing the new houses across the open green space of the Field of Dreams it is a lovely addition to the emerging Ecovillage.

It is well used by Community members as well as local artists. The many classes and workshops, exhibitions and events attract people from a wide area. www.morayartscentre.org

The Song in our Hearts

Before coming to live at Findhorn I was a professional musician, teaching and performing regularly. I enjoyed my job, but not the competitiveness of the music business and the inner emptiness that seemed to go with it. The soul of the music was lost and the name of the game seemed only to be personal success and business. Then, shortly after returning from a visit to the Foundation, I had an experience which changed my attitude to music profoundly.

I was standing in my little garden on the outskirts of Munich. It was a beautiful spring day. Soft music was drifting into the garden from inside the house. As I looked at the colours of the daffodils and crocuses, I suddenly had the feeling that each flower was singing, singing its own song of celebration and gratitude for life. Every living thing around me seemed to be in harmony; every blade of grass, every flower and every leaf on every tree seemed joined together in a big symphony celebrating life. I had the feeling that this symphony had started with the creation and had continued day after day ever since, but I had never noticed it before that moment.

The experience awakened in me a deep desire to express music as an affirmation and celebration of life, as I had seen the flowers do. Over time I found that music really was a medium for divine energies and needed to be treated in a sacred manner. When music is played with such an attitude, then something truly magical can happen and both musicians and audience become transformed and enriched.

As focaliser of the meals in Cluny kitchen where I worked when I joined the Community, the quickest way I found to inspire my coworkers was to share a song or do a dance. On those occasions when the whole kitchen sang together, we hardly noticed we were working, the team spirit was high and we produced especially delicious meals.

Over time I learned many songs from different cultures and discovered that those that touch me deepest are the songs that open my heart to God: the song becomes the bridge through which I can touch feelings of deep gratitude, devotion and joy. Singing, and especially devotional singing, has now become a regular part of our community life. When a few of us first agreed to meet to sing in the Nature Sanctuary every morning at 8am, I decided to use this time as my personal spiritual practice, even if it meant singing alone. I didn't advertise what we were doing and yet soon we had people from the Community and Findhorn village, as well as guests, coming day after day, for songs and a shared prayer in the morning. I am pleased that this little morning ritual has become a regular part of community life and that it will continue in my absence.

A few years ago I had the chance to go to Japan to present my work there. I knew very little about Japanese culture, only that it doesn't encourage people to show their feelings or to touch each other, so I didn't know what reactions to expect. For some people the term 'workshop' was misleading. Not having been on one before they came, sent by their companies, with book and pencil, ready to do 'work'. However, the mood soon changed when we began to do trust games and circle dances together. But it was the singing which created the break-through. The third song we sang together, a beautiful Russian Kyrie Eleison, left half the group in tears. Afterwards, people expressed how deeply the music had touched them and what a healing experience it was. I think it was the suggestion to allow their inner child to have fun which helped both men and women to forget cultural differences and let go of centuries of conditioning and hug each other.

Through experiences like this, I now know that music is not only an agent for personal transformation but, in helping to bridge the gaps between cultures, races and religions, it has immense potential to create peace and understanding in the world. I still feel in touch with my experience of the 'singing flowers'. I feel blessed to be a part of this community and to be able to travel to many countries to share music with others in such a way that they too can experience their voice, their heart and their part in life's symphony.

BARBARA SWETINA
One Earth

On Being a Community Musician

I find myself standing in a warm pool of light at the centre of a moving circle of dancers: gone is the stumbling self-consciousness of beginners; their faces are rapt in expression, their feet moving in rhythmic waves upon the floor. As I look towards my fellow musicians, I know that we are aware of each other as one body and that our listening has spread so as to encompass the entire auditorium in the Universal Hall. There is an atmosphere here, a great amber glow. It is so thick one can feel it, like honey. This is what a friend of mine calls 'the descent of the Muse', and what we performers live for.

There are times when I am playing that it seems as though I am blowing my entire soul into my instrument. I cultivate the experience of being possessed by the spirit of the original music, feeling what it might be like to be Bulgarian, Irish or Greek; a bit of Africa lives in the drum, a bit of turf and the peat fires in the Uillean pipes and tin whistle. These are moments that bring us together. This is the community of dance, of the song sung together, of music.

As Community musicians, we choose songs with real depth which are at the same time easily learned. Even simple dances or tunes grow in the hands of the sensitive musician, unfolding new layers of experience though they are performed many times. There is a tremendous repertoire to choose from: Sacred Dance, folk dance, the Songs of Taizé, Dances of Universal Peace, Gabrielle Roth's Five Rhythms, Jazz and Baroque and other early music. These are tailored to suit the rich palette of colours that community is, especially this community at the Findhorn Foundation.

I firmly believe that true culture cannot exist without a living tradition of art and celebration. The Muse finds it difficult to descend through the media of tape and television. The festivals, especially the Celtic ones that honour nature's round and wisdom, are the most natural times for celebration, providing themes that are ancient but ever new. Confucius says that the festivals help us to feel, collectively, our place in the cosmos, they fill us with awe and remind us that we are more than we seem. By performing dance and music from different world cultures we help to heal and weave among peoples the web of compassion and understanding. As the universe is mirrored in a grain of sand, so also is our common unity in the simple circle dance performed with love.

This communal music and celebration is a new, emerging art form. To participate in it requires no greater genius than the willingness to work with others. It is the art of loving and giving. I know of no one who has made a fortune from it, but through the doing of it, great riches are to be had.

RORY O'CONNELL
One Earth

Weddings

At weddings I usually say an introduction and welcome, on behalf of the couple and the Foundation and part of it generally runs thus: "From the earliest days a couple would cock an eyebrow at each other, grunt 'yeah, let's'—and that was their marriage. The consummation took a lot more grunting about 'your place or mine?', but the result was a couple in a live-in bond, with, as time went on, family and tribal approval for such arrangements.

If there was some kind of spiritual consciousness dawning, a blessing would be sought, in whatever was the current way, on their union and fertility. Just as family and tribe muscled in on the joinings together, as time went by religions developed, to order and control the spiritual experience of people and muscled in on the joinings too. Initially, couples would wait for a holy person to come by the hamlet or house cluster and come to them and say: "We are married, we want your/god's blessing".

Then, of course the Churches, as they developed, muscled in on the very decision to marry, insisting on blessing that before the couple could be considered married. They controlled this by instilling the fear of God's retribution if everyone did not comply—the same god whose blessing couples once freely and confidently sought of their own accord, as an outward and visible sign of the inward and invisible state they had chosen for themselves! Or, in other terms, an outward sign of the god within them as a couple. Oh, and, you guessed it, then the state muscled in on the act and now controls the whole shebang (if you'll permit the expression). Even the Church cannot create a legal marriage unless the state authorises it to do so! A marriage is complete when someone declares: "By virtue of the authority vested in me by the Registrar General of Scotland I declare that you are husband and wife..." Then the marriage can be blessed!"

So, way back in 1990 or thereabouts, Ian Pullen was invited by the Focus Group to be the wedding celebrant for the Foundation, a post he held until 1994 when I was asked to succeed him. Since our Trust Deed describes us as providing education about the various religions of the world and as a spiritual community, we fall under the Marriage Act (Scotland) as a religious organisation, we have the right to nominate a member to the Registrar General for authorisation as a Marriage Officer of the Moray District. The same officer of the law can and does authorise that person, from time to time, to conduct weddings outwith the Moray district. Within and without the home district the rituals may be held almost anywhere, so long as it is above the low water line! After that Marine Law takes over!! Could be in the Findhorn River though (if you could persuade me or Judi Buttner—more recently nominated as co-wedding celebrant and also a marriage officer in the Moray district—to wade in with you!).

Well, anyway, if a couple comes to us here at Findhorn for a 'spiritual marriage' we will guide them to the wonderful local registrar to do the essential legal preliminaries and then settle down to draw out of them the wedding within them. Then into that process we weave the simple legal requirements of our wonderful, person-centred Scottish law for wedding ceremonies. One question each: "Do you ZXC recognise and accept BNM as your lawful wedded husband/wife?", or words to that effect, to which one expects a positive affirmation! If it is forthcoming, one can then make the declaration above: "By virtue of the authority...etc" and guide them to the table on which the Declaration of Marriage waits, to be signed by wife and husband and two witnesses and the officiating marriage officer. That's it!

By the way, the wife signs in her own name. This is sometimes called her 'single name' on the assumption that she will adopt a 'married name' and usually that will be her husband's family name. In fact there is no legal requirement to do so! This arrangement belongs to an era when the wife was owned by the husband—and his family! It is an interesting thought that the couple could now agree to adopt the wife's family name as their joint 'married name', if they so wished. Or the wife might adopt her mother's 'maiden' name or her father's name and hyphenate it with her husband's— in whatever order they chose. There would be some admin to do to let everyone know; banks, changes on legal documents, electoral registers, driving licence, passport, etc., etc., etc. Maybe the reason for sharing one name may just be to save a lot of bother!

Since 1994, weddings have been celebrated in many venues around the Community. In the santuaries at the Park and Cluny and also at Newbold and at Minton House, in the Universal Hall, in the gardens, on the sand dunes at the beach, in the gardens of homes in Forres. Also on the Black Isle, in Righoul Cottage, at Geddes. And further afield in an hotel in the glens near Glen Affric, in the function rooms of old hotels from Edinburgh to Argyll, and in old castles, notably several times in the banqueting hall of beautiful Eilean Donan castle near the Kyle of Loch Alsh (watch it as the BBC balloon floats by it every night on TV!). Ah, yes, then there were weddings in the ruins of old Deer Abbey over Aberdeen way, in an enchanted forest glade near there. Then there were ceremonies in Iona Abbey's Michael chapel, by the river-side at Ardclach and also a Celtic ritual wedding at the standing stone up Calipher Hill.

Sometimes our ceremonies are 'spiritual and legal' and sometimes just 'spiritual'! The latter most usually because one family is here at Findhorn, and the other in another country and the couple wishes to include both. So, we may bless a marriage that will become legal overseas or make legal a marriage that was blessed somewhere else. But, of course, it is all in the Spirit, if it is in the spirit of the Findhorn adventure.

Timing of weddings has been from 5.00 in the morning to midnight and most times between! We were asked to conduct what would have been a registry office wedding because the date chosen was a Bank holiday and the registry was closed but expensive travel tickets had already been paid for! The couple were invited to go and look at the nature sanctuary (neither of them had ever been in a church or chapel, let alone anything like this!). The groom-to-be was 'blown over' by it and came back several times on his own before the wedding to sit there quietly. The nature sanctuary, equally quietly, taught him to meditate and meet Spirit.

We have 'held' three joint Buddhist/Findhorn weddings and even a spiritual-atheist wedding! There is a marriage coming up for a couple who want neither a religious nor a simply secular wedding and who are both of Jewish background.

One of the glories of this Community is its multi-national and multireligious nature and its tolerance. Its lack of attempts to proselytise and its cherishing and accepting of spiritual paths across such a wide spectrum. A willingness to open to and learn from the traditions of all peoples may be its greatest gift to the world.

KEN HILLS

Update: There are now a dozen celebrants in the Community who have undergone the Interfaith Ministry training and ordination. They perform wonderful weddings, naming ceremonies, funerals and various forms of commitments and re-commitments both in the Community and beyond. Most of them also offer Spiritual counseling and mentoring.

CHAPTER FOUR

IN THE SPIRIT

Many people may consider 'Spirit' to be an essential aspect of all the stories in this book. I have put these pieces into this section to demonstrate the consciousness that some people here have regarding spiritual realms, and to show that we also have a sense of humour around the subject.

The Spirit of Findhorn

People often ask me about visiting Findhorn and I also often have an intuition that people need to visit Findhorn. I also often find myself saying this:

"Even if the workshop is rubbish, even if the workshop facilitators are rubbish, you will nevertheless have an extraordinary experience. There is a spirit to the place that transcends and permeates even the worst events."

This, I know, can sound like faint praise. But it also acknowledges on of the most important realities about the Findhorn Foundation: It has an extraordinary and wonderful spirit.

The Spirit of Findhorn. What do we mean by this? We mean that there is some kind of mythical and energetic being, some essence, which is at the very core of the place. This spirit of Findhorn can equally be called the 'over-lighting Angel' of the place.

In tribal societies, in classical Rome and Athens, there was no problem about discussing the spirits, gods and goddesses, and angels. Every activity had a spirit. Every place had a spirit. Athens was over-lit by the great Angel and Goddess, Athena. There is a myth that this being went on to over-light Constantinople and then London.

If a flower can be over-lit and coloured by a fairy, if a mountain can have its sweeping and huge nature spirit, why can't a wonderful human community also have its angel? Anyone with the slightest sensitivity, if they choose to sit silently and to open their psychic awareness, immediately feels and senses this presence that permeates and over-lights everything at Findhorn.

When I first came to Findhorn and sat in the sanctuary, I swooned at the magnificence and beauty and healing nature of this wonderful angelic presence that is companion to the whole community.

Sometimes people forget that a human community is also an ecosystem, as fantastic and complex as anything in the Amazon rain forest. And like any ecosystem, it has its nature spirits. Human beings are, despite appearances in the industrialised world, not separate from nature and Gaia. We are part of nature and we too have our great nature spirits that work with us, as individuals and as communities.

I would dare to suggest that the Angel of Findhorn has a magnificent history of being involved with human communities. Within her energy field she carries lovingly tolerant and understanding patterns of how humans can behave and inspiring blueprints of how fully perfect this community can be.

Even the most cynical of visitors may quickly become seduced by the quality of silence at Findhorn. What is this quality? It is the atmosphere of the angel's energy field inspiring us to something new and more loving. Every time I visit Findhorn I am touched, moved and educated not only by the people, but by the ever present spirit of the place. I am grateful and I seek to encourage anyone and everyone to enjoy a similar relationship.

WILLIAM BLOOM

The Spirit in the Day of Francoise

My grandmother, who died ten years ago, is shouting at my mum. My mum is crying. I feel sad and powerless. My consciousness is slowly stepping out of last night's dream. It is between 5:45 and 6am. This is a November morning. Still dark. It feels warm in my bed but my nose is cold. The premature winter frost is penetrating the little bedroom of my caravan. The silence is special. I know it's been snowing. A new day is ahead and that comforts me, only a little bit. My dream is still with me.

O Master
Thou art the real goal of human life,
We are yet but slaves of wishes,
Putting a bar to our advancement,
Thou art the only God and Power,
To bring us up to that stage.

I feel embraced in God's arms. It is reassuring. I feel in touch with my faith. It took me months, three years ago, to accept this daily prayer. I fought against it and I changed the words several times. But I kept saying it inwardly because my teacher had asked me to do so and I trust him. I knew that my fight against the words was a fight against parts of myself. Now I say it fully with delight, receiving each time a dose of love, faith and courage and I feel grateful for having learnt humility during the process.

The layer of snow is thin but icy and the roads in The Park are slippery. It is fun to cycle to the main sanctuary. The 6.30 am meditation is a very special time for me. I rarely miss it. A bunch of us meditate together in complete silence for one hour. Eileen is always there. She encourages us to participate in that meditation. I like it because I share a daily spiritual 'get together' with my community while I am doing my own morning practice. I start with five minutes of inner cleansing. Once the gong has sounded, I bring my attention to my heart, let it be filled with the sensation of divine light and stay with that. If I get caught in any thought, I let it go and gently bring my attention back to my heart. I would like the meditation not to end. If death feels like that, I would like to die, to go 'home'.

In the hallway, we put our shoes and coats back on, still in silence. The sacredness of the previous hour is still with us. Outside at this point, the sun is rising and playing with pink clouds over the snowy Park. It is calm and beautiful. OK, I wouldn't like to die.

Back home, Eileen's guidance for today reminds me about willingness. At 7:45, somebody knocks at the door. That's one of the usual times I give 'sittings' My spiritual practice is called Sahaj Marg, which is a modern form of Raja Yoga. I am one of the many 'preceptors' who help my teacher in his work all over the world. He prepared us so that we can channel his 'prana' or transmission of divine energy, to any disciple, in his absence. This from the living Master is a process that helps us disciples to contact our Master within and to walk towards the goal of human perfection. Accepting the help of a Master that way is also something that took me time and taught me a great deal about humility.

The sitting is taking place in my lounge. We sit facing each other and for half an hour I let my Master send, through my heart, his cleansing and divine energy to the other person's heart. I feel blessed for serving that way and for receiving a little part of the transmission that passes through me. Afterwards the person shares how the sitting felt and we take leave of each other.

A quick cup of tea, a ride to Park Reception to check the mail, and it is time to bring the divine inspiration of the morning into the activity of the day. Outside the garden shed, the gardeners have gathered. We form a circle and we invoke Spirit and welcome the day together. There is some excitement in the air since we are responsible for the safety of the roads and paths in The Park in case of ice and snow. This is our first day of action of that kind this winter. We review all that has to be done; we split into teams and off we go, armed with wheelbarrows, shovels and grit. Hard work but we have great fun. Soon we are joined by the Maintenance team. They are going to spread some grit onto the roads from their truck. That will help! It is a job out of our routine, a job that needs togetherness and coordination. It creates a warm and playful atmosphere amongst us and we feel important. (We always are but we don't always know it.)

Before lunch, I run to Accounts to deal with some Garden bills and then I join the queue in the Community Centre. Hot soup and plenty of winter salads. Yummy! Thank you cooks!

Outside the Community Centre, I share a bench, a cup of tea and a cigarette with my friend Marietta. It's very cold but good to escape the busy dining room and it is the only way to have a smoke anyway. We talk about relationships. We both have had a heavy heart for the last few months and we have a look at how we deal with sadness, anger, commitment and Spirit. We cry and we laugh. We haven't got all the answers we wish for, but sisterhood is good. From there we drift to our relationship to the Community and the Foundation. We share how we see our own commitment, then we gossip a little bit about people whom we think are not properly committed. Sisterhood is good.

I will just give you the highlights of the rest of my day. I enjoy answering some French inquiries in the afternoon; I make a phone call after dinner and I am upset by it; I calm down after doing my daily half an hour of inner cleansing in the sanctuary and giving another sitting. I feel happy for having no meeting or other group activity tonight and for spending an evening of half lazy/half busy solitude in my caravan while listening to Miles Davis.

Before I fall asleep, my last conscious action is to inwardly say two or three times the prayer I said this morning when I woke up, so that I can open myself to the divine light in my night as well as in my day, trying to live my life as a spiral rising patiently towards the goal. Sometimes I panic when I seem to wind back down. But I always have the choice to surrender to my Master's help and to climb up again. Not always easy, but how rewarding!

FRANCOISE L'HERMITTE
From 'The life in the day of' series in Network News

F

Coming Home

"How d'you know when you're getting guidance?" I used to ask anyone who I thought might be even slightly more evolved (spiritually) than I was. I'd ask myself the question constantly—how can you tell? How would I know the difference between real guidance and wishful thinking, my imagination, or projection? How could Eileen and Dorothy have been so sure, I kept wondering. Until I heard the three short words that helped to change my life:

It was the first evening of my third visit to Findhorn. It was Good Friday, and I'd dragged a somewhat reluctant teenage daughter up to Findhorn with me for the Easter Weekend. I wanted her to see what I was so excited about, why I hadn't stopped talking about the place since my first visit three years before. We'd arrived earlier that day, looked around a bit and had dinner. So far, her enthusiasm was about as warm as the weather here that Easter—we woke up to snow the next morning! When I suggested we might spend a fun evening singing chants from Taize at a vigil in the Nature Sanctuary she politely declined (euphemism), and opted to wait alone, with a book for company, upstairs in the Community Centre.

Arriving late, I knelt in the doorway of the tiny, crowded Nature Sanctuary. The atmosphere felt magical: the room was lit only by candles and nightlights, which gave the singers' faces a special, ethereal quality, as only candlelight can. There was such a quality, too, to the silence between each song or chant—a stillness, a quietness you don't normally 'hear' anywhere but in the depths of the countryside. Nevertheless I found my mind wandering during the periods of silence between the singing. I felt a bit mean leaving Cait on her own on our first evening, and was thinking that I should get back soon.

Suddenly, from nowhere, in the silence, I heard a voice: "You've come home", it said. I jumped, startled: The words were perfectly clear, though I knew that no-one else had heard them. They were nothing like my usual thoughts, it was definitely not me talking to myself—yet if someone had asked "What was the voice like?" I couldn't have said whether it was loud or soft, deep or high-pitched, male or female. I knew it was a voice, it was inside me, but it was not me speaking. I felt a rush of emotion: my heart seemed to be bursting with joy, and I realised that tears were streaming down my face.

Soon afterwards, I returned to the C.C. to find my daughter chatting with three other teenage girls. She was happy, and wasn't in any hurry to leave after all, so I needn't have worried. From then on, we had a wonderful weekend together!

It had never occurred to me, before that night, that I might one day really be 'at home' here at Findhorn, but sure enough, four years later, at Easter, I did move here to live—and my daughter no longer worries about whether or not it's cool to be here, she's delighted to come home whenever she can. After a life-time of never really feeling I belonged anywhere, I really do feel, two years on, that I really have 'come home' at last. And I'll never wonder about guidance again—when it happens, as they say, you just know!

SOLASAN (MANDY) WILKINSON

The Angel of Findhorn

One morning, about halfway through a visit back here, I awoke to discover the Angel of Findhorn. It was very early around 4 or 5 am, and I lay in bed just observing and appreciating the beautiful flow of energy in and around this beautiful being as it gathered in the energy from the rising sun and transmitted it as a spiritual light throughout a wide radius around this Centre.

Then, there came an invitation and I found myself taken up into the Angel's consciousness. From here I could look out and from a peculiar perspective see the entire world, draw upon the reservoir of goodwill, love and peace generated by all the participants in this Community and the daily work that is done here. Also, I could see that where individuals consciously and deliberately aligned with the Angel and used their wills to focus that energy out in the world, this flow was intensified.

As I watched an interesting change occurred. The earth suddenly seemed covered with a brown crust underneath which I could see an intense, searing substance like lava. Here and there this crust was broken by eruptions that from this perspective looked like volcanoes. A stream of silvery light swept out from the Angel, and I rode upon it far out over one of these volcanoes. Looking down, I could see straight into the crater and down into this molten mass, which radiated an intensity that I could feel.

I realised that what I was seeing was a representation of a psychic condition within humanity. The searing, seething, molten mass was a deep layer of fear, pain, hatred, frustration, suffering, and other negative emotions, much of it crusted over. The volcanoes were places where this ancient stuff was erupting into manifestation, and I realised that the particular volcano over which I hovered was Rwanda. The volcanoes were horrible places, but they gave access to the deeper layer of human pain beneath the surface.

As I watched I saw countless silvery lights hovering about these volcanoes and plunging into them, right into the seething, molten stuff. I realised that these lights were individual beings, some discarnate, some non-human, and some humans who were operating in their sleep state or through meditative and prayerful projections. They would bathe in and connect with the many streams of light criss-crossing the landscape, including the one that I was in, that were being radiated out from the Findhorn Angel. As they did so, they would glow more brightly, like a light being turned up. Then they would dive into the volcano, into the midst of the suffering and pain.

To observe what was happening I felt compelled to dive into the volcano myself, which psychically felt much like it might feel to dive into a real pool of molten lava. However, as I was about to hit the stuff, I was infused with protective, cooling light, so that even though I was in the midst of this psychic material, I felt unharmed by it. Then I could see all these light-filled beings radiating in a way that cooled, transformed, and released the ancient conditions of pain and anger, hatred and fear that form the substance of that mass.

At last I found myself back in the body of the Angel, hovering over the Community. It was very clear that I had been shown one of the services that this Community provides, that of drawing upon the ongoing inner and outer work of the Community, as well as upon its own spiritual connections with the sacred, to send streams of light into the world to those who work on both inner and outer levels to heal humanity from its ancient wound and their modern eruptions.

Though the Angel did this work and drew up the Community's energy whether the Community cooperated consciously or not, it was evident that any and all acts of personal and collective cooperation with this process, as well as with the general acts of blessing and empowerment that flow out from this Angel to the larger world, would serve to enhance and intensify the various streams of light that are the Angel's—and the Community's—gifts to the planet.

DAVID SPANGLER
Network News

Spirit in Mo-tion

There was nothing subtle about Maureen Willett, better known as Mo. Her use of language, her hair, which could be coloured anywhere on the spectrum from saffron to magenta, her multi-coloured clothes, bought mostly from charity shops and put together with aplomb in her very individual style, and her bright home décor all proclaimed Mo's zest for life.

Mo was a deeply spiritual woman. Since being a young woman in the early 60s she had been meditating and investigating spiritual practices and philosophy. She was often found in the sanctuary and loved the early morning Taize singing. Even so, her spirituality was of a very practical nature.

Mo aimed herself at life, and if it was not nifty enough to get out of the way, change happened. Her ability to spot the need for change and to attempt to do something about it has been of great benefit to so many people. In her tireless work on the conscious evolution and reconstruction of this Community to enable it to become more inclusive, Mo's practical demonstration of Spirit in motion has been inspirational.

If you needed something doing you would ask Mo. When you wanted help getting a project launched, or the most appropriate speakers to address any particular issue you went to Mo. If you wanted good catering for an event you would go to Mo, who was a former restaurateur. For delicious food and convivial company with whom to explore radical ideas you would go to one of Mo's lunch or dinner parties. Those who would like to enjoy a drink or a cigarette along with their chat in uncensored surroundings would drop in on Mo.

Before the Ecovillage was built, when accommodation was scarce in the Park, visitors who needing a bed for the night would be sent to Mo and they would find her house by looking for the huge teapot with the name Moses painted on it by the side of her entrance.

If you needed someone to take care of a waif and stray or to give a few days respite to anyone having difficulties at home you would ask Mo, athough she was probably way ahead of you. When people have turned up in the Community with little money and the assumption that they would be welcomed with open arms it was Mo's arms and heart where they would most often find that welcome.

WOOFER'S, (originally meaning Workers on Organic Farms now referring to any itinerant type of work done in exchange for food and lodging) frequently turn up in the Community not realising that there are so many local volunteers and so little accommodation in the Foundation that WOOFING is not part of the culture. Mo would take them in and find someone who needed some work doing and if not would set them to painting her house, building a shed, creating a pond in her garden, mending her car, teaching her computing skills, etc.

For all her big heartedness Mo did not suffer fools gladly. She was impatient with bureaucracy and prevarication and was incensed by mean-mindedness and injustice – local or global. She stood no nonsense from people, and had little hesitation in speaking her mind about issues or concerns about which many of us were being diplomatic, sometimes to the point of cowardice. Her outspokenness and habit of barging ahead with solving problems and creating projects did not endear her to everybody. With the very best of intentions she nevertheless often left some ruffled feathers, trampled toes and bruised egos in her wake. Her friends would sometimes be required to smooth those feathers and put some diplomatic salve on throbbing toes and damaged, fragile egos. The sticker she put on her fridge which declared: 'I'm not obnoxious, I am just tact challenged', summed her up nicely.

If Mo considered you to be a friend she would be your staunchest ally. She would have your back in a fight and hold your hand through distress or despair. To our mutual delight, we called each other friend for 20 years.

Crippling arthritis in both hips did not prevent Mo from doing anything. On good days she would be seen hobbling about the Park leaning on her stick. At other times she would zoom around in her little car or her mobility scooter.

Having very little money never prevented Mo from doing what she wanted to do either. Anywhere in the World where important connections were being made, such as at a convergence of spiritual thinkers in South America or in India, or gatherings of indigenous peoples in Canada or Australia, Mo would be there – and not just to be there. Mo's way of being was doing. If there were any practical steps for improvement to be taken after such gatherings Mo would almost certainly be involved. On one occasion, being engaged in something useful and interesting in New York, she missed her plane home. Undaunted, she hitched a lift back in exchange for cooking for a crew as they sailed their boat in a cross Atlantic race.

She was smuggled in and out and around the Former Yugoslavia during the most horrific times of that region's recent past. She offered spiritual, emotional and practical support to the women there who were working to protect their communities and to bring peace to the area. Mo recognised that, although the UN Peacekeeping Forces were tempering some of the violence, there were many people existing in dangerously deprived circumstances. Returning home, Mo galvanized everyone in and around Findhorn in a project to gather foodstuffs and clothing to make up parcels to alleviate some of that suffering. Having collected a huge amount of these essentials she persuaded the personnel at neighbouring RAF Kinloss to delivery these parcels with the shipments of equipment being flown out to the Balkans.

I later learned that Mo's son, Peter, who was a tank commander in a UN Peacekeeping Force out there during that time, was called into his commander's office. On being asked who had caused the camp to be littered with boxes with his name, Willett, written on them, I could imagine Peter sighing deeply, raising his eyes skywards and replying with something like, 'that would be my mother, Sir.'

Mo had always been determined that by the time she died she would have been thoroughly used up. When she passed away at the age of 70 I hope she believed it was so. If there is a heaven, I can imagine folks up there will be getting an earful of Mo's opinion on the state of the World and what somebody up there ought to be doing about it. Down here, while I'm sure it will heal in time, we have a hole where a Mo used to be.

KAY KAY

☞

Spiritual Maturity

Q "Eileen, what is your view of this Community's spiritual maturity since you stopped giving it the guidance that you received, and what does the future look like?"

A "I think we are moving in the right direction, although it doesn't always look like that. Everything that needs to happen will happen. Before we can all attune to what we need to do, we need to continue learning to put God first and this aim is the same for each of us, everyone in the Community. I have a deep inner knowing that we are right in the middle of this process.

Community meetings are sometimes uncomfortable because the rough edges of personalities are still being smoothed away and things are coming out to be transmuted—it is not a comfortable stage, as we learn to let our personalities get in the way less and less, but I think the Community is maturing.

Sometimes I used to wonder why I am still here, especially since giving guidance is not needed any more. I know now it is because I hold in my consciousness the thought that everything is moving as it should. It is important that I continue to hold that thought until it manifests. This is where faith comes in and my faith is very strong."

Extract from an interview given by Eileen Caddy to

EVA WARD AND JEREMY SLOCOMBE
One Earth

Update: Eileen continued to hold the community until her death in 2006, aged 89. She was firmly in support of the intention to create an integrated, inclusive and cooperative community with which to face the new millennium.

In 2004 Eileen received the MBE for her, 'Contribution to spiritual enquiry'. Being too frail to make the journey to London to receive the honour from the Queen, the Lord Lt of Scotland came to the Universal Hall to represent her majesty. It was a simple, respectful and delightful ceremony in which Eileen was very gracious in her acceptance. She was quick to point out that this recognition was not just for her, it was for everybody in the community, past and present and she was merely accepting it on everyone's behalf.

Although this was obviously a very happy day for her, the day that clearly gave Eileen the most joy was when all of her family was finally united to celebrate one of her last birthdays.

Her passing touched many people with a mixture of the sadness of loss and of joy and gratitude for what Eileen contributed to the world.

When God and I Speak

When God and I speak we don't always see eye to eye
He or she has plans for world peace
I have a plan for a second cup of coffee
He or she is a being of pure light
I am a being with peanut butter stuck in his teeth
He or she is tireless
Me, I'm sometimes tired before I get up
He or she is in everything
Me, I'm in a room 12 by 10
He or she stops at nothing
I stop for tea breaks
Timidly I ask God what his or her plan is for me
The answer comes that I am to find perfection within
To live in harmony with my fellow human beings
and with nature
and to take part in a New Golden Age
it's at that point I look around to see
if God is really talking to someone else.

DAVE TILL

CHAPTER FIVE

YOUTH MATTERS

During the life of this Community some remarkable young people have grown up here. The pieces in this section will give some sense of what has supported our young people to be who they are.

Youth in Community

Love is all they want, and love is all they have to give

There I was in New York City, in the winter of 1989, sitting on a bench wondering to myself, "What is a woman like me doing in a mess like this?" I was without a job and soon to be broke. A black teenager sat down beside me and asked, "Why so sad?" I told him I needed a good job, I wanted to use my experience working creatively with kids and help them to solve their problems by learning a better way to live in harmony with one another. He advised me to check out 'Citykids' in the Soho area of downtown New York City.

The next day I was on the phone with 'Citykids' and was told that they were auditioning people to work with teenagers on a theatrical play that dealt with life issues. I jumped at the opportunity and arranged an interview.

As I entered the old building housing 'Citykids', I felt a surge of expectancy and excitement in the air. I walked slowly down the stairs towards the sound of Rap music getting louder and louder. When I opened the door, there in front of me were about fifty teenagers of various ages, shapes, colours and cultural backgrounds dancing in full tempo, flying through the air doing flips, splits, synchronicities— rhythmic pulses that blew into a fireball of movement. The music was deafening, ghetto blasters were blasting, sweat was pouring, and it was a kaleidoscope of fun.

Suddenly, someone noticed me. An exquisite woman in full African dress raised and clapped her hands and in moments a group formed a circle around me. The audition was on. I jumped over the edge of sudden fear, took off my shoes and soon I was sweating too as the kids asked me questions and wanted straight answers about why I cared about children, what art meant to me, and what I thought were the issues that mattered most. These 14–22 year olds spent an hour squeezing the juice out of me to see what I was made of.

Then I was invited to climb onto the stage and "Do something with the kids." There was dead silence in the room. In that glorious moment when life pushes you to the edge of innocence, I could suddenly hear the sound of a water tap dripping. I heard my own heartbeat strong and clear and my feet began to echo that rhythm... boom, boom. I encircled the kids with power and called out, "Freedom in the jungle!" counted to three to break the silence, and then a volcano of animal sounds burst open as they became wild animals in a forest, feeding each other when hungry, healing each other when wounded, carrying the sick, playing, wrestling, and nursing their young. I watched as a group of fifty Hispanic, Black American, African, Asian and a small minority of White (New York's sacred blend) teenagers became a smorgasbord of instant peaceful collaboration amongst each other.

I got the job and met a great group of people. I was hired as Choreographer/Stage Manager and travelled with the one-hour show *'Growing Up and Other Heroic Deeds'*, to fifteen high schools throughout the boroughs of New York City. The show was written by Jeffrey Solomon and performed by thirteen young members of Citykids. It dealt directly with issues of prejudice, racism, homosexuality, falling in love, violence and education, and there were question and answer times with the audience following each show. We played to hundreds of kids in each school who sat in gangs and loved the performance. We went on to do a big fundraiser in a theatre on Broadway and it was well covered by the media.

'Good news on the news: Citykids of mixed cultures are standing up for making a better world and telling people to wake up, stop fighting and learn to love each other.'

I had learned to love what kids had to say long before my experience with Citykids. I had spent much time during my training to become a music therapist by exploring musical expression and healing with children and when I graduated I travelled around the world with a drum and a flute, a tape recorder, journal and little else on a journey to discover more of the magic that children brought to this planet. I wrote eight journals, took photographs, recorded songs and stories, played music and danced with little ones from small villages and cities everywhere. It was the happiest year of my life and it ended with a three-day presentation, 'The Universal Message of Children' for the International Conference of Music Therapy in Atlanta, Georgia.

I had then gone on to spend two years working as a music therapist in the New York Foundling Hospital, a very old hospital for homeless children, learning that these neglected and disabled infants and older children living together in unspeakable conditions offered a clear and powerful message: *'Love is all they want, and love is all they have to give.'*

I worked with one very large Jamaican nurse's aid who would sit on a chair and hold three children across her chest and two more on her lap, jiggling, singing, laughing and displaying the depth of motherhood, community and the basic innate life energy of humanity. It was there that I learned the down to earth meaning of courage.

After the Citykids' show finished, I kept in contact with them and kept myself busy making music, giving massages, running creative movement classes for children and earning money as a waitress. It was during this time that I met Peter Garner. Peter was a former member of the Findhorn Foundation and after we had spent a year together strengthening our bond, we visited the Foundation with two members of Citykids, Jeffrey and Carmello, who both did Experience Weeks at the Foundation.

During their stay Jeffrey and Carmello gathered all the young people of the community together to perform an infamous play inspired by the sometimes too serious Experience Week. Members, guests and friends in the audience boiled over with laughter as the kids made fun of everybody. Funds raised by the performance were given partly to Jeffrey and Carmello to get them safely back to New York, and the rest were put into a new Youth Project account. We had helped to gather together the community teenagers and unite them to form a new generation of Findhorn Foundation Youth Project. The old Youth Project members had grown up and dispersed to live all over the world, but they still remain close to one another in heart and come 'home' to Findhorn to meet up occasionally.

After that rich summer of 1990 of planting the roots of the Project and days busy with childcare in the playhouse with the children, I returned to New York. I was working with the network of Youth Projects in New York assisting the teaching of troubled seven to thirteen year olds in city schools, when the focaliser of the Education Branch at the Foundation phoned to invite me to return for the summer of 1991.

I wondered if it was the right thing to do, to just pick up and leave for

Scotland without the guarantee of a substantial paid position. I wondered how many other people were already on staff, how many children there were, and what their needs were. I didn't even know what was being envisioned for the children of the community. But circumstances and timing allowed me to say 'yes' and come to see what was happening and I arrived in July of 1991 to find that I was to be the only one on staff for all of the young people.

The summer was full on and I was spiralling through a whirlwind of activities: mornings at the playhouse with the younger children, afternoons with the five through eleven year olds and intermittent contact with the Youth Project. Not knowing very much about logistics in the community, I plodded through the summer getting to know who everyone was, tapping on as many doors as possible. We went on weekly outings, formed music groups, did theatre, and creative play, art, camping trips, get-togethers and sharings. It was hard work, lots of fun and far too much for one person to handle.

After the summer the community agreed that there was a need for the children's programme to continue and to grow in proportion with the overall growth of the community. I said I would stay on and work with children and families to help create a department for children that served the whole community lifestyle. I was hired to learn the scope of the needs of families; inspire and facilitate activities; observe and find ways to support the needs and rights that would allow the children to flourish.

Since then we have seen the young people of the Youth Project raise funds for a building of their own where they can gather and express themselves creatively. It has now been built and we had a ceremony of blessing by the whole community.

The Children's Family Department has been taking important steps to assure programmes, staffing and continuity, and to make sure that children have a vital role and influence in community life. The trustees of the Foundation have requested that Education Branch address the need for education of the young people here, in the context of the developing lifestyle of the Planetary Village. A recently evolved statement of vision says part of the department's function is: *To be of service to family by creating and sustaining, within the Planetary Village, a safe, educational and supportive place for children to develop and grow.'*

This statement for the needs of the children, their families and the Foundation, has been inspired through the mysteries of the blessed lessons that the young people here have to teach us. Their ability to express creative energy, innocently and honestly, and mirror our own condition, is a gift yet to be fully realized.

The seeds of life have been planted and we are now watering this department so it will grow—through our meditations and through the discovery of our collective willingness, and by our actions towards healing our connectedness. I am excited by the creative power that the children continue to offer and I stand deeply moved to be in this privileged place with such an abundance of beautiful, healthy, endearing children to serve.

LORI SUNSHINE
One Earth

℉

Hearts and Minds

A challenge of our times is the split we are experiencing between our heads and our hearts. When it comes to educating our children, we no longer quite know how to do it for the best. Our heads can devise many different aims for education: "Let's give our children all the intellectual learning they can absorb, as early as possible—we can even begin in the womb." Or: "Small children are so full of Spirit; it flows out of them in leaps and kicks and laughter, drawings and sayings— surely if we give them more freedom it will flow even better."

The latter philosophy forgets that creating anything usually takes time, discipline, love; formative elements which bring about the true magic of a work of art when head and heart are working together. I love the words Imagination, Magi, Majestic, Magic, Imagine—they speak of an intelligence filled with pictures; the flame of thinking tempered by the rose of love. Imaginative thinking comes from a really broad, informed perspective; from being able to envisage many sides of a given task.

About 1500 years ago Christianity came to change the consciousness of Britain. It floated in to the Celts on small coracles as a mystical, nature oriented experience and a hundred years or so later it marched in with Roman clarity of thought and organization to the Anglo-Saxons in the south. It was a religion of the head in the south and of the heart in the west and north. Whenever Celtic and Saxon religions met, a wonderful flowering came about in the realm of the soul: Lindisfarne Priory, The Book of Kells, Arthurian Legends; all gave light to the ages to come. Head and heart worked together to produce these and the whole of Europe was enriched.

An enriching meeting is occurring now in Scotland in the Moray Steiner School. The clear mind of Anthroposophy, working through the medium of a Rudolf Steiner school, is currently serving some of the parents and children gathered here around the Findhorn Community, a northern community of the heart. Some years ago, when parents in the community wanted to begin a school that would embody the qualities of the

Foundation, they chose Steiner's methods to provide the most appropriate structure.

Both the Findhorn Foundation and Anthroposophy in their essence ask for deep observation of 'what is'. Steiner's aim was to bring head and heart together and induce clarity of thinking. The Foundation, in my view, is working with the split between the masculine and the feminine, looking for clarity in the sensitive feminine world of feeling. Putting aside the cumbersome, confining labels which tend to bring up a host of images, either positive or negative, but anyway divisive, it is possible simply to see the deep wisdom of the two movements as nourishing each other and bringing a greater understanding and vitality.

The gift of Findhorn

The contribution of the Findhorn Foundation to the school is the heart connection it offers, expressed both subtly through personal support and also very practically through money and organization. The school is housed in Drumduan, one of the Foundation's properties set in beautiful wooded gardens, and for which the school pays only a very moderate rent. Having a large, diverse and loving community behind us means that our Moray Steiner School not only has the fatherly support of the Anthroposophical movement to guide it, it also has the nurturing motherly quality of the community. This is something that I have been very aware of as a teacher to the school.

The community has been hosting and healing thousands of people annually for many years so there is a wide experience of social living of love-in-action brought into their daily lives. This provides the school with a great store of heart wisdom to draw on. There is a vital underlying certainty that the needs of the school will be met if we just stay present with what is happening, and this creates a sense of care in all we do. It is as though the art of social living has reached a point of real flow. Creating a fundraising May Fayre or an Open Day is a joyful adventure in trust which allows these occasions to manifest in the most astonishing way. Having in the past experienced the stress which can surround such fundraising events, I have been amazed at the results created by a handful of fairly materially impoverished people here.

Our little school of about seventy pupils of course still has many physical needs to be met. No child is turned away for lack of funds and we receive no state subsidy to help finance us. The school's entrance hall undoubtedly needs a new floor covering; the year's budget is always in deficit until some miracle manifests; our numbers are growing so rapidly that a new assembly hall will soon be needed. But in the meantime we all work together, the older children helping with the garden and the parents cleaning and maintaining the school building.

The gift of Anthroposophy

Steiner observed that children, while growing up, pass through the whole of what humanity has experienced in macrocosm throughout history. Therefore, the literature and 'idiom' of each year of his curriculum recapitulates this progress. Having myself taught children aged from four to fourteen years, I have experienced how enthusiastically they respond to this sequence as it carries them from prehistory to modern times, through mythologies and historical stories. It is a marvellous adventure for teachers and children alike.

Steiner divided child development into seven-year stages; the first is the time of growth of the Will—a time predominantly of doing. Little children are very imitative and love to copy all that goes on around them. It is not only the fascinating and powerful noises of pots and pans clanking that attracts the toddlers, they are also playing with pots and pans to do as parents do. We can use that natural imitation fruitfully by making our actions worth imitating. At around seven years a child has formed its own etheric body and becomes a separate physical entity; by this time creative energies are freed to engage in forming thoughts instead. Too much thought before this time can lead to too much emphasis on form.

The second seven years, up to age fourteen, encompasses the growth of feelings—perhaps a sort of 'birth' of the feeling body. Prior to that stage children are very much at the mercy of their surrounding atmosphere, but around fourteen they become more independent.

The third seven years is the time for true intellectual development, so that by ages 18-21, thinking becomes independent and free, if scope has been given for that freedom to develop.

Of course these stages can overlap and intertwine with each other, as rhythms within the greater rhythm, but as a general guideline they are most helpful. We have probably all experienced how, at around the age of 21, a new independence is apparent. Or noticed that our brilliant little stars at age six are just on their way into life and have not yet altogether arrived.

A school for life

When I taught Class One, we began our day like this:

"Good morning dear children of Class One."

"Good morning Auriol."

Eighteen sparkling little faces turned towards their teacher, who will hopefully be there for them for the next seven or eight years. We would say a verse together which spoke of the sun, representing the loving parenthood of God. It also spoke of the strength which lies in us to 'love our work and learn' and of the thanks we give for this strength. Then there would be songs for the season or for fun, and then fifteen minutes of playing pentatonic flutes (minimum discords, maximum softness and warmth of tone). We would go on to a time of movement, perhaps acting a play or using bean bags, or playing social games. Then came a quick intellectual sparkle, with work on mental arithmetic and multiplication tables.

At last the moment of deep nourishment would arrive: The Story. A 'fairy story' that is actually not about fairies at all, but about the great drama of life. We all, on our way, will have to encounter witches or giants which attempt to hold us in thrall and from which it will take all our courage and wit to break loose. We too, in faithfulness to the prince or princess within us, will find lasting joy.

Then, for Class One who are still so involved with 'doing', came the best bit of work of all: recalling and preparing together what was learned the previous day, all to be recorded on the large unlined pages of their books and illustrated with bright, sweet smelling beeswax crayons which give lots of scope for colour as well as line.

Reading begins with writing—as beautiful as possible. Numbers begin with movement as we walk patterns of numbers in rhythm. Number is not really learned but is born in us, we only have to awaken consciousness of it: five toes, fingers, etc. Numbers are universal whereas writing is the product of human thought and becomes much more individual.

Two hours pass quickly to 'snack time' followed by time to learn our languages, French and German. Then handwork and painting and physical activities.

Class Two will draw on the literature of animal fables counterpoised with stories of animals and saints. The fully human and the little animal in each of us is explored without moralizing.

Class Three will have stories of the Old Testament which teach law and order; the rules that God lays down. The children will learn farming and gardening, building and crafts—they are coming down to earth.

Class Four studies local geography and animals related to humankind. They will hear about the powerful and tricky Norse Gods and explore their own power to change. They will learn how the artful intellect can get us into trouble—or out of it. Fractions are included in the number work and grammar is included in language because these reflect the inner exploration which the children are experiencing at age nine or ten. The mood of this age is: "No one really understands me" or "I don't even think these are my real parents."

Class Five is the year of harmony, expressed in ancient Greek mythologies. True history begins; also botany, geometry and the beautiful forms they create.

Class Six will explore the making of laws again, this time with the civilization of Rome. No longer are laws given from above, we now have to decide together what laws are needed for our classroom. We explore law-keeping and retribution, cause and effect. Chemistry begins.

Class Seven is the Age of Renaissance and exploration, art and adventure; all preparation for the challenges which lie ahead. Algebra as pure thinking is introduced. And so it goes on.

The true 'I' of the child—the spiritual essence—comes step by step down into incarnation to rule the kingdom guarded by the Old King (parents and teachers). The curriculum fosters this journey all the way, while still preserving the creative flow which is the hallmark of the artist and the young child. 'Art' does not refer only to painting and drawing, we can be artists at preparing a meal or managing money, too. The real artistry lies in clear imaginative thinking— putting our whole hearts into the task—and then a true morality arises which encompasses not just me and you, but I and Thou and the third element, the Holy Child, in us all.

When we manage to conserve these vital creative forces of childhood and bring them to maturity in a healthy and balanced adulthood, and link them to a real respect for the Earth and all humanity, then we are redressing the balance between mind and heart, healing the split between the two. We work with the 100th monkey principle (morphic resonance), knowing that we may not be able to reach all children, but the ones we do reach will spread the energy to others of their generation. When we know that change is possible, it is already half the battle won, and when we manifest change in the present, we are safeguarding the future for our children.

AURIOL DE SMIDT
One Earth

Since this was written, Auriol has retired and the Steiner School has raised the money and purchased the building from the Findhorn Foundation. The Moray Steiner School now teaches children up to the age of sixteen. These pupils come from all over the area and are no longer predominately from the Community.

Making a Difference

"Imagine for a moment, a world filled with young, energetic people who got together regularly and communicated with each other, with heartfelt passion, about issues that affected their lives each day. Subjects such as: discrimination, unemployment, violence, the environment, AIDS, drugs, and alcohol. Imagine these young people making positive efforts to share their values with as many people as possible. Then imagine these young people being honoured for their clarity in taking action to effect social change and for their ability to care.

What would our world be like if young people were using their power, every day, everywhere, to make a difference; using the present conditions they find themselves in as their playground for doing this essential work? What would the world be like if we heard their united call for peace and for combined wisdom that could find unique and creative solutions to our concerns?

This is what the young people here can give and are beginning, more and more, to give, as they find each other, befriend one another, and support each other to be the best they can be in every moment.

A group that gathers here regularly is the Findhorn Foundation Youth Project, and we are striving to make the world a happier place for our future lives, for all humanity, and for our children's children."

LORI SUNSHINE,
Former Focaliser of the Findhorn Foundation Youth Project.

The following quote is from Shirley Barr, a founding member of the Findhorn Foundation Youth Project.

"The Youth Project put my feet on the road to the rest of my life. It gave me many, many things. Skills at 'people work', experience of coordination of all types of events. I learned the capacity to listen to people, use my intuition, share my love for life in constructive ways. But the absolute most important way I benefitted—I learned to believe in myself. And that's where, in my view, everyone has to start".

This Project was begun in August of 1984, by two Foundation members, Allan Howard and Kim Graham. Their idea was for the young people resident within the community to form a group that would provide an outlet for their own particular expression within the work of the Foundation. The belief was that in this increasingly changing world, young people need to take responsibility for their own lives and to recognise their potential for creating a peaceful world.

The Youth Project came out of an obvious need at the time to channel the anger and boredom of the community's youth into more beneficial areas. The teenagers felt a lack of purpose and direction in their lives and these frustrations had been showing themselves in many forms including petty theft and vandalism. By coming together as a group, they could develop their own support system where they were safe to air their grief and anger, and so dissipate them without harming anything or anyone else.

The original Youth Project had a lot of success in building connections locally and internationally while at the same time establishing themselves as a powerful and close group of young people, but they grew ripe to take their next steps in life, and many of them left for university, jobs, or to travel abroad. Eventually, the Youth Project's energy died down. Then the next generation of young people entered their teens and formed a group at the Foundation, which is now the current Youth Project. We began where the old Youth Project had left off: setting our sights high and working hard to turn our dreams into a reality. As the youth of the 'nineties' our purpose was: "To use our talents as supporters of each other and explorers of ourselves and our world, through communication and creation, in order to make strong local and international connections and to build respect and belief in ourselves, others, and our planet, with love, gratitude, and fun!"

In May of 1992, we excitedly unveiled and opened our Youth Building, built of timber and with a grass-covered roof. This provides the members of the Youth Project a space to go whenever we need it. Here we can meet friends, do our business, and create a space in which to work and play in any way we choose. The energy behind our building was a long held dream that began with the need for a place for the original Youth Project to house their group meetings and gatherings; we did the fund-raising for the building and helped to design what we would need. We felt very lucky to have a beautiful, ecologically sound building and our heartfelt thanks reach out to everyone who made this a reality with us. The younger children are also able to enjoy this space when there are planned and scheduled activities for them.

Our group has grown as new people from the local area continue to join us. We keep the personal closeness that we have always had by continuing to have personal sharings, and by working together. We use a wide range of creative education, networking and leadership training to provide us all with the skills experience, and opportunities to learn to articulate our thoughts and feelings on any issue that affects us. We believe that knowing each other well and feeling comfortable with each other is the key to friendship, and that friendship is the key to having a strong group.

Despite our efforts to be unified as a group, we do face conflicts from time to time. The openness of our group allows all the anger and dislike to be aired, and when the truth is told, the conflict is eventually resolved with as little pain as possible. The others in the group are supportive of those with the difficulties, and we have found that conflict is actually a necessity that leads to greater understanding and love of one another.

It is not only the members of the group who have been brought closer together by conflict. We have had discussion between the members of the group and our parents. These have been the most beneficial of our meetings. It seems astounding how little most parents know about their children and how many things that youth feel they can not discuss with their parents for fear of their reaction. Because of this fear, many young people cannot talk to their parents about important issues in their lives. Too often, if parents find out about something that upsets them, they react by punishing—which makes us even more afraid to speak openly.

The Youth Project has become a powerful group of young people between the ages of thirteen and twenty. Not only are all the youth of the Foundation Community in the group, we also have members from the local area with no connection to the Foundation other than through their input with us. In this respect, the Youth Project is one of the best public ambassadors of the Foundation and a bridge to the 'outside world'—to Findhorn village and much farther beyond.

Although none of us might still be around here in years to come, we hope there will always be a group for the young people in the community. For this reason we are constantly taking in new members and we have a wide range of ages, projects activities and interests. We try to ensure that our group never becomes stagnant. Even though we keep getting larger, it is essential that we always retain our personal closeness and safe space, while we also remain aligned with the principles of the Findhorn Foundation. We would like to see the Youth Project have a voice that is heard by all the youth in the world. It would be a voice for personal growth, intimacy, and uniting youth everywhere.

By hosting youth programmes and conventions where young people from every nation gradually unite to solve major problems —starting out locally and moving outward internationally—youth exchanges can bring people of different countries closer together by showing each other their beauty. This is the ongoing goal that all the little things we do are aimed at. While we strive for individual happiness, we are also trying to help unite tomorrow's leaders, so that the present situation of 'everyone for himself' is exchanged for a society where people try to work together for their mutual benefit. We, as young people, are all the Presidents, the Prime Ministers, and the leaders of the future, and we can achieve what our elders have not, through spreading understanding that will lead to harmony and collaboration for everyone on our planet.

JENNIFER BROCKBANK and TOM RAYMONT
Written while they were teenage members of the Youth Project
One Earth

People Start as Children

Before arriving in Findhorn, I travelled to approximately 25 international communities all over the US while trying to learn all I could about children and education in such settings for my PhD dissertation in Child Psychology. This piece is an attempt to summarise some of what I have learned.

In the typical nuclear family, a child lives within several overlapping social contexts. First, there is the nuclear family itself, generally consisting of a child's biological parent(s) and siblings living together. Next, there is the school context where the child is typically taught in age-segregated classrooms with his or her friends and peers, and siblings are typically taught by different teachers and with different peers. In the social context of the peer group, most children have friends outside the school setting who are generally different from his or her siblings' friends.

In addition, most children's parents also participate in their own work and social contexts, which are far removed from their children's social contexts. Consequently, these children typically have little contact with adults who are not their parents, close relatives or teachers.

In a generalised model of an intentional community, we find a much closer woven network of relationships within the overlapping social contexts of family, school, friends, and work. While nearly all children in communities live with one or both biological parents, most spend much of their time with various nonbiologically- related adults, and friendships tend to develop informally as adults interact with children during mealtimes, community events, or chance meetings in their homes or around the community. I believe that such friendships are incredibly profound for children (and adults!) and are one of the most important benefits of community life. Furthermore, in communities with their own educational programmes, children tend to know their teachers outside of the school setting and their teachers tend to be friends with and/or colleagues of their parents. These factors allow students and teachers to relate on more personal levels and be more aware of each other's needs and idiosyncrasies. This can mean more individualised instruction and personal attention for the students.

While most intentional communities do not offer formal schooling to their children, diverse informal learning experiences for children are ubiquitous. In every intentional community I have visited, children are exposed to, and learn from, many complex and subtle aspects of adult life that tend to remain 'behind the scenes' for most children. For example, through exposure to their community's economic and political systems, children learn directly about such things as fiscal planning, budgeting, the use and abuse of power, negotiation and conflict resolution, leadership, voting and/or consensus building, etc. When children are able to effect changes in their community, it can be a positive experience for all concerned.

Other examples of adult activities frequently available to children include seasonal ceremonies and rituals, spiritual practices and meditation, tree planting, craft activities, cooking, and multitudes of formal and informal meetings and gatherings. Furthermore, as most contemporary intentional communities are concerned with developing a certain degree of self-sufficiency, other practical skills such as composting, food storage, organic gardening, recycling, and incorporating solar energy into building designs, are also commonly available learning experiences for these children.

So children see adults building houses, building political structures, and building relationships. Some last, others don't. In the process, parents and other adults become demystified and more human in the eyes of children.

Adults, both with and without children, also benefit from the close network of relationships frequently found in intentional communities. For example, in mainstream society it is typically difficult for childless adults to create meaningful relationships with children. In community the wide range of involvement available to childless adults lets them participate in the joy and the work involved in caring for children without assuming the awesome responsibilities and obligations of becoming a parent.

Furthermore, through sharing childcare and related tasks such as cooking, laundry, shopping and cleaning, adults with children are freed to pursue activities other than parenting and to be more fully involved in the work and activities of the community.

Now, just so you don't think having children in community is all peaches and cream, I will also briefly mention a couple of disadvantages frequently associated with integrating children into community life. First, with so many adult–child relationships, parents and children have to contend with many different theories and expectations about everything from nappy changing to the budding sexuality of adolescents. From a parental perspective, whether it's trying to enforce a particular diet or bedtime, or trying to locate their child's shoes in the morning which could be in one of a million places, this lack of control over their children's behaviour and environment can be extremely frustrating. Conversely, from a child's point of view, inconsistency and miscommunication among multiple caregivers with respect to discipline and expectations can also be extremely confusing. Some people have even given a name to this phenomena calling it the 'Cinderella effect' as in "Cinderella, do this!" "No, Cinderella, do this!"

Secondly, because of their large amount of free time and their limited mobility, resources and private space, children are frequent users of communal space and, consequently, are frequent violators of rules or norms involving noise and neatness. This can be especially frustrating in crowded communities and for adults who do not particularly enjoy the company of children. Also, for children, the omnipresence of social interactions may make it difficult for them to find time or space to be alone.

So it seems that children present particular challenges and opportunities for intentional communities. On the whole, I believe the pros of integrating children into community life far outweigh the cons. Through such efforts, children are provided with nurturing and holistic environments in which they can learn to share, endure and generally live with others. Given the rapid pace at which our world is progressing, empowering children with a de facto understanding of group processes and adaptation to change is likely to be one of the most important contributions that contemporary communities can make to children and to the world.

So, what does this all mean to the Findhorn Community? It means supporting children/families financially and socially even though they seem to take time away from what some may consider to be 'more important' activities. This does not mean abandoning a spiritual focus. Quite the contrary, it means opening ourselves to the spiritual gifts, lessons and challenges children constantly offer.

To care for the child without is to care for the child within. I firmly believe that fully welcoming children and families into its heart is the critical next step this community must take if it truly wants to become a 'planetary village'. It has been said many times that instead of growing 40-pound cabbages, the Findhorn Foundation now 'grows people.' People start as children.

DANIEL GREENBERG
Extracted from an article for One Earth

Postscript: Daniel lived in the Findhorn Community for eight months as a 'workscholar' in the Children and Family department. He and his wife, Monique return occasionally. They now have children of their own.

PeaceTrees

"...*People working together can reach a common goal and make a difference to what's happening in the world. When we accept each individual for who they are, what they look like, what they believe in, what they feel and what they think, then we will have unity. When everyone listens to what their hearts and minds are saying, they can do the right thing and we can have peace. We all live in this world with all its wonders, beauties, hardship and decay. We all need to respect the world, each other, and ourselves. We are all responsible for what we do to each other, ourselves and the world. Why not make a better situation? After all, we can.*"

MARCUS AIGNER, *a PeaceTrees participant*

The Camden PeaceTrees project was organised by two ex-members of the Findhorn Foundation and people from the EarthStewards Network, who had set up other PeaceTrees projects in many countries. Eighty people from all over the world gathered to work in this run-down North American city. Thirty of the participants were from various rehabilitation centres around New Jersey; they were just finishing their sentences and were soon to be released.

Not everyone in the Findhorn Foundation Youth Project went to Camden, but the whole Youth Project helped and supported the group who were going by joining in with fund-raising activities like car washing, a pizza service and a jumble sale. When our big day finally arrived we were bundled onto the bus as we bid our farewells to family and friends, and we started off on our long journey to the States.

We arrived starry eyed on an eighteen-mile-long, golden beach island just off New Jersey, where we stayed for the first two days in utter bliss. This was what we had all pictured America to be: beach, big cars, beach houses, good looking men, '7-elevens' and sun.

We left Long Beach Island and arrived at one of the worst ghettos in the United States. Gathering in the car park of Rutgers University where we would be staying for the next three weeks, we met some of the people we would be working with—what a shock, to say the least.

There were big dudes from the rehabilitation centre, twice our size, with huge afro hairdos. With unusually quiet voices, we said our Scottish hellos.

There were also young people from many different countries such as India, Russia, Costa Rica, Canada, Ireland. What we didn't know in that first moment, was that in the next three weeks we were all going to build very close friendships with these people.

After we settled in and began to get to know each other, we started our first day of work. We woke up at 7 am, had breakfast at 8.30 and started work at 9 am sharp. Once or twice during our three weeks, work was delayed because we had transport problems, and on these days we would fill in the spare time hanging out, getting to know each other. We always seemed to be busy.

When we began work we found ourselves on a littered square patch, a barren plot between two buildings in the middle of the city —which we were going to transform into a flower and vegetable garden for the local community. We started with a blessing for the opening of the whole PeaceTrees project, and the Mayor of Camden and the media joined in with the official ceremony.

We were all assigned to one of three working groups: the garden group, the tree planting group and the cooking group. We rotated through all of these groups over the three weeks so that in this way the responsibilities were shared.

The garden group had the task of removing all the glass, metal and litter that had collected on the site over the years, and then the ground could be weeded and prepared for the planting of trees and shrubs. The tree planting group were assigned to smash up squares of concrete and dig holes along the sidewalk to make space for the trees. Manure and fertilised soils were then layered down in the holes to provide a healthy start for the young trees to grow.

The cooking crew were led by an amazing black man called Thomas, who worked voluntarily, full-time for the whole three weeks, preparing and cooking meals for all the 80 PeaceTrees participants. He grew increasingly more loving and open to our group as the days passed, and he served the simple, institution-type food with a smile. And he always provided a second helping if we wanted one.

We ate our meals in a cafeteria style room with plastic utensils and plates and school-like benches and tables. The food was always some kind of meat, bread, and fried potato, and a canned dessert.

As well as doing a lot of hard work we still had some time for fun. We had a block party, where all the neighbourhoods related to what we were doing came together and joined us for a huge pot-luck supper outside. We also had a dinner party at our base (a nearby church). We went to see a American baseball game, and a youth theatre production called Love All People, which was about youth empowerment and respect for all people.

A nearby pizzeria donated boxes and boxes of pizza and we took these and all of our 80 participants across the Delaware River by boat to Philadelphia harbour, where we spent the evening eating pizza, singing Lori Sunshine's children's songs, listening to Irish folk songs, and laughing and dancing the night away. The evening ended with a splash when we found ourselves in the middle of the biggest lightning and thunder storm we had ever experienced, and we ran whooping through the deep puddles, giggling and soaking each other in a huge water fight. It was a night to remember.

Towards the end of the first week we split into groups of men and women; the women were to spend a day at an assault course in Pennsylvania and the men were going to participate in an American Indian ritual sweatlodge.

We arrived at the assault course after another original yet wonderful breakfast from Thomas and the cooking team. We filed out of the vans, and found ourselves at the bottom of several extremely tall telegraph poles, hanging from which were numerous ropes and harnesses. There was stunned silence.

When we caught our breath, we blurted, "Get real!" "No way!" and "You can't make me!"

We were then told by our instructors that there was no such word as 'can't'.

"What about 'won't'?" we asked, but we knew it was useless and we'd be up there on those poles before the day was through.

We started with some easier games; one was called 'Trust', where we had six people in a line holding hands with another six people across from them in a line, and one person standing on a high tree stump on their own, with their back to everyone in the lines. When the hand-holding people were ready, the standing person let herself fall backwards into everyone's waiting and supporting arms. The games lasted until lunchtime.

During lunch we mixed and talked with the girls from the rehabilitation centres and also with the girls from other countries. At first this was extremely difficult because the 'corrections' girls looked mean and rough and didn't seem too enthusiastic about getting to know us. But within half an hour we were all sitting around the picnic tables, eating pizza and talking like old friends. They turned out to be such nice people— compared with our first impressions. Now they were gathering around us enthusiastically to find out where we came from, what Scotland was like, and what we thought about America. It was a breakthrough in communication.

Lunch was over and then it was back to the rope course. Some of us headed back towards the smaller rope courses, only to be directed back to the extremely large telegraph poles, where we then stood paralysed with fear. The harnesses were handed out and we were instructed in how to put them on.

We then did everything from walking along ropes forty feet above the ground, to doing a final trapeze jump from a platform at the top of one of the poles. The day was unforgettable and proved to be a confidence building and eye-opening experience.

Another eye-opening experience was just living on the campus of Rutgers University (a State University of New Jersey). Since it is situated in a ghetto, there was maximum security provided all the time —undercover police, security guards patrolling the premises with guns. We had to have personal identification cards so we could enter the main building. All of these precautions were taken for our own safety.

It seemed everyone wanted to help and get involved with the PeaceTrees project, from locals in Camden to the US Army. One particular member of the US army (who befriended many of us and went by the unforgettable name of Captain Yesko), was always willing to help out in his spare time and contribute as much as he could.

The local church, that was our daytime base, was looked after by Father Michael Doyle, and he gave much of his time to help with the PeaceTrees project, encouraging young and old to work together harmoniously. He had dedicated his life to healing and helping poor people.

Although planting trees was our main purpose in the project, there were many other things we ended up doing: looking at our attitudes to each other, our sexuality, our beliefs and our religions, and we were able to use and express our attitudes and emotions.

The PeaceTrees Project drew to a close, our bags were packed and it was time to say our goodbyes. The Department of Corrections bus came and collected the young people from Camden, and warm loving hugs and promises of friendship were exchanged. There were tears filled with the sadness of saying goodbye. Eventually everyone left. As our plane took off to leave America, we all felt as though we had left a part of ourselves behind.

IVY WILLMOTT, ZOË ISAKSEN, ERGA and
SHEERA SUTHERLAND
At the time of writing aged 16, 14, and 16
One Earth

Update: PeaceTrees Projects became annual events in several parts of the world until the death of the coordinator, Danaan Parry, in 1995. These years covered a period of economic and social change in Russia and violent upheaval in the Balkans and areas of the Middle East. I was privileged to help facilitate several of these projects and was inspired by the way the young people from these and other areas of the world and with different ethnic and social backgrounds worked cooperatively together to complete each project, to understand one another and to develop lasting friendships. Kay.

Community Studies

In January 1995 the Findhorn Foundation, in partnership with Pacific Lutheran University in Washington State, USA, created a popular fifteen-week programme in community studies, based here at the Findhorn Foundation. The programme has grown steadily since.

After many years of hosting short-term student groups and some independent long-term graduate students, the Community Studies Programme is a milestone in creating closer collaboration between the Findhorn Foundation Community and the academic world. The programme, developed by Professor Lawry Gold and several Community members, provides students with the opportunity for an in-depth experience of community life, while maintaining the academic rigor required by universities. The result is a truly holistic educational experience, where intellectual, emotional and spiritual development is integrated within the context of living in community.

As the 21st century begins, the problems of our world threaten to reach crisis proportions. Today's youth will inherit the economic, ecological, social and spiritual problems of tomorrow's world. Traditional academic education often falls short in preparing young adults for the challenges of our world while alternative education centres such as the Findhorn Foundation tend to be less accessible to young people. Students need educational experiences which prepare them for the enormous challenges and responsibilities that they will collectively face.

The Community Studies Programme is a response to that need. It aims to help prepare students as potential leaders of tomorrow by attending to their spiritual and emotional development, as well as their intellectual development. The emphasis is on integrating concepts and theories with real life experiences, through written reflection, discussion and practical application. Reading and writing are integral parts of the programme and students send weekly essays, via the Internet, to Professor Gold, who monitors the academic progress and standards of the programme.

This community is an ideal setting for such a programme. The Community itself becomes the classroom where students can develop an holistic world view. Here, they learn some of the basic ingredients for creating a sustainable future, through the study of psychology, human ecology and other subjects, within the context of a spiritual community. Students can also engage with the wide variety of exciting projects, such as Trees For Life and the Moray Steiner School, as well as many other community activities such as pottery, art, music, dance and theatre. Community members share the skills and expertise they have developed here over many years. In the Findhorn Foundation Community, the available 'faculty' outnumbers the students! Students also join in the communitywide activities such as conferences, festivals and meetings, where they can benefit from the extraordinary talent and wisdom of our visiting international faculty.

Students become part of the fabric of the Community, working in the kitchens or gardens, in addition to attending classes, workshops and events. As a group, they also become a community within a Community, grappling with such issues as group decision-making, trust, intimacy, and dealing with differences and conflicts. The process can be intensive at times. However, this intensity of experience is what most students come looking for. They want something that is 'hands on' and teaches them skills that will help them deal with a wide range of situations in life. The day to day joys and challenges of living together combined with the rich diversity of activities available on our 'campus' make this a unique environment for students to develop the awareness and life skills they will need to become agents of change in the world.

The programme also takes students into the wider area, where they can explore more of Scotland. They spend several days in Edinburgh, visit Celtic and pre-Celtic sites, and stay for a week on Erraid. Some students have even traced their family heritage to a local clan and found their family tartan. They also use their mid-term week to travel independently and many take time to see more of the UK and Europe at the end of the semester before heading home.

The Community has warmly welcomed the students and many friendships have been formed here. They bring to us energy, youth and vitality that enliven us. Their questions and observations help keep us reflecting on what we do, while their unfolding and blossoming as aware young adults inspires us. They remind us of what our work here is really all about.

BEN FUCHS
Network News

To Russia with Love

A few years ago a colleague and I were privileged to shepherd a group of 16 young people between the ages of 15 and 18 from the Findhorn Foundation Youth Project to the Kitezh Children's Community in Russia for two weeks of work, play and learning.

We spent our first night in Moscow and spent the next morning sightseeing. We visited Red Square and the Kremlin. The sizes, colours and lavishness of it all took our breath away. We left for Kitezh late that afternoon, on what we discovered was a 'good' Russian bus. We arrived just before midnight after a long, hot eight-hour journey. We spent the first night in houses rather than set up camp in the dark. We pitched our tents the next morning and spent most of the day preparing what were to be our homes for the next twelve days.

A typical day at Kitezh went something like this: we were up by 8.30 am with morning exercises for mind and body at 8.45. At 9 am we had breakfast and then began work. The routine at Kitezh is that boys and men do the building and work in the fields with the hay, while the girls and women do the gardening and cooking. Being from the West, we challenged this idea and some of the girls did building and worked in the fields as well. We worked until 12.30 and then walked to the nearby lake, 3–4 kilometers away, for a swim.

Lunch was at 2 pm. All meals were prepared and eaten in a big old canvas tent. It was unbelievably hot inside and when it rained outside, it also rained inside the tent! On the highest beam in the centre of the tent there was a birds' nest which had four chirping babies in it.

At 3 pm we gave English lessons to the children who either lived at Kitezh or were staying there for a month or two as a break from a Moscow orphanage.

We worked in small groups—usually two of us and three, four or five Russians. It was quite a challenge to teach English, especially as we could not speak more than a few words of Russian. However, the adults of Kitezh said that the children all made real progress with their English speaking over the time we were there.

We often found that just by spending time with the children, playing games, swimming, etc, their confidence was built up, and then they were more inspired to learn English and thrilled to teach us some Russian. We all laughed together as we struggled with the Russian pronunciations.

From 4–7 pm we were free to do as we pleased, We might spend time with the children and the adults of the community. Some of us took part in sports, arts and crafts, cooking, and teaching English to adults. We also used the time to relax at our campsite playing cards, reading or sleeping.

After a 7 pm dinner we took part in various activities. Some nights there were discos in the schoolhouse, singing by the campfire, and one night there was even a special Russian celebration at the lake. We also organised evening activities including Scottish dancing and games, and a prizes night for the children. Friendships were made in the most unique ways: sports, singing (everyone knows the Beatles' songs!) and hand and body gestures became normal means of communication.

We learned a lot during our time at Kitezh. It was very hard not to when we were surrounded by 50 orphaned or unwanted children. Also, Russian country life is so different from anything we had ever experienced. The importance of people working together to make sure there is enough food for all the people and animals, and firewood to keep warm in the winter, taught us so much about living day to day. At Kitezh they don't spend hours thinking about who has a nicer house, car or job. This made us consider the materialistic culture that we all live in. We realised how much we take for granted, for example, when on the third day of our visit to Kitezh the well ran dry. It was scary not knowing where the next drop of water would come from. It was often a physical challenge for us. The food was unusual for us as the temperature was around 28–30° C. However, not only did we connect well with Russian young people, but the time at Kitezh brought our own group closer as well. We really supported each other through hard times. There were lots of tears and laughter.

To end our trip we spent three days in St Petersburg seeing the sights. We visited St Isaac's Cathedral, the Hermitage Museum— Peter the Great's

Summer Palace, and the War Memorial from the Siege of Leningrad. We went to see 'Kapella', incredible Russian folk dancing and singing, and we also saw 'Swan Lake' (wow! a real Russian ballet!). We even had time for some souvenir shopping on the main street, Nevsky Prospect. St Petersburg was breathtaking and it was intriguing for us to see the way the West has so strongly impacted upon this city in recent times. There were times when we could have been walking down a busy London street if we judged by the shops and fashions that we could see. By the time we were on the bus to the airport we were all completely exhausted and ready to come home.

All of us are grateful for our experience. We are thrilled at the prospect of having exchange groups of Kitezhians come here to the Findhorn Community and Scotland.

JESSICA ABRAMS
Network News

Update: Kitezh is so-called after a Russian folk tale that tells of a time when, after years of great struggle, the country will once again have hope for the future.

The project continues to offer this hope as it expands. There is now a second village, Orion, where more orphan children are helped to thrive and to grow into remarkable beings. This does give hope to Russia and to many people around the world who are inspired to be involved in the vision. We know the old saying: 'it takes a village to bring up a child'. Through the Ecologia Youth Trust community members and others continue to support, both practically and financially, these newly forming villages.
Discover more at: www.ecologia.org.uk

F

CHAPTER SIX

JEWELS IN THE SEA

Iona and Erraid are two small islands which lie close together off the larger island of Mull on the western coast of northern Scotland. The Findhorn Foundation was given a house on Iona which is used a retreat house for members and paying guests. Erraid, a smaller tidal island, is owned by a Dutch family who enjoy being there for a number of weeks in the summer. For the rest of the year the island is lived on and cared for by the Erraid Community, which is a satellite of the Findhorn Foundation.

F

Retreating to Iona

Saturday, four-twenty a.m. My alarm clock wakens me to a bright June morning. Today I'm driving the Community bus that links us here at The Park, Findhorn with our sister community on the isle of Erraid, and with the island of Iona and the Foundation's retreat house, Traigh Bhan.

Each week one or two Foundation members volunteer to drive this 350mile round trip. Today I'm going just one way and will stay for a week on Iona. Someone returning from the island will drive the bus back.

At 5.10 I'm at the Foundation's Community Centre collecting several of my passengers—a mix of Foundation members and guests and a young mother with her two year old child—then to Cluny Hill College to board the others. A total of eleven people going today. Food and other supplies

113

for Erraid and Traigh Bhan have been loaded on to the bus the previous afternoon.

We briefly join hands to ask for a blessing on our journey, then it's off through Forres and the quick run to Inverness. From there the road winds south along the shore of Loch Ness—if the passengers aren't too sleepy they will likely have a look for 'Nessie', the famous Loch Ness monster, reputed to haunt the depths of the loch. A stop for a brief stretch at Fort Augustus, and then on past Loch Lochy and through the Great Glen. Skies are clearing now, giving us a view of Ben Nevis, Scotland's highest peak, still with some scattered snow patches on its higher elevations.

As we approach Fort William I glance at my watch: it's 7.40 and we are in good time to catch our first ferry. This ten-minute crossing marks the transition point from busy highways to the emptier and rugged beauty of western Scotland. Soon the road narrows to 'single track', with driving speed governed by how far I can see the road ahead. I need to be on the alert for oncoming vehicles. The road wends its way along the shore of sea-lochs, then climbs steeply as the bus crawls up in low gear. It's now a sunny day as we cross rolling hills to plunge again to sea level and our second ferry.

Again our timing is good and we'll be on the 9.30 departure for the Isle of Mull. After this fifteen minute crossing it's another hour's drive across the wild and beautiful, sparsely settled countryside of Mull. Our destination is Fionnphort, here my relief driver is waiting. He will deliver the remaining passengers the short distance to the jetty opposite Erraid, and take returning people back to The Park at Findhorn.

Those of us going to Iona make our way to the pier where we join the other dozens of travellers eager to touch Iona's shore. This small western Scottish Island was home to Druids in Celtic times. Here St. Columbus brought Christianity from Ireland to Scotland in the 563, founding a monastery on a site where today, fourteen centuries later, a Christian community flourishes at Iona Abbey

After the crossing we walk from the small village by the jetty, past the ruins of the 13th-century nunnery and the familiar presence of the Iona Abbey. Twenty minutes later we are at the north end of the Island near the white sands at the edge of the sound. Across the open fields amidst pasture land dotted with wild flowers is Traigh Bhan.

Traigh Bhan had been gifted to the Findhorn Community in the 1970s by Jessica Ferriera, a spiritually sensitive woman who set aside one of the rooms in the house as a sanctuary in which she did regular meditative work for the uplifting of the planet.

Since the Foundation acquired the use of Traigh Bhan, much work has been done to preserve and improve it. The outer fabric of the house has been extensively rebuilt, and the interior has been renewed, including new kitchen equipment with a Rayburn stove that provides warmth, hot water and coal-fired cooking. The house has been comfortably furnished.

The sanctuary remains a clear and beautiful environment for meditation and personal introspection as one looks out beyond the images of the dove and the Celtic cross, and across the turquoise water of Iona Sound to the hills of Mull.

Over the years Traigh Bhan has provided a welcoming environment for renewal and relaxation to scores of Foundation members and guests. The Foundation's Management group has an annual working retreat at Traigh Bhan which provides a vital space for the group to work with its own interpersonal relationships as well as to draw on the inspiration of Iona to clarify Community goals and direction. Indeed, Traigh Bhan can serve this function for all those who spend a week there.

I shall always cherish the time I spent alone at Traigh Bhan, being nurtured in the peace of Iona and in the nourishing environment that Traigh Bhan provides.

CHARLES PETERSEN

Iona Most Ancient

Iona, most ancient,
The stony heart of the world,
I will chant your name
Like a mantra.
I will tell your stones
Like rosary beads,

Stone like fired and fractured clay,
Stone black and smooth,

Flowing down to the sea,
Shaped to fit the hand
To touch and stroke,
To lie against and press
The mouth to.
There is nothing in this world
But rock and water and sky
And always the light,
Present or absent,

In its absence most present,
Imminent, on the point
of breaking through.
What is hidden will be revealed.

ℱ

No Ferry Today

The white waves leap up
On the dark rock
And fall back,
Leap up and fall back,
White waves racing
Up the Sound of Iona.
No ferry today.
Who would want to be elsewhere?

LYNN BARTON

ℱ

Growing on Erraid

I first encountered the Isle of Erraid in February 1990 on a one-week visit. I felt at home immediately, resonating with the bright, rough rocky land and salty wind. Childhood experiences of annual Irish holidays, a year on Malta and three years near Dartmoor, had instilled in me a cellular understanding and love of granite, shore, transparent sea and changing light.

At the time of this first visit I was near the end of a 10-year sojourn in landlocked Midwestern USA, so I was hungry and thirsty for this landscape. My inner being, however, had an even stronger appetite for what the Findhorn Foundation's spiritual school had to offer, so I spent 5 years there, going through a period of exhilarating (sometimes painful) transformation, discovering what was 'mine' and what was motivated by my perception of other people's expectations. It became clear that Motherhood was my Holy Grail.

A single man arrived (they occasionally do!), also looking for a relationship and I latched on to him. We struggled to find a way together on-off-on-off for about a year and a half. We got (accidentally or unconsciously) pregnant. Shock! Hallelujah! My womanhood suddenly made sense to me, at 40. Eleven weeks along, I miscarried. Such sadness. I experienced the terror of death and loss as my tenderest dream was wrenched from me. At the same time, I was utterly blessed by the care and support of my friends and community and could create the space I needed to integrate what had happened.

Later, my man and I took a week off to go to Erraid to ponder whether our relationship was strong enough to embrace parenthood consciously. Within two days of arriving I knew I had to extend my stay by another week. The next day a special prayer circle was held at Full Moon. I prayed "to live my deepest dream, NOW!" The day after that, clambering alone on the heather hills, I heard, felt or knew this: "I could live on Erraid." Next thought: "What a privilege!"

Dave seemed amused or bemused by this but had no particular reaction. We parted at the end of the week with no conclusions drawn and he returned to our home in The Park at Findhorn. So I let it sit, gently, though I told one friend on the island of my inspiration to live there.

The following week, I was on my way to Iona for the day, thinking things over. At the time I often used the DMA technique of 'Creating Your Own Reality', by stating personal choices as a first step in making positive changes. That day my heartfelt choices were: I choose to play guitar, I choose to live on Erraid and I choose to make a commitment to Dave. Whoosh! The last one had a lot of energy! That afternoon the February weather changed suddenly and a storm blew up. I became stranded on Iona. In the evening on our telephone date, my boyfriend declared his decision to call a halt to the relationship. My world imploded. Alone, I spent a desolate and panic-stricken night holding on to life and sanity by praying and trying to breathe.

The next day dawned ludicrously calm and bright. I got home to Erraid feeling as fragile as paper. I fell weeping on a friend. He said, with his wonderful clarity, "Katie, it sounds funny to say this now, but I can't believe the timing. You're free to live on Erraid!" In the blur of grief I could acknowledge that Spirit in its most Shiva-like ferocity had flung wide the door of my life and blasted me to the threshold of a new path forward. I had asked for my (soul's) deepest dream to be realised and here it was, apparently—NOW!

I was living on Erraid three months later, having substantially completed the former relationship and travelling light. I hadn't lost everything—I had health, sanity, wealth, direction and a fundamental trust in Life. But I was liberated from the Dream that had haunted me for so long and so intensely. Sitting on the high point of Erraid the day I arrived, I heard, felt or knew that I was on the island "to give, to love and to serve."

What are these qualities if not those of Motherhood? Circumstances, or Spirit, had forced me to surrender utterly to a greater wisdom and in doing so I effortlessly entered the stream of service within the Angel of Findhorn, within Life. Formerly service had always sounded servile or grandiose to me, but now this energy guides me constantly: to do the accounts when boating and gardening were my love, to learn to milk the cows, though I was truly scared of animals of any size; ultimately to focalise the community, shouldering real responsibility for the first time in my life and learning to stand tall but flexible in my truth.

The experience of Erraid has many aspects in common with pilgrimage. Those who are drawn to live here are seeking a powerful, transforming experience, opening to the unknown. We don't move through space as you would on a journey towards a sacred place, but there is a measure of deprivation in the rugged lifestyle, simple food, limited privacy and absence of distractions. We are in a way trapped together, our Master is the island, the elements and the community. We receive tough lessons via personality clashes or elemental extremes. This one-stop pilgrimage is purifying and enlightening.

There's no back seat on Erraid, so it's impossible to stay on the island without being fully present and committed. I feel quite strongly that in our situation, personal needs must always be considered in the light of community needs and, if necessary, take second place. I feel blessed that this has flowed for me during my four or so years on the island, and yet now I sense the door marked 'EXIT' subtly opening. Why now? It's a sense that I have learned the major lessons Erraid can teach me, that I have given everything I could and that it's time to step aside and let others shape and be shaped by this magical place. If you had asked me to leave any earlier I would have thrown a major tantrum, but now I'm fulfilled and ready to open to new horizons.

The gifts I take with me are: a commitment to serving the planet by living lightly and close to the Earth, more self-confidence, deeper self-knowledge and acceptance of my limitations, broader understanding and tolerance towards others, better listening, respect for animals, scores of practical and group skills, more joy in simple things, hope, inner peace and—hey! guess what?—a really nourishing partnership! I might have learned all these things at the Mothership of Findhorn but it was at her precious offshoot that I met the Angel in all its glory, for which I am, of course, endlessly grateful.

KATIE LLOYD

F

The Life in a Day on Erraid

It is hard to get up on a cold wintry Monday morning here on Erraid, but the alarm clock is persistent! It's 6.30 am, time for meditation and my herb tea before heading off to the byre.

A serious dose of Monday morning blues is upon me. I drag myself out of bed, stick the kettle on, pee in my bucket, light a candle and sit for an hour. My meditation practice is simple: just connecting to my breath, centering and entering the stillness, preparing for the day ahead and allowing time to be with myself.

By 7.30 I feel a bit more ready to go, as stumbling out into the dark street, changing into overalls, milk pail and cow bucket in hand, I head for the byre. A brilliant, crispy clear, still morning and no other signs of life, not even Goosey who's usually standing outside the byre demanding his breakfast in a very loud voice!

We have five cows. Two are milked in the morning, Maeve first, a very large heifer. I brush her and sing to her, and perch on a stool to milk her. It's a bit of a movable feast as we shuffle up and down the stall together, with me, a bucket in one hand and teat in the other, trying to anticipate her every move! And then there's dear old Rhone who stands meekly chomping away on her bucket of goodies— what a joy she is to milk!

Time to get everyone out of the byre including the chickens that live in the back section. Cows manage to produce vast quantities of dung in just a very few hours, so there is lots of shoveling to be done. I look up and notice the dawn heralding a beautiful day and my spirits lift.

It's a rush to make it for 9.00 singing in our little sanctuary on the hill, overlooking Iona. It's a lovely way to come together in the morning, singing Earth chants, Sufi chants, and Taize songs. A familiar sound on Erraid is the bell which announces morning meetings and at 9.30 all the residents and guests gather in our communal lounge to plan the day. There are meals to cook, wood to split, candles to make and polish and seaweed to collect.

A great morning for seaweed collection—low tide, gorgeous clear weather. Five of us head for the beach to await tractor and trailer, pile up the seaweed with pitchforks and head back up to the Community, where the seaweed gets tipped at various strategic points ready to be spread on the gardens and pastures. This is a great muscle-warming jovial activity down at the strand by Christine's croft. Christine is the only resident on the island who is not part of the Findhorn/Erraid Community. She has owned her croft for thirty-six years.

We manage three loads of seaweed before midday meditation—a service meditation following Findhorn Foundation themes—then it's back down the hill for lunch. Piping hot soup and winter sprouts and salads, mostly gathered from our own gardens. We try and grow enough to see us through the year.

My areas of focus are the kitchen and accommodations but I spend a lot of my time working in the garden, as well as milking. I love the variety. Every day is different and can be tailor made to suit the weather. Today the island is really calling me, so straight after lunch, I head up to the High Point, past the brand new observatory which was helicoptered into place a couple of months ago, replacing the old original rusty worn-out version. Erraid was built as a shore station for lighthouse keepers in the 1850s. They also quarried stone to build the whole settlement as well as the lighthouse of Dubh Arhach. The observatory was used to signal to the lighthouses in the days before radio.

The view is breathtaking. I love to see the winter sun, the clarity of light is extraordinary and the colours superb. The combination of the low sun and pink granite is quite magical. You can see for miles—so many other islands dotted on the horizon. The whole of Erraid is more or less visible from this point and I stand in the stillness with not even a puff of wind!

I had planned to do my accommodation letters in the afternoon, but I can't bear to go inside on such a glorious day and decide instead to make hay while the sun shines and get some of the seaweed onto the newly prepared beds. It's so nutritious for the garden and I spend the afternoon happily plodding up and down with my wheelbarrow and pitchfork, loading and unloading.

We knock off at about 16.00 in winter, but today it's still light enough to be outside for longer. The water is so still, the sky is turning a glorious colour. I feel like going for a row. So I trundle down to the pier and launch the row boat from the ramp. Thankfully the tide has come in now, which facilitates an easy launching. As Erraid is a tidal island, we live closely to the tides which dictate our every move. We spend a lot of time glued to the tide timetables.

I head up the bay towards Christine's croft, and decide to tie up at her jetty for a visit. It's wonderfully normal at Christine's; she has a gin and tonic and cigarette in hand and we have a jolly good old natter! Christine reckons Erraid is her own version of Coronation Street. The 'Erraid Street' provides the best local gossip in the neighbourhood and she keeps her eye on all the comings and goings. A visit to Christine's is such a change of scene from the Street. She has lived full time on Erraid for about twenty years, so knows all the old faces and is full of stories about the early Findhorn days.

On Monday evenings Katie (another member) and I go to choir practice in the local village church hall. Another outing in the boat, this time in the dark! This is always a bit of an adventure, especially when there's no moonlight and it's difficult to pick out the jetty on a full tide. Choir practice is a very sociable occasion, meeting some of the local women and singing at various events. The next one in the pipeline is the annual Burn's supper tribute to the great Scottish poet, Robert Burns.

Finally, home to bed and thank God for electric blankets is what I say! Some people think that life is very primitive here, but actually I find it most luxurious! A hot bath and bed brings my blessed day to an end.

GWEN ATWOOD
Network News.

CHAPTER SEVEN

HEALING

*The healing of Mind Body and Spirit is a strong thread
running throughout this Community.*

I am with you that I might heal.
You are with me that you might heal.
We are together that we might heal.
We are healing that we might love.

Lyrics by PHYLLIDA TEMPLETON

Sophie's Smile

I only saw Sophie smile in a dream, and it was always the same dream. I
would be walking in the darkness and could see, at the end of a tunnel, a
rose garden in the most brilliant light. Sitting at a table is Sophie. She sees
me, waves a hand and smiles.

Maybe she did not have much to smile about, for at the time I met her
she was 28 years old and had cervical cancer. She had been told by a friend
to go to Findhorn and ask for my help. I did my best to convince her that
she had come to the wrong person, but Sophie insisted that her friend (of
whom I have no recollection) said that I was an Explorer and would know
what to do.

Sophie believed that there just *had* to be a natural solution, somewhere out there in nature. If there wasn't then she would die, rather than return to face conventional treatment for her cancer. So the question was, "How do I behave like an explorer at Findhorn that may guide Sophie in the right direction to heal herself?"

It can be said that explorers are only Boy Scouts without a woggle, who can keep a promise and are sometimes capable of a good deed. The solution I decided upon was to do what grown-ups sometimes forget to do: go and have some fun. We'd have a picnic by the sea...

In that summer of '81 we had more than our pick of sunshine days. However, finding our way to a deserted beach by the long walk through the Culbin forest, made Sophie very uncomfortable.

"I don't like being here", she said.

"It's the forest, it makes me very nervous," she explained. I drew most of her attention with non-stop chatter about commitment: the commitment of holding on to a vision and never letting go.

Before we descended out of the forest she saw before her all the brightness of sand and sea. It made her cry "Yippee!" and run ahead.

There was an empty beach without a stone, and a sea without a ripple. All this, and a sun in a cloudless sky. Sophie danced barefoot where the sea ran in and washed over the untrodden sand. She seemed to be looking for life as she kicked at the water to fill a need for action. Her fancy took her to bring in the wood and tend our fire. There was freedom to saunter for miles, and she did. She took with her the company of sun, sea and sand, and the caresses of a warm breeze.

A big black bird flew low over the sea. Sophie stopped tending the fire and watched its flight.

"That's a cormorant, isn't it?" she asked. It tickled her even more when she learnt that the bird, like us, could be having trout for tea.

We filled the belly of the trout (I had bought them from the fishmonger in Forres that morning) with almonds and mushrooms, and laid them on the fire. Then came the watching and waiting upon what our own expectations might be.

With daylight fading, the fire drew more of our attention. We stared at nothing but the magic of the flames and let them steal our cares away. I told the story of a holy man to keep darkness at bay.

It concerned the lama who lives mostly in a monastery in a place known as 'The Valley of the Moon', north of Junbesi, that lies beyond the trail to Mount Everest. When a new moon comes with a new season, the lama leads pilgrims to where the valley runs out and the moon stands still at the holy lake of Numbur, and it's there, at the water's edge, that people stand and ask for deliverance.

So we had our twelve hours of picnic—and it was just a picnic— but according to Sophie next morning "It was the most wonderful day in my life". She may not have been smiling, but her whole persona was abuzz with life. While I was trying to work out exactly what caused her glowing transformation, she asked:

"Didn't we walk home in the dark through that forest?"

I nodded.

"Imagine that," she went on. "Me in a forest, and in the dark."

Then she went on: "Couldn't we both hold the vision of me getting well?" I gave her a promise, and a hug. And that was the last time I saw Sophie, until the dream of her sitting smiling in a rose garden.

This all came about a year after our beach picnic. She telephoned asking if I could arrange for her to go to the holy lake with the lama, and stay with him in his monastery in the Himalayan foothills. I asked Sophie— as one would—how her health was. She wouldn't tell me: and that's how the dream of Sophie came about. For years it was all I had to hold on to, but hold on I did.

So much came out of that day that I played being an 'explorer' at Findhorn. It took me a time to work out the extent that Nature played in Sophie's transformation, but finally I did. The first step was admitting the depth of my ignorance about the full effect that Nature might have on her. With this out of the way it became all plain sailing, and a lot of fun.

I became such a convert, impressed with each new discovery of the nurturing spirit of Nature that I had a tent permanently pitched in the forest, close to our original beach fire. And as the years went by, I would go and acknowledge the boundaries of Nature, and especially the simplicity of it all. It felt as if it was all mine and I could share with whoever I wished the extraordinary calming effects of a smooth sea on the body and soul, the feeling of being safe and secure with a fire, being connected with all there ever was, walking barefoot on sands that are timeless, and a body getting the freshest and cleanest air to breathe.

Thus the gift I was given by the one who had nothing to lose but her life gave me confidence and a knowing that when I think of others, miracles *do* happen. In 1982, for my work in Iceland and the Arctic, I was made a Fellow of the Royal Geographical Society. But for my time as an explorer at Findhorn, I was given the biggest prize of all: the discovery of feeling part of Nature, and the knowing that the true explorer lies within all of us. And all this from a picnic on the beach!

Life went on, as it has to, and in 1985 I was in Kathmandu getting ready for another Himalayan adventure. I took a stroll to my usual eating place for breakfast. Unable to find an empty table, I ambled about in the warm sunshine outside until I came to a sign by a stone archway. It read: 'Come and have breakfast in our rose garden'. So I did. I entered the darkness of a passageway, at the end of which I could see a rose garden bathed in the most brilliant light. Sitting at a table was Sophie. She saw me and waved a hand, and yes, of course, she was smiling.

As far as I know, today, Sophie is smiling still.

BILL GRANT
From his Autobiography

ℱ

Going Through Some Stuff

When you see a head lowered and the shoulders are round
When the brows are all furrowed and the feet drag the ground
Then few words are spoken and life it seems rough
You're aware of a person who's Going Through Some Stuff

With looks like a dagger and thoughts like a mole
It's easy to see these Dark Knights of the Soul
They eat Sauerkraut for breakfast and drink Vinegar for sweet
Then move like shadows as they walk down the street
They're sombre and silent so don't call their bluff
Just please be aware that they're going through some stuff

When your Mind it says one thing and all seems to go
It's strange what then happens when the Heart it says NO
Then the third force of Spirit comes into the light
How your poor body struggles in this three-cornered fight
Your awareness is heightened and from others you huff
They're aware of a person who's going through some stuff

So what is this stuff that we are writing about
That makes us keep silent...or Burst Out and SHOUT?
It's all Wheels and Circles that work in the Mind
You seek for an answer and inwardly find
So if your shoulders are round and your voice is gruff
Needs be aware that you're going through some stuff

But at last comes the Dawning by day or by night
When the mist clears away and everything's bright
Once again meet your friends with that normal warm smile
As you relate of the days when your body held Trial
How you hit a bad patch and the going got tough

125

And the best word description "I've been going through some stuff"

When you see a head lowered and the shoulders are round
The brows are all furrowed and the feet drag the ground
Then few words are spoken and life it seems rough
You're aware of a person who's Going Through Some Stuff.

SANDY BARR

Winnie

My thoughts and feelings about death, dying and especially living more consciously have changed a lot in the last four years.

Starting with the discovery that I had cancer of the colon, (successfully removed by surgery) I was thrown into confusion about my life: fear of how to live now so that the cancer doesn't come back. The quality of my daily life, interactions with people, and being honest with myself about what was really important to do now became paramount.

After a healing period of convalescence and 8 months travel, I returned to the Findhorn community in April '97 and found out that a previous neighbour of mine, Winnie, had leukemia.

I started spending more time with Winnie, as part of a mutual support group that Cornelia Featherstone, our community doctor, had started up for anyone with a life-threatening or life-changing condition. I went with Winnie several times to Aberdeen for some of her difficult visits to the hematology specialist. (Having previously worked for many years in hospital laboratories I was quite familiar with the medical scene.)

Sometimes we talked a lot, other times not, just knowing that each of us had some special understanding of the other's situation, fears and feelings—an ally when faced with sometimes insensitive hospital personnel or bewildering hospital tests and controversial drug regimes.

In April '98 I participated in a conference at the Findhorn Foundation called Conscious Living, Conscious Dying. I hadn't really looked at death in such a frank, open way, probably denying its obvious reality, especially in my own situation, as I now seemed to be basically free of disease.

We listened to and discussed ideas about living wills, dying at home, do-it-yourself funerals and woodland burials. These new ideas of a more personal, accepting, natural approach to death were exciting to many of us, including myself. Although Winnie was not able to attend the conference, some of us talked with her about the ideas we had received there.

Finally, the day came, a few months later when Winnie decided that hospital was not a comfortable place for her, no more blood transfusions or chemotherapy could help, she just wanted to rest at home. So very informally a few of us decided to help look after her there.

Starting with one friend 'A' who had been living with her for a few weeks, another friend, 'V' and I decided to take time offering our support as and when Winnie needed it. I didn't know what I was getting into, but I felt I had made some kind of unspoken commitment to Winnie to see her through this experience of leukemia whatever happened.

Winnie got rapidly weaker, and more uncomfortable with fever and bed-sores and grief and fear over leaving her 11 year old son Corin. (Corin's father came and took him away for some holiday time, checking back in frequently for visits). A long-standing difficult family situation was on her mind, and needed to be dealt with sensitively with various relatives.

Our team of 3 friends plus the part-time social services home help 'D' was increased with a cousin of Winnie's and many more friends lending a hand.

Cornelia was an excellent support getting in touch with and coordinating the help of various health professionals: the Macmillan cancer nurse, district nurses, Winnie's GP and various complementary therapists who had been treating Winnie. Winnie, who had been a nurse, was very much in charge of her own care, what and who she wanted at any one time.

I felt it a privilege and honour to be able to serve and help such a brave and honest woman, in whatever way was needed and with gentle care and respect for her wishes, and compassion and unconditional love. Just to witness and support her through her different stages and feelings: at one moment, hoping for a recovery to be with her son, and the next moment wanting a peaceful release from her weary body and emotional turmoil.

I came to realise the importance of looking at the priorities in my own life, of dealing with unfinished business on various levels— physical, emotional and spiritual.

As I witnessed Winnie's last breaths early one morning, it seemed like she finally passed from a deep sleep to a much deeper peace, without any struggle or pain. I felt my tears composed of grief and also relief at the end of her journey.

In accordance with Winnie's wishes, Cornelia and I laid out her body, in her home, and we all kept a vigil there for 3 days while we made the funeral arrangements. The simple cardboard coffin was painted and decorated by friends of Winnie and Corin and family members came to help plan the service. Local friends dug the grave under some trees on private land nearby as Winnie wished.

I was very moved by the depth of feelings of so many people who came to share in honouring the life of this friend who has touched so many people's lives. The service was full of children supporting Corin, of music and home grown flowers.

When I hear of the many people who die alone, or in institutions with no caring friends who finally are themselves paralysed with fear and grief, I feel very saddened. We all have to die, so let's prepare for it with an attitude of calm and acceptance and openness, with our friends and family, and truly live consciously right till the end.

I am now pleased to be involved with the work of Alanna, where we seek to offer respite care for those facing death and those who care for them, in a holistic, loving way.

FAY BLACKBURN

Home for Healing

Findhorn turned my life on its head! One moment I was living a quiet domestic life as a wife and full-time mother-of-three in rural England and the next moment (less than six months later) I found myself purchasing a vast pink mansion (Minton House) and seven acres of land on the edge of Findhorn Bay with the aim of turning it into a Healing Centre.

In between these two stages came the Experience Week!...a week when the reality of my life did a total about turn. That was a week that, for the first time ever, provided the safety for me to review my life and to dare to consider making some changes to it. And I knew that drastic changes needed to be made. I had just lived through two medical crises in my family and that more than anything indicated to me that I needed to take stock of my life. Two years prior I had been admitted to hospital with a growth the size of a football. I was one of those fortunate patients who awoke from their operation to be told that the growth was benign. I felt I had been given a second chance in Life. Then just over a year later (a few months prior to visiting Findhorn) I had nursed my 4-year-old son out of another grave medical emergency resulting from a badly burst appendix and life-threatening complications afterwards.

These two events caused me to question my family's lifestyle and to acknowledge the spiritual emptiness that I felt at the heart of the family. That sense of desperation was what led me up to Findhorn at the age of 33, knowing absolutely nothing about the place, purpose or culture of the community and my only previous experience of God coming from our dry and arid family services in the local parish church.

I was yearning deeply for a more vibrant spirituality and for a more meaningful and community-orientated environment in which to bring up my young family. And that week I found it. I found it in the smiles and in the eyes of all those I encountered, I found it in the oneness of the Sacred Dance, I found it through the extraordinary support and love of my group and I found it instantly in the twice-daily meditations that connected me to the souls around and to my own inner world.

Having made these discoveries and connections, I knew that I needed to return to this environment for a longer stay. My husband Peter-John was going to work abroad for a while, and the deal was that I should take my three children (aged 5, 3 and 1 at the time) and explore whether we might move up here.

So that September, I strapped my three children into the back of my Renault 4, tied two suitcases onto the roof-rack and drove north into the unknown. When Peter-John came to join us that Christmas, I had by then already put in an offer to buy Minton House! So that's how our family found ourselves buying and moving into Minton House on April Fool's Day 1984!!

I had seen Minton a few weeks after I arrived in the area (it had been on the market for 18 months) and as soon as I looked over the house I knew that was why I had felt this strong pull to move up to Findhorn. I instantly knew that it was my destiny to turn Minton into some kind of healing centre and that this would be my life's work. Even before I saw Minton, when somebody was first informing me of the big pink house that was for sale, there was something about it that 'rang bells in my head'. Now, looking back, I realise it wasn't me that discovered Minton, it was Minton that found me!

And here I am, 17 years later still feeling that the vision of Minton is only beginning to really reveal itself and that the potential of this beautiful project is only finally being manifested. It has been an arduous 17 years—a time of struggle, hardship, many tests, but also many wonders, joys and achievements. There have been a few occasions when I have felt pushed to my limits in holding responsibility for this undertaking, but whenever I have walked beside the ocean, I have always heard the same answer from God that I should continue to "hang in there". Which is one thing I can proudly claim to have done. I have hung in there through thick and thin, constantly baffling my business friends by managing against all odds to make ends meet, always having faith that we would get through the next financial crisis and somehow always managing to! It has been an enormous learning curve for me and an even greater test of faith.

Over these years, I have witnessed the Findhorn community change dramatically. Minton House was probably the first independent project to start up around the Foundation and now we boast almost 40 small businesses and organisations in our community. I have seen (and been involved in) the birth of our Steiner School, I have experienced first-hand the isolation of keeping a business going outside of the Findhorn Foundation, felt the pain of the 'them and us' situation that existed in our growing community over more than a decade, and now celebrate and welcome the radical structural changes that are coming about through the governance of the New Findhorn Association, reflecting the major shifts towards collective co-operation and unity that are pushing our community through into the next millennium.

Through all this time I have had the pleasure of bringing up three wonderful children, and now find myself at the stage where they have all left home to pursue university education elsewhere. Now it's the moment to focus fully on Minton, taking it into an era of healthy financial sustainability and abundance of activity, and it seems that I can hardly keep pace with all that is growing and expanding here now. Minton hosts some of the Alanna respite and hospice work, it is the venue for many inspiring retreats, a place where the healing power of music can be experienced more and more, and somewhere where many thousands of guests have enjoyed its tranquility while visiting Findhorn.

I feel greatly honoured to have been the caretaker of this beautiful house all this time, and feel particularly blessed to be witnessing the many miracles that are taking place currently in the process of manifestation of Minton's vision as a Centre of Healing. I feel humbled that amidst my personal confusion at the age of 33, I was able to listen to that original inner call and I feel privileged that it brought me up here to be involved in such a graceful part of God's work.

JUDITH MARTIN-MEYNELL

Update: Minton House played an important and valuable part in the Community for many years. Even so, the time came for Judith to cease her valiant efforts. Minton House was sold to people who were able to restore it to its former glory. When they decided to move back to the United States a few years later it was bought by the Shambala Trust and became Shambala Retreat Centre. The building returned to being available to the Community and although strongly Buddhist was open to people of all faiths. The Shambala Retreat Centre closed in 2010 and the house has once more become a private property.

F

A Healthy Community

I came to Findhorn in 1987 because I was yearning for a spiritual context for my life. In the community I experienced a homecoming which was so deep and precious that I had to come back and do the 'student programme' in spring 1988.

I made this decision out of the fullness of life and a wealth of choice—I was at a stage where I had achieved a lot of what I had set out to do—I had managed to get through medical school and was a qualified doctor ready to take up my place as a GP. Yet, what I had thought would be the fulfillment of 'Life's purpose', left me still missing an essential central aspect—'IT' as I called it for the lack of an appropriate name. And I found 'IT' in the Findhorn Community— even though (or perhaps even because?) I was not working as a doctor but in Cluny Garden and later in the kitchen there. After a year people would ask me what would make me stay beyond my student time. The answer, which came, was two reasons: I would stay if I would have a child and if I would find work, which would allow me to use all of my potential.

Within a few weeks of saying that, I was in a committed relationship with Alan Watson—and we do now have a child together— although it took a few years before Kevin joined us. And I had the vision for a holistic health centre in the community, which would use all of my skills and experiences as a doctor and much more. So I was to stay—and I did stay, happily.

Community and health became my main work for the next nine years. By 1990 I was the Focaliser of the Health and Wholeness department, which looked after members and guests, and I started a small private practice to allow people who wished to see me for medical services. Our facilities at Cluny were wonderful with the Bodhi Room for massage and bodywork and a counselling room. However the premises at the Park were not ideal. 'Merlin' the trusty old caravan was beyond its best and if you were unlucky water would drip onto your face when you were having a massage during a rain shower. At that stage the staff of the department had expanded and attracted a number of enthusiastic people. We made the commitment to find a beautiful and healthful healing environment. This we manifested in the most remarkable way with the help of many generous and inspired supporters. By August 1991 we moved into one of the first ecological houses built at Bagend and called it 'Meridian'.

In the coming years the core group of the re-named 'Holistic Health Department' organised four successful international conferences named 'Medical Marriage', and ran an educational programme and the community health scheme in the Findhorn Bay Holistic Health Centre. This scheme allowed us to provide daily reception services, the treatment facilities at Meridian and many other health and awareness promoting services.

Because our work had expanded and blossomed the Findhorn Foundation felt that it was time for the fledgling to leave the nest and set up its own charity. We founded Holistic Health Care, a registered charity, in 1993.

In 1994 we bought a beautiful old house in the centre of Forres and set up HealthWorks, a complementary health centre, where I worked as a doctor together with a group of complementary practitioners.

One more highlight of the network and co-operation established over the years was the publication of the book, Medical Marriage. Over 40 people who either lived in the community or had participated in one of our conferences wrote contributions for this textbook for health professionals. It is now used by many students and practitioners and even government committees in Norway and in London. For me it is one of those seeds of the spirit of Findhorn which spread out and affect change in the world.

As it is with many organisations, time brings change and after expansion comes consolidation. So also for Holistic Health Care. Since 1993 I had planned to go on a Sabbatical journey in September 1998 for my 40th birthday— to have a break rather than a midlife crisis. Due to many circumstances neither the staff nor the money were available to continue the work of the Findhorn Bay Holistic Health Centre and so we decided to close it in May 1998. Whilst many people feel sad about the loss, many of the services are still available in a more decentralised form. Individuals have stepped into the breach and taken up specific aspects of the work. Groups, like 'Alanna' (offering respite and hospice work) have joined together to serve the community. And there is an overall feeling of a germination time for a new phase of health care provision in the community.

Whilst I was on my Sabbatical in Australia it became clear that the best way for me to serve the community was to join the National Health Service as a GP. In that way I can apply the lessons of Medical Marriage in the 'real' world.

So at the moment I am working as a GP down the coast from Findhorn—re-learning the skills of orthodox medicine—especially drug use. To my great surprise and happiness I feel welcome and appreciated for the different medical care I provide. My 'fringe' experience with complementary therapies is seen as an asset and both colleagues and patients are happy for me to provide care which integrates the more natural and self-help approaches with orthodox medicine.

I hope that eventually I shall be able to work in Forres so that the community members can see me on the NHS without the strain on their finances which private care presents. It is still my ideal to work with people who know me and who I know well, where the roles of patient and doctor are not the only ones we hold for each other. For me healing happens in the relationship and that relationship is formed in community.

CORNELIA FELLNER FEATHERSTONE

F

Alanna

After the conference called 'Conscious Living—Conscious Dying' a small group of women began to meditate together and discuss how we could work with the concepts we had learned in the conference. It soon became clear that the group had the purpose of offering a heart centred holistic service for conscious living and conscious dying. This would include: compassionate support and respite care; care of the dying; care for the carers; education & training; the use of music and the healing arts in assisting integrated medical care; and provision of a resource and information centre.

Phyllida Templeton, a newcomer to Findhorn, who had been a presenter at the conference, suggested the name Alanna. It is a Celtic word which, roughly translated means, 'Greeting the beauty of the soul shining through the human being'.

Our first respite project was to host, in Minton House, six women from Northern Ireland, who were experiencing cancer in various forms and stages. What a magical week it was! Many people in the Community helped us to raise funds, and offered time and skills towards the care and healing of these courageous women.

These women relished every new experience: vegetarian food, complimentary healing methods, meditation, circle dancing, Taize singing, and stripping off for the sauna and the hot tub! We laughed and cried together, sang and danced together, meditated and went to the pub together. They returned home relaxed and refreshed. We all learned the benefits of living for today.

Many of those who had volunteered to support this respite week asked to be included in future work. This enabled us to make the respite week a regular programme, and to offer similar weeks for carers. We could also offer respite care to the sick and their carers in their homes.

With Phyllida Templeton some of the group began creating education programmes embodying the concepts of Conscious Living and Conscious Dying and this has led to the formation of the Alanna College. We intend these workshops and trainings to be made available here and in other parts of the world.

The theme of Hospice had been with us from the early days of our meditations. Being aware that developing a purpose built building would require a long-term commitment, we began to investigate how, in the meantime, we could offer this special care in the facilities available to us. We wanted to work with the concepts of conscious living and conscious dying by providing care for dying people in a place where everyday life was going on. We hoped to remove some of the mystique and fear of the dying process and to bring awareness to it being one of the aspects of life.

Judith Meynell, a member of Alanna and the owner of Minton House, offered us the use of a beautiful room in Minton at a reasonable rate. Minton is a large building run as a business offering Bed and Breakfast and Workshop space and is situated in spacious grounds on the edge of Findhorn Bay. We were grateful to Judith and her staff for their willingness to have a part of Minton used for this purpose.

We have several medically qualified people in the group who have experience of caring for dying people. Phyllida holds the overall responsibility for this aspect of the Alanna work. She trained with Elizabeth Kubler-Ross, and combines that training with Celtic Spirituality and her own inimitable style of caring, which is based on being real, being honest and being in the moment. She specialises in helping people to heal their emotional wounds by expressing their unexpressed feelings of anger or grief.

Our commitment and competence were soon tested when Mair, a member of the Community, was diagnosed with an inoperable, voracious cancer, and asked to be cared for by the Alanna group at Minton.

My role in the group was recruiting and organising the volunteers into a rota to provide 24-hour care for Mair. We were not short of people with willing hearts. However, it was important that these were paired up with people with experienced hands. We also had to be careful not to overwhelm Mair with too many people. It was a delicate balancing act. We had the professional support of Mair's GP and the Community's doctor, Cornelia Fellner-Feathersone. In addition we were relieved on some of the night shifts by Macmillan Nurses.

For those of us who had no experience in this work it was a steep learning curve. We were anxious to be as professional as possible and soon had efficient systems set up for all aspects of care for Mair.

I have rarely witnessed so much love and selfless care being extended by so many people. This love permeated the whole house and affected everyone in it. The staff, who were not expected to take part in the work, insisted on doing everything that they could to help the volunteers in their tasks. Some B&B guests felt privileged to have stayed at Minton at this time and offered help if it was needed.

Mair's son and daughter had taken leave of their work and had travelled to be with their mother. Naturally they were engaged in her care and the rota of volunteers revolved around the times that they and Mair wished to spend together. The circumstances they found themselves in must have been difficult for them but they did their best to help Mair live out her remaining days in the way she wished.

After a few short weeks Mair's journey came to an end. She died gently in her sleep, pain free, at peace with herself, with her family and with the world.

During her time at Minton Mair had often expressed her gratitude for the love and care she had received from the people in Alanna. We all feel it is we who have so much to be grateful for. Mair offered us the opportunity to grow beyond our fear of death. She allowed us to witness her strength, courage and willingness to go through this process being consciously aware of every moment. She gave us the chance to give unconditional love to a fellow human being.

The work of Alanna will evolve in whatever way it is supposed to do. I have come to realise that Alanna is above all an attitude: the attitude in which we 'Greet the beauty of the soul shining through each other'. It is not so much what we do but how we do it that really matters.

KAY KAY

To the Dance

I asked a friend about holidays with an alternative dimension and she gave me the address of the Findhorn Foundation. I decided to go. What was calling me? I am on some sort of a soul search, looking for something that will touch me at essence. This search probably began earlier than I ever realised but in the last year it has taken on a more intensive nature and I still don't know what it is that I am looking for. I was diagnosed with M. S. and have opted to take the alternative path to healing and avoid all conventional medicine. This factor further catapulted my already searching soul to seek to live at a deeper level. I still don't know what that level is. Every week I meet with a group and we dance the Gabrielle Roth 'Five Rhythms'. So when I received the programme of events in the Foundation and discovered that I could attend the Sacred Dance Festival without having done an 'Experience Week' I reckoned it was for me. The friend, who had initially given me the Findhorn address, also decided to come and to do an Experience Week.

I was completely unprepared for what lay ahead. I knew nothing about Findhorn and assumed it was a meditative Centre with a strong ecological tendency.

We arrived a day before the Festival began and I threw what I now call 'a wobbly'. I was expecting a small Centre with only a few people. We seemed to ask all the wrong people for information. Finally we arrived in Cluny College, where my friend was to stay, and there things seemed more organised. The receptionist was able to give precise information and showed me the registration list for the Dance Festival. It seemed to me that there would be about 100 people there. I was further thrown. The receptionist was also able to give me my room number in the Park. So we returned there and walked all around in vain looking for G.7. Feeling very disconsolate I eventually suggested that we abandon the search and I returned the following day at the appointed time. How wrong I was about all my forebodings.

When I arrived at the Community Centre the next day all was in superb running order. I was shown to my room, which was lovely, and given a quick tour of the park. After lunch and introductions, the dancing began. Such wonderful music, such excellent dance teachers, such delicious food, and such superb organisation. Our schedule was so tightly packed that it would be almost possible to overlook the efficiency and excellence underlying the Festival and assume it was just the natural flow of events.

At another level something major was going on inside of me. I began the week with enormous resistance. I felt I should not be there. There is a strong spirituality underpinning Findhorn, of which I was previously unaware, and I was unsure where I fitted in. What is spirituality and what is my God? What—if anything—do I believe in and what right did I have to be at a Sacred Dance Festival, and to be in such a spiritual Centre when I was struggling and at times in such doubt?

The week progressed with surprising outcomes. By Tuesday I was entering a state of complete exhaustion due to my M.S. Every moment of the day was accounted for, and I didn't want to miss anything. But I could feel myself slipping into a state of desperation. Tiredness and an exaggeration of my symptoms were frightening me. However, on Tuesday night we were going to dance the 'Five Rhythms' to a live band and I had been looking forward to this since my arrival. The music was wonderful. The hall was huge and there was freedom to move as one saw fit. I was dancing among strangers and some very newly made friends so I had the freedom to express myself as I wanted, and I took it. I could feel the emotions of fear and desperation rising and rising. It was very frightening. The reality of my M.S. diagnosis was engulfing me. Usually I have some sense of other people having bigger problems or more serious illnesses than me but on this occasion there was no escape from the reality of my own situation. I danced on and on.

The following day we met in our small group and I decided that I would have to talk about how I was feeling. Many of them were foreigners with varying levels of English and I was nervous about being understood. I also had the concern of being thought a complainer, or that maybe this wasn't the place in which to dump my worries. But I did so and the group was wonderful to me. Everybody was tired by this stage of the week so the focaliser decided we would end the session by singing an angel song. I was placed in the middle of the circle and those who wished placed their hands on my body. At first, it was difficult for me to receive because I felt I was taking up space and time or somebody else's place. But finally I decided to relax and accept the gift. It was such a comfort!

The following day we had a free afternoon and this is when the magic of Findhorn began to emerge. It's almost too precious to put in words but I'll try. I felt I needed space, time, peace and quiet. I decided to just follow what I felt I needed to do. First I went to the labyrinth which had been made by our dance teacher Gabrielle Wosien and some of the dance participants. I walked the labyrinth in serenity. Then sat in the centre and did a painting. Afterwards I went for a walk along the beautiful shore and then returned to the Park and went into the Nature Sanctuary. It was here that something strong and profound occurred. It's hard to describe but it was like an awakening of a part of me that was dormant. I found myself becoming deeply in contact with nature. It was as if I was making a connection with the Earth at a level I had only fleetingly experienced once before. Then the forest called to me. It was almost like a need to climb into the earth, be as one with it. Something had touched me at a level that it is difficult to name.

These experiences were new to me and it was hard for me to leave at the end of the Festival.

What is next? I just don't know. I can say that life is now unfolding in ways that I would never have expected and I'm open to the possibility that new paths will present themselves—if I stay open and trust.

JEAN TUOMY

The Man who Healed Himself

Some people say that by all the laws of modern medicine, I should not be alive. In 1983, with a wife and three children and a career in solid state physics, working in the development of semiconductors, I came close to killing myself. Not by any deliberate act, but through what I now believe was my own ignorance concerning my lifestyle.

I was a workaholic. Few breaks; no holidays. Drinking 10–20 cups of coffee a day. Eating and sleeping badly. Hardly seeing my family No time even for my beloved cello. I'm told I looked so pinched and unpleasant that maybe I wasn't a very nice person to be around.

In 1982, I suddenly came down with a fever that lasted several weeks. Then I found blood in my urine. Mainstream medics said nothing was wrong; even my wife (a doctor who specialises in ageing) could get no sense out of her profession. Only Koshiro Otsuka, who is a holistic medical counsellor, came up with an open and direct diagnosis. He believed there was something wrong with my kidney. I sought more medical advice and the doctors at the hospital recommended a course of injections. By the third day I felt terrible. On the fourth I looked in the mirror and found my beard had turned white overnight. Chemotherapy, I realised; radiation treatment.

Stick-thin and weakening, I had a dream: My body was lying in a coffin and I was looking down from the ceiling. Many people were coming to see me. Then just before the lid was closed, I screamed, "No, I'm alive." I shouted so loudly that I woke myself up. When I told my wife, she cried, because she'd been told I was dying.

The experience proved to be a turning point. I felt some kind of physical change, which included the heightening of sensation that many people experience when near death. One night my sense of smell became so acute that I thought I would go mad. Crawling out of bed, I made my way up to the hospital roof, where I thought the air would be fresh. There was panic when the nursing staff discovered I had gone; finding me on the roof, it was assumed I was considering suicide. I was told, "If you want to stay here you must follow the rules, otherwise…" The following day I checked out.

I decided to take responsibility for my own healing. I accepted that the cancer was of my own making, that I had created my cancer, no one else. I was responsible for my sickness. Western medicine regards cancer as alien, an invasion to be battled with but I came to believe that my cancer was a part of me that needed to be loved. It's not an enemy; it's still my body. And I created my cancer. I said to my body, "I made a mistake. Oh, I'm very, very sorry. But you are here. So I love you." I loved it with all my heart, and I began to heal. I thank my cancer always because I changed so much because of it.

I switched to a macrobiotic diet, as Koshiro Otsuka had recommended, and I spent much more time playing my cello.

An extremely vital part of my healing process was my first visit to Findhorn. Although I still had a shadow on my lung, I accepted an invitation to speak at a conference there in 1988. I actually stayed for 40 days. It was here that for the first time in my life I was hugged by people I hardly knew. This is a very beneficial therapy with absolutely no side effects! Usually Japanese people are very shy and it was wonderful for me to experience so much love every day. By the time I had returned from Findhorm the shadow on my lung had disappeared completely. I am now happy to help organise for many of my fellow Japanese to come and experience this special place.

As I healed I began to share with others what I had learned. I did this in many ways. Between 1988 and 1995, I became executive director of the Japan Holistic Medical Society based in Asagaya, Tokyo. This society has 600 members (4,000 if you include those counselled by phone).

As part of an international network of holistic medical practitioners and supporters, I am privileged to travel extensively. I go to Israel, for example, where there is a tremendous amount of cancer. People there are raised in an atmosphere of acute stress to think, 'Fight, fight, fight!' No wonder they fall sick.

I counsel many cancer patients, charging what each can afford. I try to change their attitude to their diseases. I try only to get them to accept that they are responsible for their condition. Even if they can't go all the way to loving their cancer, acceptance of their cancer, acceptance of their part in its creation can bring about revelation and peace.

"It's up to you," I say. "It's very simple. We all die. So isn't it better to live well until we die, rather than in a state of fear and angry resentment? Treasure each moment, don't waste the time you have left!"

SHINICHIRO TERAYAMA

CHAPTER EIGHT

WHO'S IN CHARGE ANYWAY?

Surprises, coincidences, miracles, these are words often used to describe happenings that are extraordinary or remarkably timely. In this selection of stories the writers relate events that have amused or affected them and made them wonder about divine intervention, and the wider scheme of things.

Angels Laughing

Thirty years ago in 1971 I was living in a spiritual community in Central London. One of our members had just come back from Findhorn and was full of it. He suggested that I go. I replied (without a trace of spiritual arrogance) that I was going for the real thing. I was off to India. The real thing gave me Sai Baba asking me to leave the ashram, hepatitis, a near death experience which gave peace beyond understanding, and a massive depression.

Many years later I wanted to move out of London but it was proving difficult, so I resolved to spend every birthday in Scotland. We were house hunting in Edinburgh, and for my birthday decided to have a day's skiing in Aviemore. We arrived just after the ski lifts had closed because of high winds. Joan, my partner, was furious as I had dawdled that morning. We returned to our bed and breakfast and the owner suggested we visit Findhorn. I picked up a brochure there and decided to go on a writing week. I knew I had to do their experience week before I could do the writing week, but tried to wriggle out of it, protesting that I was very experienced. No dice. Reluctantly I turned up and made it clear that I was not happy. I would ring Joan every night and complain (without a trace of spiritual arrogance) about this New Age twaddle I was being subjected to. Friday night was a party celebration. I could not wait to leave and my now friend from the bed and breakfast in Aviemore was coming to collect me. The group wanted to say good-bye and as they did I felt surrounded with love. I am quite an experienced group leader and know about group highs at the end of workshops. This was quite different—the love was coming through them from another source. I rang Joan and announced that I wanted to come and live here. I can still hear the angels of Findhorn laughing.

When we did move here, I made friends with Ben Fuchs, another Jewish therapist. After he had returned from a workshop where revenge had been a theme and I had shown interest, he suggested we write book together. It was a nightmare. At that stage in the relationship he felt intimidated by me (all things pass unfortunately), and was reluctant to commit himself to paper as I was an established author, and he did not yet trust his writing abilities. I got very irritated. We fell out and I finally managed to get him to write by provoking him with angry letters to which he replied with plenty of fluency—considering he thought he couldn't write! We lived the revenge. We dropped the project and were cool with each other.

About a year later he called me and said he was not happy with the relationship and could we meet. Reluctantly I went to his house and he started by saying that he was not the person who had messed me around. He had changed. I looked at him and immediately saw he was different. How could I be angry with someone who did not exist? I knew I had to let the past go. But I still wanted to write this book and told him so. His reaction was very powerful. He looked dismayed. He obviously wanted to be my friend, but equally obviously did not want to write with me. I was stuck for a moment.

And then out of my mouth came the words. "OK, no book, but how about a conference on forgiveness?" He said "yes" immediately, and since then we have had a very co-operative, easeful relationship, which I really value.

The angels now have stitches from laughing so much.

ROBIN SHOHET

Postscript: The Findhorn conference on Forgiveness organized by Ben and Robin in 1999 was a tremendous success.

Update: Robin has inspired many people to take up their pens. His persistent encouragement and support finally persuaded me to start writing in the late 1990s. On his advice to begin by working with other writers my first project was to be the guest editor on an issue on Children's Self-esteem for Self and Society, a journal for Psychologists. The second project was the first edition of this book, Growing People, published in 2001. I am now a full-time writer working on three series of books under the heading of Making the Difference. Robin's work can be found at:
www.cstd.co.uk/supervisors/28-robin-shohet-cstd-tutor

F

The Key to Opportunity

In 1974 a friend handed me a copy of the magazine section of a local newspaper. The article was entitled, 'There are Fairies at the Bottom of your Garden',—an article about Findhorn. He asked me if, in my upcoming travels around Great Britain and Europe, would I stop in to see what Findhorn was about and report to him.

I had been anxious to make the trip for a couple of months and planned to 'just follow my nose,' but, since this was a specific request, while touring Scotland in a rented car, I headed in the direction of Findhorn.

Unfortunately, I sailed right past the turn-off to Findhorn from Forres and thought, "Oh well, I've missed it, I'll carry on", but several miles later, I had a nagging feeling to turn around and headed back to Findhorn.

I arrived in the village of Findhorn about 5pm and got out of the car to ask directions to the community when I realised my car keys were neatly dangling from the ignition behind locked doors. By the time some local fellows had gotten me back into the car and I had recompensed them at the pub, it was after 6pm, so I had missed tour time in the community.

I stayed overnight in Findhorn Village and, next morning, I arrived at the shop in the community, asking for a tour. As luck would have it, David Spangler's father, Marshall, was passing by and someone, thoughtfully, called out to him from the shop, asking would he mind showing me around. I had my own individual guided tour. In the course of the tour, Marshall said to me that I would never really understand the place unless I stayed overnight and experienced it for a few days. I felt that he was right and did so.

Although I didn't stay long at that time, I came back a year later and stayed for four years. If I had not locked myself out the car and had made it in time for the 6pm tour, it is possible I would never have experienced the community in depth and would have missed out on one of the highlights of my life.

A SMITH

F

Gender and Deep Ecology

JOHN SEED: I was at the Findhorn Foundation in April 1989, helping Joanna Macy with a deep ecology facilitators training when I met these women who invited me to help prepare the Beltane ritual.

Beltane is the festival which falls between the Spring Equinox and the Summer Solstice where in the olden days people made love in the fields to invite fertility. We were preparing for this joyous celebration with couples holding hands and jumping over a bonfire. There were a couple of local women, another woman from California and myself.

It was then that I visited the neighbouring town of Forres and first saw the Witches' Stone. I was walking along an ordinary kind of pavement with a retaining wall about 5 feet high between it and a grassy hill when suddenly there was this boulder blocking half the pavement. It seemed that when the pavement and retaining wall had been built, they had carefully left this boulder half-buried there which now emerged out of the pavement and the wall. There was this old corroded bronze plaque embedded in it. In raised letters, the story was there told of how, not so long ago, when a witch was discovered in the town, the people would take her to the top of yon Cluny Hill, place her inside a barrel, drive iron spikes into the barrel and then roll her down the hill. The barrel and it's mangled contents would then be burned. This stone was the site where one such barrel came to rest. Interestingly, the solid brick police station was built right across the road from this.

Later I learned that Forres was one of the last places in Europe where the witch hunts took place and also that the old people in the town still had the habit of spitting over their shoulders when they passed the Witches' Stone to fend off evil spirits.

I was deeply disturbed by this and discussed it with Marian Rose, the American woman who was designing the Beltane ceremony with us. I wanted her to come visit the stone and incorporate this into the Beltane ceremony.

MARIAN ROSE: I was visiting Findhorn during the spring of 1989 when a Scottish woman in the community came to me and said she had heard that I knew about the Beltane dance ceremony. She wanted me to help her lead one in the community so she could connect with the ancient ceremonial traditions of Scotland and her ancestors.

I was shocked to learn that no one at Findhorn knew the ceremony because I myself had learned the ceremony in the states from a former Findhorn community member. It just goes to show how fragile sacred traditions are and how easily lost. I agreed to reintroduce the ceremony at Findhorn and John Seed heard about our efforts and joined us.

We only had a few weeks to prepare and I was very busy with other projects, but John kept asking me to come see this witches stone that he had discovered. I was not too interested. I didn't want to get into the whole oppression of women issue since I was taking a break from my feminist identity. John however insisted so reluctantly I went.

From my native American teachers I had learned how to listen to the rock people who are the keepers and holders of energy. So when we got to the stone I knelt down and touched the stone to connect with it. The minute my fingers made contact with this stone I felt zapped. Images of fire and feelings of terror filled my body. I usually don't have big waking dreams, but in an instant I saw the land scorched and scarred from the fires, children screaming in distress. All of this happened in a flash before I even started to meditate as I had been taught. I had never had such a profound 'shamanic' experience. This witches stone indeed held much energy and it was an intense jolt which deeply changed my life forever.

Since we were in the middle of a busy street, John drove me back but we didn't talk much about what happened because I was so overwhelmed by the images and feelings that I was in a trance.

That afternoon, the experience and teachings from the stone kept coming. I just cried and couldn't do anything else. I couldn't go on with my life. I must explain that it was not new information that was shocking or distressing me. I had read accounts of this burning time, but having an intellectual understanding is not the same as feeling it and living it in the body. That stone had stopped my life and taken me into a place of death, change and transformation. That night I told my colleagues planning the Beltane ceremony that I didn't see how I could go on with the ceremony given my despairing state.

The Beltane is traditionally a joyous ceremony full of leaping for joy and dancing with the spirit of creativity represented by the fire. The fiery attraction of men and women served to support the fecundity of the earth and regeneration of crops. Any children born from this ceremony and sacred unions belonged to the whole community, and lived in the temples. I felt that it was impossible to lead a Beltane ceremony where love and joy between men and women were in support of the earth given that the women's' faith and trust in men had been so deeply wounded, and the land itself was scarred by fire being used against women who tended the fire and hearth of the home. Moreover I felt my faith and confidence in ceremony itself were suddenly shattered as I considered the fact that these women, my elders were truly connected to a spiritual tradition that worked with ceremony for healing and protection on a regular basis. They were not like me, a Western woman disconnected from any indigenous tradition and groping in the dark trying to learn how to honour the land, heal and live in a sacred way. How could I serve the earth's healing through doing ceremony if these wise and powerful women elders who had community and tradition to support them couldn't use ceremony to save themselves and each other? If ceremony had any access to magic or power at all how could this tragedy have befallen them?

Despite my sudden crisis of faith in ceremonial tradition the Scottish woman and John convinced me to go forward with the ceremony— which was only one day away—since the community was looking forward to it. We then revised the ceremony to address the death of the women who had been burned on that land, and prayed for the healing of all women and of the feminine energy itself and the healing between men and women so we could truly do Beltane ceremonies to support the regeneration of the earth in the future.

JOHN SEED: This was April 1989 and as a rainforest activist, my mind was filled with the fires that were then raging in the Amazon. An area as large as Germany was going up in flames and I suddenly realised that there was no way that we could extinguish these fires as long as our culture continued to repress the burning times.

In my experience as an activist, it seemed that we were always shoving sexist behaviour and patriarchal conditioning under the carpet, too busy trying to save the planet to take the time to work through this difficult material.

As a deep ecologist, I was wary of the human-centred agenda constantly trying to re-assert itself. I had dedicated my life to the interests of ecology as best I could understand them, to the web itself rather than any strand in the web. If the tree of life itself was dying, what was the use of tending to any of the leaves? Sure there were all kinds of social issues concerning justice and so on, but to my mind, this was all taking place on the Titanic and it was time to cry out, "Iceberg dead ahead", and "All hands on deck", and leave these other issues aside till we had at least secured our life support systems.

But now I realised that the burning of the witches and the burning of the forests were two sides of the same coin and we needed to deal with both, that the ecological age could not dawn unless we dealt with our gender wounds at the same time as we worked for the Earth.

To cut a long story short, we revised our ritual. We still jumped over the fire, but first recounted the story of the Witches Stone and I sang

Charlie Murphy's 'The Burning Times'. Marian and I agreed to facilitate some workshops that we would call Gender and Deep Ecology. We did so a couple of years later in California and I have since facilitated this workshop on many occasions with a variety of co-facilitators.

MARIAN ROSE: When we did the Beltane ceremony a very interesting thing happened at Findhorn the next day. Several men from the community came to me and were concerned that by doing the 'pagan ritual' we had hurt the land where the ceremony took place. In a strange way I felt like a witch who was being psychologically burned at the stake for doing ritual magic that wasn't Christian in origin. I left Findhorn feeling that much work needed to be done to really heal the land and all women who work for the healing of the earth.

Several years later when John and I led the Gender and Deep Ecology workshop we learned that during the week we were leading this workshop the Oakland hills were burning in the most devastating fire the Bay Area had experienced in years. Since we were on land where there was no television we heard the stories of the land burning from the people who came to join us over the weekend. That synchronicity of the fire speaking so loudly was difficult to miss. Since fire represents spirit and the creative essence, I believe that we must all learn to work with the essence of fire— our creative spiritual selves—to birth a world that honours all life, not just human life. Fire carries the essence of transformation which includes facing and accepting death and rebirth. As humans we must become like the fire to cleanse and transform our human world so we can then birth an economic system and lifestyle that supports and generates life.

JOHN SEED and MARIAN ROSE

Eastern Promise

The Summer 1994 Newsletter of the Friends of the Findhorn Foundation arrived on my office desk in Oman. It had been opened— which happens occasionally (by the censor I assume). Within the hour I had a phone call; my name had been recognised.

"Hope you didn't mind, I found it like that." No, I didn't mind the open envelope.

"Have you been there?"

I answered that I had been only twice, once to participate in programmes and once just 'being there'.

"How did you find it? Do you have more information?" The brochure changed hands once again. Silence. Energy.

A week later: "I booked an Experience Week, many thanks."

What did I do?

What a joy to be a channel, especially when unexpected and unaware. Miracles do happen. Life, the power of awareness, change.

HERMANN BOYNG

F

The Hitch-Hiker

I met Michael B. when I was hitchhiking. I have never before missed a bus between Cluny and Findhorn.

A man slightly younger than myself, maybe 35, Michael had just broken up with his live-in girlfriend in London. He was bleeding profusely from the heart...well, metaphorically speaking.

"Funny, you should be the one I pick up," he said after a few minutes of gabbing.

"Why?" I asked.

"I just saw you in my dream," he admitted after hesitating for a long while to hide his bewilderment.

"Me?" I asked.

"Yes, you and you shouldn't have been there."

"Oh, was it something you can talk to me about?"

"No, not really."

He kept driving and we continued our "who are you"? "What brings you here?" chatter. He was doing experience week. This was my second trip to Findhorn and I was a Working Guest. I'm from New York City; he's a Londoner.

"I might as well tell you," Michael let slip after a few more fumbling seconds of evaluation. "I had a terrible break-up with my girlfriend and I prayed all night to every high power I could think of, for answers. The Angel of Findhorn, Gods, Saints. But, I kept seeing your face, and I didn't get any answers."

"Humm, maybe they were too busy," I added.

"How are you going to help?" he asked.

"I don't know."

"What were you doing in my dream?" he asked out loud to the windshield wipers.

"Tell me about the problem."

147

Mike looked at me perturbed.

"Who knows?" I said, shrugging my shoulders.

Mike's story was very similar to my own divorce a year ago— which brought me to Findhorn. I had worked out the main issues during this year and I told him of my solutions.

"I think you're right" he said.

Two days later I had missed the bus again...something I tell you I never do and along comes Michael. We talk and he's had another dream. He describes it and a vivid symbol he's seen in the dream. I'm hearing my heart pound away. He's describing the Egyptian winged Scarab I've got around my neck, under my undershirt. Where did I get it? Greenwich Village from an Israeli jeweler who informed me it was the last one he had. I believed him, since several of my 'Insight Meditation' friends had told me to buy the silver scarab from this shop, after they had discovered it. I took the scarab off and handed it to Mike.

"Did it look like this?"

Mike looked agog.

"Yes" he said.

"It's yours. Don't feel you're taking something from me. I hate it. Every time I run it bounces up and down and hurts. I don't like to wear jewelry. Keep it. You need it and it...needs you.

" Every time after that, when I needed a ride or needed a 'talk', I just stood by the side of the road and Mike showed up. We both decided to look each other up for anything. In the next week we took rides to Pluscarden Abbey for talks.

I called Mike a month ago. It's been twenty years. I got his name from the Acupuncture Association of England. I knew he had become licensed and was practising in Wales, somewhere. Mike's married to another Acupuncturist. I'm a Findhorn Resource Person and married to a Frenchwoman. He said, "You know I still have the piece of jewelry you gave me, and I wear it every day."

IRWIN ZUCKER

Staying Open

My friend Christian, who is the farmer where we live here in Norway, asked me what my relationship was to the Findhorn Foundation these days. I replied by saying that the separation I feel at this time is good. I have gifts to offer but have not yet found my way to offer them to Findhorn. So it is best that I continue on my path while letting go of any concern for acceptance or rejection— and simply continue to take responsibility for the development of my skills and vision.

Like so many who have been close to the flame that is at the essence of Findhorn's magic, I too have been burned. And it is in the carrying of that wound that I learn my lessons. As I find the courage to allow the wound to remain open, I find myself maturing in ways that I did not realise were necessary. I heal and the world heals around me.

"Thank you Angel of Findhorn."

GEORGE KOSTVEIT GABRIEL

𝓕

Relationship
An Enlightening Experience

It was Christmas Eve and I had just returned from a wonderfully joyous Christmas party at Findhorn. Half the community had celebrated with Christmas carols and dance in the famously exuberant Findhorn style of the mid-1970s.

However, I had chosen this particularly happy occasion to break up with a community member I had been dating for several months—my second failed relationship since I'd joined Findhorn the summer before.

In those days (and maybe today as well?), Findhorn was one of the special places on the planet where untold legions of members and visitors had met and fallen (or should I say 'risen') in love. Romantic expectations were fairly high among the young members—and truth be told among some older ones as well, as Findhorn had a mischievous way of rekindling youthful fires.

So here I was on Christmas Eve, feeling very sorry for myself and my unhappy relationships, as community members filed into the sanctuary for a special midnight meditation. After the silent meditation ended, I sat there with tears streaming down my face, as I reviewed the seeming dozens of failed romantic relationships in my life.

"Why is it so difficult for me to find the right relationship?" I asked myself or more precisely, I asked my soul or higher self. I always thought I wanted a long-term committed relationship with someone who shared a similar spiritual path, ideally someone with whom I could share a common purpose and work together. But somehow this had always eluded me. So since my soul mate hadn't shown up, I found myself responding to an endless series of physical/emotional attractions with men that never worked

149

out.

In fact, the irony was that the latest disastrous relationship was as much a mental attraction as a physical or emotional one. (Even our astrological charts indicated we were well matched). But this didn't work either.

I sat alone in the sanctuary after everyone had left, my personality deep into the 'poor me' syndrome, as I prayed and meditated about why I had such a problem with relationships.

Then suddenly, something shifted. It was subtle at first, as it began to dawn on me that the purpose of my life was not just finding the perfect relationship and walking off into the sunset together to live happily ever after. (Growing up in Hollywood and seeing too many movies in my youth may have damaged my sense of reality until then).

I realized later that it was this moment on Christmas Eve in the Findhorn sanctuary when my soul finally had broken through the personality cloud of melodrama and self-pity. It was as if I suddenly woke up and saw very clearly for the first time the decision I had made as a soul before I was born. The purpose of my life was to serve, to help others and to help the world, not just to seek personal nirvana in the arms of some romantic hero.

As this new insight hit me, blinking through my tears, I vowed to focus primarily on my spiritual growth, on my work and my service, and to release my endless search for the perfect soul mate. In fact, I bravely committed myself to releasing the need for a relationship for the rest of my life, and living alone if need be. (This was a huge step for a woman like me, who in my formative years had absorbed all the messages of my culture that women were not fulfilled without men—a message later transformed by the women's liberation movement.)

As I re-chose this pre-birth soul commitment, an astonishing thing happened that I'd never experienced before nor since. An intensely bright light suddenly burst inside my head. With each breath that I took a light bulb seemed to turn on in my head. Light circulated throughout my body, down through my feet, then around and up through the top of my head, then spiralling down and around again.

I couldn't believe what was happening. It felt like something was permanently changing inside of me as the atoms of my body were electrified. It felt as if God was sweeping things clean inside of me renewing me, transforming me. The spiritual power of Findhorn provided the right environment for this incredible experience.

A million new insights went through my mind...I felt elated and transformed...re-energised. The light went on for some time and then gradually lessened and ended. I slowly walked home, feeling very unusual, and really curious about the meaning of this powerful experience.

I noticed that in the weeks following this experience of light, I actually did focus more fully on my work. I wasn't so distracted by men, endlessly searching for the right one. For the first time, I really enjoyed my work and became absorbed in it. I began to accept that my single status might be permanent and that was OK with me.

But as you know, the spiritual path is about avoiding attachments to things, to people, and as I was soon to discover, to ideas and beliefs. A few months later, as I was enjoying my path of celibacy and being alone, I met a visitor to Findhorn who really affected me on a deep soul level. He awakened a new type of love in me: the spiritual love that grows out of a shared purpose. His name was Gordon Davidson, and he had just left his work with a spiritual group at the United Nations to join Findhorn.

Soon he and I began to live and work together, and a year and a half later we left Findhorn to co-lead seminars around the U.S. about our experiences there. We then were guided to co-found a spiritual community in Massachusetts based on the principles we learned at Findhorn. We've co-led hundreds of seminars and written two books together, and four years ago we started a spiritually based leadership institute in Washington D.C.

Our co-creative partnership has unfolded and deepened over the years. We didn't walk off into that sunset of eternal happiness. We've certainly had challenges in our relationship and in our work but our lives have been very creative and fulfilling. A profound bond has grown between us that is richer than any purely romantic relationship could ever be.

That was 24 years ago, and we're still together today. I know I never would have drawn this type of relationship to me if I hadn't made that difficult decision in the Findhorn sanctuary on Christmas Eve many years ago.

CORINNE MCLAUGHLIN

Be Careful What You Wish For!

On my experience week back in August 1992 I went on the usual outing to Randolf 's Leap, a local beauty spot, where we were told about nature spirits and that here the veil was thinnest between the two worlds. I remember thinking that much as I would like it I was not the sort of person who saw nature spirits—too earthbound! However I liked the idea of being out in nature and set off alone along the river. Almost immediately I heard a splash and saw a salmon jump. I sat by the river for a few minutes watching the magical sight of the salmon running.

Then I set off again and not long afterwards I saw a dark shape moving along on the opposite bank. It was an otter! Wow! I had never seen an otter before. I watched entranced as it went about its business totally oblivious of my presence. Ah, I thought to myself, nature spirits. And because of my earthbound side they are turning up as embodied rather than in their spirit form. Wonderful! Then I thought to myself well all good things come in threes, so what will be my third nature experience?

By now it was coming close to time to return to the group. In fact because of someone with unsuitable footwear the time for the walk had been shortened. I had minded this so had stretched the time a little for returning and imagined I would probably be the last. Although we were quite a large group I had not seen anyone else during my walk. As I was walking back the path divided, one dropped towards the river, the other climbed slightly uphill. I found my feet taking the uphill path and about a minute later I heard what sounded like a twig snapping. Ah, I thought, my third nature experience. I heard another crack and looked to my left downhill towards the river to see if I could see what I thought was an animal moving about. Then suddenly there was a great roar and about thirty trees went crashing down onto the path below - the one that I did not take! Somewhat shaken I went to look at the debris and sure enough there was a tangle of trees across the path. I certainly would have been injured if not worse if I had taken the other track. I hurried back to the rest of the group thinking that the next time I get greedy and engage in manifestation I must remember one of the laws of manifestation: to be very specific about what one wants!

JOAN WILMOT

CHAPTER NINE

IN CONFERENCE

International Conferences are held here at least twice each year. They are usually topical, often life changing for the participants, and always inspirational. They have covered a wide variety of subjects. Eco-Villages, Forgiveness, Holistic health, Peace Education, and Angels are but a few. In the following pieces two people relate their reasons for initiating their conferences and participants describe their experience of them. There is also a transcription of an address given by Patch Adams during the Power of Service Conference. This gives a taste of the inspirational quality of these events.

The 'Western Mysteries' Itch

In response to the question, "Whatever possessed you then, dear RBD, to do this thing on 'The Western Mysteries: Which Way Today?'" I offer this tale.

A large part of what drew me to the Findhorn Foundation 20 years ago was the first 'mystery school curriculum' offered by the community under the focalization of Francois Duquesne and Michael Lindfield. I had recently completed my doctoral dissertation on Plato and Aristotle's theories of art, an exploration which had in turn led me personally, intellectually, and spiritually to the Arcane School teachings of Alice Bailey. As the Bailey material comprised much of what was on offer here, I felt that I had come to my 'spiritual home'. The experience of working with it in the company of other 'seekers' in the experiential context of the community at that time was quite simply one of the most exalted, challenging and joyful periods of my life.

Since that time, I have come to feel that the 'non-dogmatic, nonsectarian' aspect of this spiritual community is at once its greatest strength and greatest weakness. Although it is clearly a place where all spiritual paths cross, a junction point which can evoke profound experiences of self-discovery, the absence of definite core teachings and traditions basically leaves the question of one's continuing development up to the individual's own discipline and/or imagination. This 'core void' has been filled with a wonderful variety of independent, if connected, initiatives related both to indigenous and world-wide developments-everything from Eastern gurus to eco-villages. I couldn't help feeling, though, that 'something had gotten lost in the translation' of Findhorn's original inspiration into modernity.

During my 1992 stint as a Programme Director at the New York Open Centre, I was responsible, among other things, for booking British presenters including John Matthews, R J Stewart and R A Gilbert. All struck me as gifted, knowledgeable teachers on various aspects of the uniquely Western mystery tradition, those perennial teachings often embodied in myths and legends, which both antedate and circumscribe Christianity. It was there that it first occurred to me how wonderful it would be to bring these people together at Findhorn for a common exploration of this tradition, if only because it represents a significant aspect of Findhorn's own 'spiritual legacy'. After all, it is the tradition in which nearly all of the community's founders, including the late great Peter Caddy, and many of its early members had been steeped.

Upon my return to the community in 1993, I checked out this idea with David Spangler who I occasionally consult on such matters. Happily, he not only agreed with me but had independently come to something like the same conclusion himself, even to the point of personally inviting John and Caitlin Matthews up to join him and his family for a summer holiday at Findhorn! As it happened, their visit was also to coincide with that of one-time community focaliser Sabrina Dearborn and her partner Dr William Bloom, coordinator of the 'Alternatives Programme' at St James church, Piccadilly, in London.

Once the idea had been shaped and approved by the Foundation's Education Group, it was simply a matter of putting our heads together over that spring and summer by phone, e-mail, and eventually in person in order to 'flesh out' the original inspiration. Before we knew it, we had quickly and almost effortlessly amassed 20-plus first class presenters to bring the impulse towards new life, particularly by focusing not simply on its past but on its current manifestations and future directions.

So, dear reader, the fruits of this collaboration were on offer at Easter 1995. The Western Mysteries Conference featured lectures, artistic events and experiential workshops. We saw it as a way of honouring not just our own roots here at Findhorn but of re-exploring the larger context for all our myriad journeys within contemporary Western culture towards a vision of oneness and wholeness that celebrates the divinity in all life.

ROGER B DOUDNA

A Conference Diary

Well, here I am in sunny Scotland, not far from Inverness, a short walk from Findhorn Village, next to Findhorn Bay, which leads to rolling skies and the distant hills of the North Sea and the Scottish highlands. The weather is pleasant and cool and the flowers are in glorious bloom, everyone is busy now at one of the two daily communal work periods— from 9:00–12:00 and from 2:00–5:00—my work it appears is to communicate the joys, hopes and experience of the Findhorn Community. So here I am typing away, trying to find the words to describe this place and more importantly, the people and their goals.

When you imagine in your mind's eye this place, visualise a place of beauty, surrounded by distant dark hills and the nearby ocean, the grasses bright green and the yellow flowers of gorse, mustard and broom full bright and glorious. Then envision driving into The Park where you see many small bungalows each with its own little yard and carefully nestled flower and herb gardens. Drive straight ahead and stop at the Phoenix Shop—a bookstore with sundry grocery items (excellent health food!), including alternative music of all types and many an interesting book title.

Park your car and go for a walk. You are walking up a small landing strip for airplanes (used to be part of an airfield) now a main road in the Park. As you face the Phoenix, to the right are many caravans (trailers) and to the left some interesting wooden buildings with grass roofs. Walk up the centre road past the Community Centre (meals and meetings), and you can find the original trailer that was the home of Eileen, Peter, and Dorothy (very small!) and see the original gardens, still producing (including a lettuce patch in the shape of a heart), surrounded by flowers of many a variety and other bungalows.

A bit further on is the Universal Hall for community discussions, lecture-presentations, and artistic performances. This is a gnomish hive of sorts, packed with many enterprises—a visitors centre, a cafe serving excellent food, audio-visual department, dance/exercise room, computing centre, actors dressing rooms, music room, and others—a beautifully designed and lovingly built building.

Walk on across the main street and you come to all the craft workshops, the nature sanctuary, the straw-bale house with straw walls and mud-plaster coating, the recycle bins for waste, more gardens, the development office, a row of studio buildings for weaving, sculpture, arts of various sorts, the eco-housing where one of Eileen Caddy's sons lives, and the whiskey barrel houses—round barrel structures with a certain elfish look (initiated by Roger Doudna, a long-time member of this community).

One of the memorable spirit dwelling places is the nature sanctuary—no description can do it justice—a small elfin stone and earth building used for meditation and early morning Taize singing, round, with a circular meditation bench and a mandala carved into the floor with a central altar of the four elements—the power in this room put me immediately into a mild trance state, and the longer I stayed the deeper it got—very powerful place. In the Park there is also the Main Sanctuary, a building strictly for prayer and meditation.

Other memorable items: a huge windmill that generates electrical power, there being a constant sea breeze of significant force; and a reed bed recycling plant for human waste that produces good water and is a cutting-edge technology; a guest lodge for visiting groups; a shop that produces Findhorn Flower Essences; various exquisite wood sculptures; greenhouses; a holistic health centre; a bakery. Up the road a bit is the Cullerne House and Gardens, very large and productive, row upon row of organic gardens (many of the communal meals are organic).

Sunday @ Findhorn Goddess Ceremony

Just returned from an invocation of the goddess, one of the best I have ever attended. It was held in the Universal Hall (the large domed building with seven walls)—projected on to the centre wall was a large painting of the veiled goddess, seated and surrounded by numinous forms and energies, dressed in white. In the centre of the stage floor was an assembly representing the elements and the fruits of the earth—candle burning, lights very low, a Celtic harpist playing in a minor key soft songs invoking feelings of quiet and yet, joy. We entered and sat in the tiered seats facing the stage on three sides. After a while, we heard a drum playing, with cymbals and rattles and wooden sticks, all beating together in time to a slow march and in came the ceremonial leaders, mostly women with David Spangler and John Matthews. The women led the ceremony—they all marched in slowly and around the inner circle and we chanted with them the words to their song.

Then the instruments were laid on the hardwood floor and we were asked to rise and perform the first part of the ceremony—we all stood and faced East, and the power of the east was invoked in the name of the element of Fire, the rising of the sun, of light, illumination and spiritual awakening. Two beats of the wooden sticks, a ring of cymbals. Then we turn to the South and invoke the Earth, mother of us all, goddess, holy source of life, stability and foundation. Two beats of the wooden sticks, a tomp of drum, and we turn to the West, invoking Water, the power of inspiration, openness, adaptation, a surrender of rigidity, a letting go of old forms. A shake of the sistrum, rattle, and two clicks of the wooden sticks. We turn to the North, facing the veiled Goddess image, invoking Air, breath of life, the energy of communication and communion, the open free space of the higher energies. A click of sticks, a cymbal resonates through cool, dark air, reverberating in our souls—this is a holy place, this is a Chalice we have opened. We face the centre, envisioning a centre of gathering energy in the name of the Goddess—there is deep silence and elemental energy is building into beauty.

Then bowls of pine seeds are passed out and each participant takes a small seed or two and holds them in his or her hand, envisioning this seed as a focal point for spiritual growth, for the inner seed that we carry in our heart, in the place where the Goddess touches us (the blessing of the mother. She enwraps us in her skirts, covers us with Her veil, holds us entranced)—the seed we must grow to transform our lives into that which will bear good fruit and abundance in Her name. We hold this seed in our hands and a deep silence descends, filling all the empty places of our hearts, we meditate together in that womb of silence, feeling the pulse and beat of our own hearts as echoing the sacred rhythms of the living cosmos. We sit in long and comfortable silence, breathing slows, mind empties, becomes concentrated without effort, rides easily on the currents of shared energy, hovers over us in a protective embrace. After a time of long and peaceful silence, with eyes closed, a voice is heard—a voice of profound purity and beauty, a young woman sings an ancient Celtic chant in the old tongue, so lyrical and touching that tears come to my eyes, that Spirit is so tangible and present, so very real in the voice of the song carrying reverence for the Goddess. She sings with delicacy and a gentle rhythm, touching many with her song.

Then we hear the drone of a many-stringed instrument and we all begin to vocalize the drone in a humming, energizing sound—the sound builds toward peaks and valleys of sound, a sea of waves of sound, rising and falling in rhythm with breath and inner harmonization. The sounds build and then softly fall away to silence. A woman harpist, Lori Sunshine, comes forward and sings a chant to the Ancient Mother, invoking Her presence. Sung with a Celtic harp several feet high, she plucks gently at the strings, stirring us—the woman beside me is crying, touched in her longing for the old songs of the goddess, the reaffirmation of the female spiritual presence, the strong contact with Her Blessings.

After this song, we are invited down to the floor of the theatre where we sit with the others in a circle, with an opening to the north. We chant songs to the earth and the children of the community are all brought in together, even the youngest, and carried into the centre of the circle where they are surrounded with the love and warmth we are feeling, into the protective centre of the community affirming the mother's gift of children and the responsibility of their spiritual nourishment.

We sing together, all the children are smiling and a little awed— happy and wondering. Then we stand and form interconnected circles and begin to chant and sway in a line around the centre altar—the circle moves and we circle facing each other and smiling and greeting friend and stranger alike. The feeling is high and happy, the children are nourished and the adults are joined. Afterwards, we go outside and plant our seeds—we eat them! Wanting to give birth to this beauty, to conceive its wonder and to find ourselves planted in the Mother's sacred depths. Her arms are about us, Her song within us, Her joy tangible and manifest. May She bless us all and find these words worthy of Her love.

Thursday Night June 21, Findhorn

A strange thing happened—the presenters got together and were asked to construct a solstice ceremony for the Universal hall. We debated this and that, and then Fiona, the Celtic harpist, was asked to construct the ceremony in terms of the Celtic traditions, with John Matthews helping. A couple of American presenters were brash, trying to push their own non-Celtic ideas, this did not go down well (this American was quiet)...ebb and flow, finally, Fiona clearly had the idea that we should enact the legend of the battle of the sun and the dark as symbolised by the solstice ceremony. To do this, we would have to have two men to enact the battle with staffs and fight it out on the floor of the Universal Hall. None of the presenters wanted to do this, maybe we could find some Findhornites to do it. Finally I decided to volunteer to be one of the battling gods. Things clicked into focus, several other presenters volunteered, we settled on Lee Irwin and William Bloom.

Strangely enough, even though I carefully said I would be one of the gods, everyone immediately assumed that I would make a great Lord of Darkness—so be it I thought, this is my role, no doubt, to live in the shadows and to embrace the stars. So we worked out the details of a quite beautiful ceremony. It began by everyone (150) gathering at the Universal hall and while they entered, being given a candle. Then in low lighting with the skylight closed overhead, the four directions were opened with one presenter with painted symbols on the face chanting to the direction and invoking the power— John Matthews opened the way with that deep, sonorous voice, power of the wind to the east, then Kevin Ryerson with fire to the south, Barbara Hand Clow with water to the west and Serena Rony-Dougal with earth to the north. Each direction was opened and then a picture of the great goddess flashed on the huge front screen, veiled and dressed in white. Then Fiona in that amazing Bardic voice, told the story of the battle of the Sun god against the Lord of Darkness, how they struggle and fight and how the Dark Lord wounds the Sun god whose strength then grows dimmer and dimmer over until the next solstice.

The lights went out, total darkness—the spot comes on, there is the Lord of Light, resplendent in yellow costume with a painted sun face. Then, out of the shadows, creeping low comes the black caped Lord of Dark looming up over the Sun god and using his staff to throttle him, his grim face painted with dark lines and blackened eyes and a red gash on his cheek. They struggle, they clash, staffs whacking away, whack! whack! whack! The Lord of Light is driven down, he springs back, whack! whack! the energy is moving we are getting into it—whack, whack! The Lord of Light loses his staff! Whack! He grabs the Lord of darkness, they struggle and the lord of darkness loses his staff, they circle warily, they rush at each other wham! they hit the floor rolling, wrestling, struggling, they separate, wrestle again— the lights are pulsating, the energy very high, the crowd is screaming— suddenly, the Lord of Darkness pulls a long red silken scarf from his pocket and whirls it around his head, it whizzes in the air, the Sun God rears back and snap! snap! He is wounded on the thigh and the red silk falls over his leg as he lies writhing on the floor—the Sun God is wounded and the Lord of Darkness fades from view.

An attractive woman of exceptional beauty and youthfulness comes forward, her long silver hair gleaming, holding a lighted candle, she helps the Lord of Light to rise and then they both kneel before the great image of the Goddess. A harp is heard and a beautiful song symbolizes the turning of the sun back on its course under the protection of the Goddess. The vibrations fill the air, the music hums—Fiona calls the people forth to come down with their candles and light them from the lighted candle of the woman who helped the Lord of Light. A Gaelic chant begins, with complex drumming—oh yes, throughout the fight there was drumming and the deep wail of the digeridoos—a procession heads for the Field of Dreams, and we go out to light the solstial bonfire, which is huge and meant to burn all night until sunrise (3:00 AM!).

There we dance around the fire and a long narration is given about the white buffalo calf woman, intermixed with dances of many sorts, dances also being celebrated on the Lakota reservations and we all look to the moon to pray and offer thanks, the same moon that shines on the Black Hills and the same blessing that falls on those who open their hearts to the Goddess. They are dancing now as I write this, the fire flickers in the sky, and the Lord of Darkness sits alone, doing his midnight work, far from the dancing throng.

Finally it is time to leave Findhorn—there is so much more I could say, indeed, most of what I take with me can't be put into words. Is there magic at Findhorn? Yes! Not figurative or speculative or theoretical— but actual, real, transformative magic. This requires respect and deep appreciation for the fullness of the experience when contacting magical places. What is the magic? Mostly it is the co-operative and seamless way the community functions and the large number of people who accept and live alternative perspectives as normal and everyday realities, a place where singing and dancing is part of the daily round and group prayers and the goddess are not uncommon; a place where you can go to the earth lodge and chant or sit in the Hobbit House to meditate or go to the sanctuary to pray and no one will think anything of it—a place where people dress in any and every style and no one bats an eye, where you can dye your hair bright red or wear a three hour perm and it makes absolutely no difference, a place where dancing to rock and roll (which we did several times) is not incompatible to listening to Celtic harps and Scottish bagpipes. A place that has a position for a professional storyteller as well as a professional chef or financier—a place of just plain people who want a better life, who are young and trying to find out what it's all about or older and trying to make new changes or recovering from trauma and illness. It is a place of opportunity, alternatives, possibilities of all types mixed with a strong dose of practicality and down-to-earth work, effort and sweat-of-your-brow commitment.

It is not a place for people who want to impose ideas or demand changes for their own good, nor is it a place for people who want someone else to give them answers, who want someone else to do their own work. It is a place that demands your full attention and energy and a place in which human relationships are primary and inescapable—here, one must relate and be willing to experience life through community and living with others in a great adventure. It is a place that burns people out—that is, a place that absorbs energy and creates circumstances that test the limits of personal capacity— and yet, it is that very test that provides that possibility for real transformation and spiritual healing, awakening and illumination— when actualized from the deepest centre. Without that actualisation, it means a constant pressure to give what you can and then, to move on if necessary. Speaking as a short term visitor, it acts with great force to open the potential of the future, because, as David Spangler said earlier today,

"Findhorn is a place where the future is being enacted, a place where what is coming is already here and what is possible is taking form."

LEE IRWIN

𝓕

Matching Up

It was a conference, sometime in the 80's. I had come up, with some colleagues, from our Centre for Alternative Technology, in Wales. We were allocated groups, with a focaliser.

It always takes me a few days to shake off the Big Bad World and tune in to the magic of Findhorn, and I felt uneasy with myself, with the group and especially the focaliser, a woman I had never met. We just did not click, and she knew it too. There was obviously some kind of karmic link that was trying to tell us something and needed sorting out. It got worse, and after a few days we decided on a lunchtime showdown. As we talked and ate, I could feel the logs starting to move, but suddenly I realised I was late for my afternoon workshop. Damn! But so was she, and as it happened, it was the same workshop. It was a big one, in the Universal Hall, and we had been asked to bring clean handkerchiefs. We crept in just in time and sat next to each other.

As part of the 'warm up' or re-connection process after lunch, the workshop leader asked 80 people to wave their handkerchief. It was a fine sight, made me giggle a bit, so many different kinds of handkerchiefs. Mine was very faded but I was fond of it. Blue with white spots and border, and in that assembly, unique—I thought. I glanced at my focaliser neighbour's handkerchief, which was bright blue, then when she lowered her arm I saw that it was in fact identical to mine, but new. I spread mine out to show her, and we exchanged a glance, which sealed our reconciliation. Nothing else needed to be said.

Is there a moral to this tale? Perhaps it is simply that the magic of Findhorn has the power to put the colour back in your hankie.

PETER HARPER
www.cat.org.uk

Business for Life

Re-consecrating Our Work

I first visited Findhorn in 1974 and worked briefly on the building of the Universal Hall. It was not until 1987 that I arrived on a permanent basis as a 'successful businessman'. The bracketed statements are necessary as their interpretation between the conventional and spiritual value systems are markedly different. Findhorn, often referred to as the 'graveyard of the ego' had first to work its alchemy on the transformation of those values.

It has however always been my strong conviction that the ethos of Findhorn only had relevance to the extent that its philosophy (loosely defined) was relevant to the world at large. It was to take over 10 years to convince a doubtful community that business (loosely defined) was not only a legitimate activity but one that each one of us was engaged in every day of our life. Where, how and what we spend our money on in the local Phoenix store makes up our local economy and, by extension, the global economy. Business is no less a potential spiritual path than the monastery, just harder. The Foundation, like any other legally defined charity must market and manage itself on a businesslike basis or it will simply cease to exist. A charity, like any business, has to be financially responsible to remain viable.

I remain profoundly grateful that the Foundation, as a spiritual community, agreed to hosting a conference that recognised business as pivotal to the transformation of our world. My personal story starts from the other end of the spectrum in that I was educated through a materialistic world view. The feeling of inner emptiness that resulted could not be filled through the normal trappings of business and social success. I went through various shades of green, wrote long ethical statements and finally came to the conclusion that my crisis and that of our affluent western world was not about environmentalism or social responsibility per se but was essentially the crisis of the human spirit.

The Conference, *Business for Life* was never meant to be 'business as usual'. We recognise there is still a large gap between right livelihood and much of current business practice. Our subtitle was to *re-consecrate our work*. This acknowledged that we needed to re-embrace the spiritual reality and purpose directing our lives. Only from that deeper understanding and basis for our business and charitable activities would arise the solutions to our pressing problems. From the perspective of our Essential Nature we will naturally create work that is life enhancing and inspiring, rekindling a sense of meaning and purpose in our collective lives. The transition period is fraught with potential upheaval but transit we must.

At the root of the problem is the rise of materialism, defined as the denial of a spiritual reality behind our material existence. The flip side of that coin is the poverty consciousness that often arises in a spiritually focused environment with its implicit judgement and/or denial of a material reality. So 'Business for Life' focused our attention on how we can mend the rift, how we could marry spirit and matter and so have our material and spiritual needs fully realised. How we might experience the mystic and the pragmatist and not have the one deny the other. This tension remains as part of ongoing collective work and is beautifully summed up in the words of the late poet laureate, Ted Hughes:

'The real problem comes from the fact that outer world and inner world are interdependent at every moment. We are simply the locus of their collision. Two worlds, with mutually contradictory laws, or laws that seem to us to be so, colliding afresh every second, struggling for peaceful coexistence. And whether we like it or not our life is what we are able to make of that collision and struggle. So what we need evidently is a faculty that embraces both worlds simultaneously. A large, flexible grasp, an inner vision which holds wide open, like a great theatre, the arena of contention, and which pays equal respects to both sides. Which keeps faith, as Goethe says, with the world of things and the world of spirits equally'.'

For 500 years we have developed rational, analytical thought to a new peak of perfection. Alongside this development of the masculine principal has flowered the age of Discovery, the Industrial age and now the Technological age. This same period has eclipsed the world of mystery and metaphor so that now we live in a spiritual vacuum. This is graphically displayed in the Anthroposophical metaphor of the traveller to the city of 50 years ago. What welcomed him on the horizon was the cathedral spire soaring into the sky pointing heavenward. Today any traveller to every city in the modern world is confronted by the towering block of the international bank and the transnational corporation headquarters. St Paul's cathedral is finally obscured by the NatWest tower and Lever Brothers. The transformation is almost complete.

The 'almost' is important because as Carl Jung succinctly sums up "Man cannot stand a meaningless life". As we enter the new millennium a new spirit of business is emerging. Business is beginning to look at the crucial role it needs to fulfill if we are to move gracefully into the next century. Presently this search is largely driven by fear: the fear for survival, both personal and planetary. This is manifesting itself in the grudging 'greening' of business. We are now ready to start the next major shift which is to experience business as sacred space and give meaning to the oft quoted phrase that 'our work is our love made visible'.

Business is one of the most potent forces in the world today and holds a vital key to its transformation. The choice is ours as to which way we turn it. This is a dilemma we all face. Doing nothing won't do it. The time for ambivalence is over. How will you conduct your next business transaction? Will you consciously choose the organic, fair traded product over your usual favourite variety? Will you smile at the person on the till and thank them genuinely or curse them under your breath for taking too long? How, where and what you buy creates our world. It is no good blaming the supermarket, they always supply what the customer wants—that is their business. Our business is to start choosing wisely.

JOHNNY BRIERLY
Extracted from the Business for Life files and updated for
'Growing People' October 1999

F

The Bottom Line

The origin of the word business means 'to nourish life'. Our word implies 'busyness', rushing around, our life consumed by our jobs, a lack of space for the rest of our lives. But what would it be like, asked one participant at the Conference 'Business for Life', if our business truly did nourish our lives? What sort of a world would we then inhabit?

This Conference, *Business for Life—Reconsecrating Our Work*, was the realisation of one man's dream, eight years in the making. The idea initially met with some resistance at the Findhorn Foundation. Questions were asked as to whether it was appropriate for a spiritual community to host a weeklong conference about business.

But Johnny Brierley, coming as he did from a business background, knew in his heart that a spiritual community is an entirely appropriate place to debate the reconsecration of our work. He'd tasted the success of business and found it wanting, known that however successful he became, the yacht would never be long enough. And then there was this yawning hole inside him and the more successful he became, the wider it yawned. From the vantage point of his personal crisis, Johnny had clearly seen that the crisis of the western world would not be solved merely by greater social responsibility or sustainable options. It was much deeper than that, it was truly a crisis of the human spirit.

And so they came to share in Johnny's dream, some two hundred participants from around the globe, committed to dialogue on the relationship between business and spirituality. They came from as far afield as Hungary and Japan, from Africa and Iceland: consultants and employees from the world of business and finance, individuals whose declared interests encompassed personal development.

They said that they wanted to connect with the deeper purpose of their lives, to bring a sense of the divine into their work, to form win/win relationships with colleagues, to make both work and personal life more meaningful, to develop a sense of right livelihood. Many of them spoke about leaving behind their emotions and their true selves, along with their hats and coats, at the office door. Some were deeply frustrated in their working lives, others had already begun to make the transition, leaving empty jobs to form consultancy companies engaged in bringing spirituality and creativity into the workplace. Many participants had already undergone such deep inner crises in their working lives that they had radically changed the nature of their work or their approach to it, or both.

Others were still struggling with all this, facing the dilemma between work which cramped and stifled the soul on the one hand, and the scary and insecure world of self-employment on the other. For them, there were sharp and practical questions. How to find work which truly made the heart sing? How to follow that impulse and still provide for the material needs of families? Downshifting and the adoption of more simple lifestyles had become a popular choice. Many had joined communities both small and large, others were engaged in setting them up.

In his keynote speech on the first night, Jonathon Porritt talked about the doubling of the gap between the world's richest and poorest people over the last thirty years. Today a third of the world's work force is un- or underemployed, and those in this group who manage to find work, do so under the worst labour conditions since the 1930s. If we are conscientious about such things we can no longer feel comfortable going about our daily business as usual.

Yet it isn't a question of lack of resources. Many speakers referred to the ten trillion dollars which circulates around the world markets every day, inaccessible to any elected government. In Porritt's view the plethora of economic alternatives now available in the domains of food, energy, pollution control and finance were an inevitable and radical response to the overarching phenomenon of life in the developed world-Universal Consumerism. The Moray LETS System and the Earthshare Food Co-operative are two of the local responses created by the wider community associated with the Findhom Foundation. Such un-subsidised and unsupported community based initiatives are now springing up everywhere. They are new forms of creating economy and wealth, shifting the energy from disempowerment into win/win situations. According to Porritt "We're in the middle of a huge paradigm shift to a community- based empowered economy that creates and defines wealth differently".

So-called 'ethical banking' is another such response. Glen Saunders,

Managing Director of the Triodos Bank (formerly Mercury Provident) talked about offering people a place to put their money outside of the ten trillion dollar a day in circulation. His anthroposophical bank aims at transparency—people knowing what is being done with their money. Investments are used to fund socially and environmentally positive community projects, from Steiner Schools to organic farms, as well as lending micro credit to the world's very poor. It isn't difficult to measure the value and accountability of such a banking system, it operates on the good biblical tenet of "by their fruits shall ye know them". It would be somewhat difficult to apply such a principle of assessment to the World Bank. Yet one of the most uplifting and encouraging presentations at this conference came from a World Bank employee. Three years ago, responding to an inner call, Richard Barrett put out an e-mail around the bank offering to dialogue with colleagues about the deeper meaning of work. The result was the birth of the World Bank Spiritual Unfoldment Society. What began as tentative and fearful discussions among a tiny group in the cafe has now blossomed into a thriving lunchtime venue, each attended by about fifty employees from all levels and hosting top guest lecturers from all over Washington.

In 1995 the Bank supported Barrett's initiative for a World Bank Conference on Ethics and Values, attended by 350 delegates from 20 countries. A central objective was to bridge that discontinuity between personal and institutional values. Barrett was walking his talk and acquiring something of a reputation. When asked in the elevator how he felt today, he'd simply beam out, "Bordering on the fantastic. How are you?". For the first time in its history, World Bank employees were using the word 'love' in their conversations with colleagues.

It wasn't an easy road to travel. Like Johnny Brierley, Barrett had to live into a dream which seemed hardly possible, with very little support at first. Now he's at the forefront of transformation of work and business in the world. All the presenters had similar stories: ordinary people who'd found the courage to live extraordinary lives, and who were committed to making a difference. Their presentations were uniformly excellent. They spoke from their hearts, and it was the quality of their speaking, as much as the rich abundance of information they imparted, which carried us along on our personal journeys throughout this week.

These speakers led by example. In their own lives they had found ways of entering that deep personal stillness from which a truly new and creative approach to life and work can emerge. It wasn't superficial, their lives were dedicated to nurturing that space. Professor Chakraborty from the University of Calcutta told us that we didn't need brainstorming to solve our management problems, what we needed was 'heartstorming'. He spoke of the Eastern seers (literally, those who are able to see) who came not from the city universities but from the ashrams of the forest. At tea, his wife informed me that he joins them every year for a retreat and that he dedicates each Sunday to silent reflection.

Such dedication to truth doesn't come merely from the mind. As Ellen Hayakawa, a tiny lady whose courage and inspiration moved many of us to tears, told us: "If you want to hear God laugh—tell God your plans!" It was emerging for many of us who'd brought our sharp and practical questions to the party, that the answers were to be found on the inside. Every now and then someone would strike a Tibetan Bowl and signal a minute's silence to remind us of this. As we entered the Conference's Open Space, one answer to all our questions seemed slowly to be emerging. That answer was Love.

In many different ways we had been shown how it was indeed possible to live out of love and to transform work and business from that centre, in the most unlikely workplaces. And was that so surprising? Perhaps not to this audience, but the message is also out there, in that murky world around which the ten trillion circulates daily. Jack Hawley told us that a recent survey of the richest readers of Fortune Magazine concluded that the public figure they most admired was Mother Teresa. Another ordinary person living an extraordinary commitment.

It is surely this, and this alone, which will transform our lives and the world of business and work. Indeed, it is the only thing which can. And the idea is empowering.

The speaker who most stole the show at this conference was just an ordinary shopkeeper. David Hoyle, who runs the Phoenix Community Stores here in The Park, told us how he hadn't grown up imagining that his mission in life was to become a grocer. And yet, as he'd travelled his personal road, he'd realised that there was no better way to express right livelihood in this world of 'Universal Consumerism' than through conscientious shopping. A recent poll indicated that 80% of the population believe in God and 70% consider shopping to be their favourite activity!

Hoyle's approach is to offer people a choice to exercise responsibility, to buy goods that are local, organic, fairly traded. The consequences of what we buy, he reminded us, can be profound. What we buy can determine whether local businesses flourish or go under, whether growers in the third world live or die. He offered us all a commitment sheet in which we were invited to fill in one change in our shopping activity that we would implement when we went home. Spirit in action, something demonstrably practical.

What touched us all so deeply about David's presentation was the depth from which he shared his heart with us. It seemed to be the bottom line. It was what participants from all walks of business and work had been saying all week. They just wanted an opportunity to share their hearts in their daily work.

I talked to a freelance business coach who said that what he'd heard would encourage him to come out of the closet with his clients, to be more open about what we're all really talking about loving each other. He already knew from experience that the lowering of barriers in his clients was a direct response to his own courage to be totally open hearted, as well as open minded. What then transpires comes out of a place of deep value and is always of direct benefit. Results he gets for his clients include promotions, changed job descriptions, more efficiently run departments, more honesty and greater willingness to share personal problems with colleagues.

A recent study of corporate culture and performance compared companies which make explicit values of care and concern for employees and customers, as well as for their shareholders. The performance of over two hundred major companies was analysed over eleven years. Those with explicit value statements consistently outperformed the others by very high margins. It seems then that balance and harmony in our personal and corporate lives also equates with success. As Richard Barrett asked, "Now, is this or is it not a spiritual message?"

JUDITH HAMPSON

The Power and Joy of Service

The first visit of Patch Adams to the Findhorn Foundation was in September 1992 for the Holistic Health Conference; he came back for the Power of Service conference and enthused us all again. He's big, bright, beautiful and breathes fun. A doctor in the Gesundheit community in the USA, and a clown, he is a magnetic person who has a dream and fulfills it, and he sweeps us up into his passion with him.

You may see him walking down the road with his pants on his head, hand outstretched to greet you, or you may see him weep recalling the murder of his friend and closest colleague, who was killed by a patient living in their medical community. What inspires most about Patch Adams is his great compassion—he says 'yes' to everyone who comes, opens his doors to all, driven by a quest to reach the hearts of everyone he meets.

He introduced his talk for the Power of Service conference by clowning, dressed in bright yellow pantaloons, a coat of many colours, a big red nose and enormous curly-toed shoes, and he carried a fish.

"I would like to start with a quote from Victor Frankl, a Jewish Psychotherapist who had been imprisoned in a Nazi concentration camp.

He said:

'We who lived in the camps remember the people who walked through the huts comforting others, giving away their last crust of bread. Though they were few in number, they offered sufficient proof that everything can be taken away from a man but one thing, the last of the great human freedoms: the ability to choose one's own way.'

Caring is a choice. I believe in individual acts of will, and that is the basis from which I give this talk.

I entered medical school 25 years ago to use medicine for social revolution. Not only did I want to deal with physical illness, I was also interested in dealing with the diseases of our society. I found greed at the top of the list. In America, medicine is the most expensive thing and I wanted to take this most expensive thing and give it away for free. Not only for free, but with no sense of debt or barter, because I felt that if we are ever going to heal our planet we must recreate tribalism and community and give people a sense of belonging. We cannot have a sense of belonging unless we fundamentally care for one another, and at least care for each other's medical needs.

But free medical care wasn't the only thing I wanted; I also wanted medicine to be free from concerns of malpractice, which is a multibillion dollar problem. Beyond malpractice being an expensive problem, it is also a spiritual nightmare, because when you carry malpractice insurance you are telling your patients: 'I am afraid of you, I don't trust you.' There isn't a hospital or a clinic in America that doesn't carry malpractice insurance - except ours. We refuse to have anything to do with it; we would rather lose what we have than be a party to fear and mistrust.

Another problem is that most medicine in America is paid for by insurance companies. They tell you what kind of care you can get, how long you can get it for, and they create a multi-billion-dollar pile of paperwork and labour that has absolutely nothing to do with caring for a patient.

And very important, we also have a crisis in de-humanising experiences; not only for the patient—which is obvious and well written about—but also in the much less written about, possibly more de-humanising situation for the care giver.

There is not a happy hospital in America. I look. I travel all over the States and challenge them to find me one, and in 22 years I have not found one. I get hundreds, if not thousands of letters every year from doctors and nurses who are crying because of how much it is hurting them to practise medicine, and yet they are doing the greatest work a human can do—they are serving humanity. But their suicide rates, their addiction and alcoholism rates, their divorce rates, are dangerous. (And the fact that hospitals treat their patients with seriousness and solemnity is dangerous too.) Applications to go to medical schools are down by 35 per cent.

To address all of these major problems, a group of us got together and asked ourselves, "Where are we most human?" and we discovered that we are most human in our friendships. This told us that intimacy was the most important medicine we could offer, particularly at a death bed or to someone in intractable pain or with a chronic disease, and so our ideal patient became that person who wanted a deep, intimate friendship with us for life.

Our next question was, "Where do we do friendships?" The answer to that was that we do it in our homes, and so twenty of us— three physicians and a support staff of seventeen—moved into a large home after we graduated from medical school, and made our home a hospital. We never charged fees of any kind, or permitted any sense of debt. We never accepted medical insurance or carried malpractice insurance.

In our first twelve years we had five to fifty overnight guests per night. If you can picture a large, single-family dwelling with twenty adults and their children living in it and all those overnight guests every night—you could just say that we lived in a workshop! We had 15,000 people come to us, 3,000 of whom had prior mental health histories—and we never gave psychiatric medication—so we can say it was an interesting workshop! We let wonderful people stay with us, and we let profoundly disturbed people be with us. My closest classmate was murdered by one of our patients, and yet we still decided to keep our doors open for everyone.

After twelve years and serving a huge number of people, we realised that, politically, we had to build a hospital. We could no longer admit our pneumonia patients to be in the hallways of our very crowded and non-technological home So, in 1980 we bought Gesundheit: 314 acres of wooded, mountainous, waterfalled, springfilled, breathtaking country in Pochahontas County, West Virginia. It had a small four roomed house, a barn and countless outbuildings, and there we set about building our dream of a health care community.

But for our first nine years we paid money for the privilege of being doctors: the staff worked at outside jobs to pay for us to do medicine. Besides this, and even more challenging, was the fact that we had no privacy. Yet in those nine years we lost no staff members —because we were a silly hospital! Humour was tremendously important and we made it fun and a joy to be there. However long, arduous and difficult the task, there is joy in service, and this is the message I want to bring.

What I had noticed, as a social activist, was that every group that was helping people had a very high burn-out rate, and so it became our priority to find that which in the work sustains us—to find, in the act of service, in the act of work, a joy that not only prevents burn-out but feels like a glorious celebration.

First let me give you a sense of what I mean by the words caring and service. To me these are action verbs: to project a countenance and action of compassion and empathy over time, without regard for reward. We can just call it basic friendship. I'm not speaking here of the rhetoric used in the media for service organisations—hospitals or hotels where the ad says, "We care." 'We' never cared. 'We' cannot care. Individuals care, because caring is an extremely personal act.

For me, and I think for a lot of other people, there comes a time when we look at the world and feel a dramatic sense of the need to serve. For some people this moment is a natural outgrowth of growing up with wonderful parents in a wonderful neighbourhood. For others who had a horrible upbringing in a horrible neighbourhood with horrible events going on around them, something had to happen to awaken them—they took a workshop at the Findhorn Foundation and came out saying "I'm going to care! I'm going to step out of my complaining, out of my suffering, and insist that I care in some way."

But I want to eliminate the concept that service is a struggle. Horseshit to that concept! George Bernard Shaw had this to say:

This is the true joy of life. The being used for a purpose recognised by yourself as an almighty one. The being thoroughly worn out before being thrown on the scrap heap. The being a force of nature instead of the feverish, selfish, little clod of ailments complaining that the world will not devote itself to making you happy.'

At the top of my list, and why I am an intoxicated human being, is that I have found that in the act of service is the greatest gold we ever dream of—the gold of intimacy. Is there anything more important to you in your life than friendship? It astounds me as a physician that no matter how I look—and I don't look the way a lot of normal doctors look—when I walk into a patient's room and hold a twinkle in my eye, a countenance of joy and an obvious projection of caring, even in a first encounter, the patient will give me more of themselves than they have ever given to another human being, even if they are sixty or seventy years old. My initial interviews with patients take three or four hours and I often find that patients are shocked that I am giving that amount of time - they are almost unnerved, embarrassed, apologetic.

During our lifetime we seek, hoping to find a few friends who will open up, respect us, trust us and love us. I was getting this contact with others in less than an hour! There was a body of people, who simply because I cared instantly gave me my greatest dreams. I was in awe from the very beginning to see how this can work in medicine, and then I was flabbergasted to realise how universally true it was. It was intimacy! Those of you who know me at all know that I want to skip all of the first, second and third steps and I want to be your most intimate buddy now. I want to have no privacy—because I love intimacy!

Through intimacy and service I have been given so many gifts. I graduated from medical school book-smart and an egghead; since then I have been a farmer, a goat herder, learned to juggle, ropewalk, unicycle, produce a number of plays and make a number of movies —and these are just a small part of the gifts that have come to me through intimacy and service; just the first way I have benefitted, and there are so many more.

The second is that I have also had the satisfaction, thrill and privilege to be part of the answer and not part of the problem. In service, you can look at the front page of a newspaper, feel the pain and suffering in the world, and amid all the horror—don't dare deny that there is gigantic horror—you can say that you are part of the solution. This means you have self-esteem and it is a gift more rare than platinum, more precious than gold.

The basis of self-esteem is the fundamental concept that you are great. Every single day you can look at yourself in the mirror, eyeball to eyeball, and say, "I'm great!" Not, "I'm greater than you", or "I am the greatest" or "the best"; it's not a comparison. You are simply joining the human race and all the other creatures. Dare to feel it. Dare to love yourself as much as you love the greatest thing you love. Stop paying lip service to "We are one" unless you add yourself to that love.

Next, with service, there is contentment and ease about life. Potentially, in the privilege, intimacy and thrill of giving, there is perhaps the greatest stress reducer you'll ever bump into. In the actual doing—more than all the treasures you could ever dream of —in the giving and the service is the potential for stress reduction, because in the giving you are the solution, you are love.

Number four: it is a chance to love. The core belief within most faiths is service and Christ's message to us is to serve - he said, "You do it, you be me, you serve." So our job is not to worship him or anyone else. Never adore me or anyone else more than you adore yourself.

In service you can have the physical experience of being love. Can you handle it? Can you actually, while shovelling manure, feel the love? Most of you feel strongly connected to a spiritual path, but how many of you even remotely think that someday you might be Christ? Or Sai Baba? Or Buddha? How many of you allow yourself even one second of that knowledge that you are the Christ? Jesus is nothing unless He lives in you—He wants you to get out there and work your butt off; in fact, He wants you to die doing it—that's what He did. Die with your boots on and your heart on your sleeve. It is pointless to have anything to do with Jesus unless you are going to spend your lifetime serving. And if you like Him for doing it, why not like yourself for doing it?

Benefit number five: a reputation for caring. I have been here in the Findhorn Community for less than seven days and I am loved to an embarrassing level. I can't want for anything that isn't there before I want it. I'm afraid to ask for anything because I'll get it back tenfold. The interesting thing is that, whether you have a reputation for humour or joy or caring, that reputation is your food and water. The entire security of Gesundheit, our hospital, is based on karma - we know you will take care of us.

To have a reputation for caring, you don't have to do anything, people worship the servant and they impose that reputation upon you. It is difficult to take because you do not give to get anything back—in fact that would completely fog the giving. You give because the intoxication is in the giving, but yet, in giving you get so much back. True givers' reputations expand not by something they do, but simply because people like to hear about givers; they make a big deal out of it. In truth, I think that at the heart of the formation of a religion or a spiritual sect is the fact that people collect around givers: 'holy' really means 'giving'. Please let yourself open up to the fact that you have done good, that you are givers. I have never met a person who told me they were feeling burned out, who wasn't really a fabulous person, a giving person. Just take the average mother—if you are a mother you are the holiest person ever, because you serve.

Number six: we have an antidote to boredom. With the complexities of our problems, the size of our difficulties, the overwhelming lethargy there is—and the colossal nature of the horror—there is room for experimentation. You spit in the face of life if you have one bored moment; you are really saying, "Up yours, flowers! Poetry! Kissing! Ice cream! Bicycles!" I consider boredom to be a medical emergency!

Your imagination and the rest of creation are enough for you to be ecstatic for the rest of your life. Why do you waste time walking around with your head not full of wonder and curiosity? What makes you want to put old socks in your head and walk around with that kind of odour up there? Be creative. Be enthusiastic. Do you remember that great song from the musical version of Don Quixote: 'To dream the impossible dream, to right the unrightable wrong, to be willing to march into hell for a heavenly cause'? It's so beautiful to go into the quest.

There is a little poem by Kabir, translated into English by Robert Bly:

'Friend, hope for the quest while you are still alive.
Think and think while you are still alive.
Think and think while you are still alive.
What you call salvation belongs to the time before death.'

If you don't break the ropes before death, do you think you will join with the ecstatic when you are dead, just because your body is rotten?

What is found now is found then: if you find nothing now, you'll simply end up with an apartment in the City of Death. If you make love with the Divine now, in the next life you will see the face of satisfied desire—so plunge into the truth. If you want never to burn out, find passion in its most raw and native state. To be passionate is the natural state.

And finally, there is the medical part: I am going to suggest that living a life of service round the clock could be one of the greatest things you could ever do for your personal health. Because, indeed, if you do live a life of intimacy; if you do live a life full of satisfaction and knowing you are great, bathed in self-esteem, if you do live that ease and contentment about your privilege to help other people, knowing that you truly are able to serve God by loving every moment of your life; if you feel the karmic qualities of service, the thrill of your creativity, the depth of your passion: those things will be great medicine for you. Great medicine. It will make the quality of your life breathtaking."

PATCH ADAMS
Transcribed and edited by Jane Macduff for One Earth

CHAPTER TEN

RIPPLES

A pebble thrown into a pool creates more ripples than the eye can see. Through the books that have been written, outreach work and organised journeys, more people than we may ever realise have had their lives affected by this place. Some of those people have never been here and have only read or heard about the place. On the other hand, there are many places around the World which have links to this Community. From London to Nepal, from Russia to South America, Centers have been developed by people from here, based upon inspiration gained here or visited by individuals and groups from here.

Mining for Hearts of Gold

"I've been a miner for a heart of gold"
NEIL YOUNG

"There's someone you have to meet!"

It was Sunday Brunch in the Community Centre, during the 'Creating Sustainable Communities' conference (October, 1998) and I was half way through my scrambled eggs, enjoying the opportunity to relax with my partner,Gill. Suddenly Michael Shaw, our boundlessly enthusiastic Chair of Trustees, was at my elbow pulling me away and thrusting me through the crowds in the direction of a Very Important Person.

Apparently some guy called Jonathan Smales had just given a talk about some Earth Centre project he was setting up in Doncaster

175

(Doncaster!?) and he had mentioned the word "reinvention". As I had been charged with focalizing the Foundation's reinvention process for the previous two years, Michael was convinced we had to meet. Frankly, it all seemed pretty thin to me...

Anyway there he was - a tall, gentle, earnest man, mid-40s, and as Michael continued shepherding us, this time in the direction of the Living Machine (doubtless Jonathan had mentioned the word "living" at some point in his talk). I managed to stumble out enough to ensure that an invitation to spend a day with Jonathan and his Training Officer would be winging its way towards me in the next couple of days.

A few weeks later I found myself sitting with Martin Winter, the Earth Centre's Training Officer, in portacabin office accommodation by one side of the river Don. The other side? The 430 acre-site that would become the Earth Centre, a vast visitor attraction for up to 500,000 people per year dedicated to promoting sustainability and currently being built atop the disused Denaby and Cadeby coal mine. The project had already attracted £42 million funding and was to be the first of several Landmark Millennium Commission-funded projects to open. It represented employment, and therefore new hope, to the people of this economically depressed part of South Yorkshire. It was built in response to calls emanating from the United Nations for "vast campaigns of education to correct the course of development". Good place to start, Doncaster.

Currently it was a sea of mud and little else. The plan was that, in about six months' time it would open to the general public and that in the six weeks leading up to the opening day all the new staff, some 120 in total, recruited from the local area and comprising a high proportion of ex-miners, would pass through the Earth Centre Training Academy, emerging a highly-motivated, cohesive team, imbued with the Earth Centre's values and bursting with enthusiasm.

Martin, it later transpired, had been told by Jonathan to spend a day with me to see if we could work together and if the Findhorn Foundation had something to offer the Training Academy. We spent several hours brainstorming and pooling ideas, at the end of which Martin, a bluff South Yorkshireman himself commented that it had been a "surprisingly good day". Why "Surprisingly" I asked? "Well, to be honest", he ventured, "I said to my partner last night that I had been told that I had to spend the day with this bloke from a spiritual community. "What are you going to talk about?" she said, "Jesus?"

I must have left my beads and sandals at home that day, as we got the job—running the bulk of the first two weeks of the training. Our task was to spend the first week opening hearts, building the teams, and developing a shared sense of purpose and then, in the second week, to build on this and look at group dynamics, leadership, decision-making and related themes, interlacing all of this with ample opportunity for creative expression.

Coming back I had to act fast and build a team that could do the work, drawing on the wide variety of skills and experiences that lie in our rich community. Jonathan Smales had been particularly struck by the music and singing he experienced in the Conference—cue Barbara Swetina, our all-singing, all-dancing musical angel. We needed people who would not be phased by working with people at a time, who had a deep understanding of groups and an ability to communicate in straightforward non-jargony language and who could think on their feet. An understanding of sustainability would be helpful too.

So the teams began to form: Gill Emslie, 10 years in community, and a highly experienced group facilitator, with a huge heart and a singing voice that could melt an iceberg; Jane Hera, more recently arrived, steeped in facilitating large group processes in various local communities in England, a very clear communicator and a permaculture expert; Judy Buhler-McAllister, recently Foundation focaliser, years of group and Foundation experience, also an excellent communicator and with a wealth of wisdom gleaned in part from years of working with the Game of Transformation. And me—three years in the Foundation, a former trainer and educator and the person who, for some reason, Spirit had called to hold the focus for this venture. That would be our first week's team—complemented, we trusted and invoked, by the presence of the Angel of Findhorn and our deepest sense of inspiration. We meditated and sang together as we planned our course material...and trusted and prayed that all would be well. The second week, Judy and I would stay for overlap and continuity and be joined by three other longtime community members: Mary Inglis, extremely well-versed in facilitating groups of all shapes and sizes and the Foundation's very own deva of the Transformation Game; Ben Fuchs, a freelance consultant to businesses and organisations, a group leader and conflict facilitator and a definite calming presence, and Andrew Murray, often to be seen co-working with Ben, supervisor to almost all the Foundation's management team, Process Oriented Psychology group worker and multi-talented individual.

And so it was that, on February 23rd 1999, Gill, Barbara, Jane, Judy and I entered the smoke-stained Denaby and Cadeby Miners Welfare Centre to begin our work, greeted by the words "Unity Is The Key To Our Future" emblazoned on the banner of the Yorkshire Region of the National Union of Mineworkers. I was transported back to the marches I had been on in my student days in the 70s, of standing shoulder to shoulder with the miners during the crippling strike of the early 80s; of joining together in 'the struggle' for peace, against the Criminal Trespass Act, for squatters rights and against nuclear power. Now, here I was in the heart of this mining community, standing alongside my colleagues from the Findhorn Foundation, hoping to help release the joy and creativity that lies at the heart of each one of us , and to build teams and a sense of community and common purpose within this awesome education project that, if successful, would serve not only to promote sustainable futures on the planet, but to rebuild the area, struck down by the pit closures of the mid-80s.

How did we do? Brilliantly! Yes, we had our edges—would a dance be too much to begin with? What about a moment of silence?—maybe we could get away with it if we called it a "pause before the next thing"? Would they understand us? Would we understand them? (One of them gave Barbara, the Austrian member of our team, a dictionary of common Yorkshire expressions to help her cope with the language and accents...). And so on. Yes, some things didn't work. One exercise that involved lots of eye contact was too much and a piece of theory about feedback turned out not to be the perfect after lunch activity, but 95% of what we offered landed, and landed really well.

Each exercise, sometimes each word, needed to be carefully considered before being offered. This was not a regular Foundation workshop, where people choose to come and pay to do so. This was a compulsory part of basic job training for all new staff at the Centre—from security rangers to actors; gardeners to exhibition interpreters; kitchen assistants to cleaners and recyclers. And while some were open and keen to engage from the off, others were mystified, horrified, petrified and even feared they would be crucified by friends and family if word got out that they had massaged one another, sat on each other's knees, or danced man to man. There was some nervousness and suspicion about the Foundation in the first couple of days. One young man started his sharing, after an exercise in pairs, by bluntly asking, "Can I blow that bloody candle out? We don't need it. It's not dark in here IS IT!?" Good point— everything needed to be explained, needed the group's approval... And, what's more—"What the xxxxxx has this got to do with my job??" "Work's work and play's play" one of the middle-aged male gardeners told me on the first day. "I don't come to work to dance." But he did—by the second day and third and beyond ... and now when I phone they say, "Oh, we miss all the dancing..."

Little by little people started to see the method in our seeming madness. We learnt too and began to ask them, "Why do you think we did that?" and they started to reflect and understand—"So we can all look daft together?"; "So there's less them and us"; "We're all in it together"; "Touching each other builds us as a team"

There were so many high points. I will choose just a few:

- On Thursday morning of the first week we provided an opportunity for small groups to work together and create something of value to the Earth Centre. The outpouring of songs, posters, maps for visitors, TV adverts and more was truly inspiring as people started to tap into depths of talent that had lain dormant, like the coal seams nearby, for so long. This was mining again, but this time for the riches of the creative heart...

- The one black person in the group, leading us in a circumcision dance and song after lunch—so free and open, even in declining the knife so eagerly offered by another participant!

- One of the kitchen assistants, a woman with very difficult home circumstances and with a slight learning disability, standing in front of the group and courageously reading a poem she had written that week.

- Amazing contraptions being built in answer to the challenge of building a "Canine Eco-Shelter" (or "doghouse") out of newspaper, string, pins and tape.

- A burly Welcome Assistant volunteering to lead a warm-up after lunch. "Great!" I said, "What will it be?" "Yogic breathing through alternate nostrils", he replied. And we all did it, at least for a while...

- And the final afternoon, when the Earth Centre staff had an hour in their working groups to produce a creative interpretation of what the last two weeks had been about, and we saw a team of 14 male security staff march to the front and sing a song they had just put together. Then one of them shyly and bravely, with trembling hands, shared a poem he had written. We saw collages and posters, and songs paying tribute to how far they had travelled together and what a team they felt now—confident, open-hearted, ready.

We closed with the dance we had started with—the Shetland Wedding Dance. Despite missing Barbara's wonderful accordion playing (we had the music on tape instead in the second week) they all leapt into this lively and vigorous Scottish fun-raiser. They cried for "More! More!" and we knew that was a good time to leave...at least for now.

I close with one of many benchmarks I could cite: Each Friday they went on bus trips to different visitor attractions to see how other people did it. One was to the National Coalmining Museum and involved travelling 1000 feet underground and standing in pitch black at the face of a coal seam. One of the participants admitted she had some anxiety about this. To which one of the others, an exminer himself, replied "Well, we've all learnt to hold hands now. So we'll just hold hands in the dark and support each other."

Postscript

Since doing this work, I have often wondered how long-lasting the effect of our activities has been. A few days after writing this piece (some 8 months after the work was carried out) I received a letter from the Earth Centre's Human Resources Manager, Katie Thorpe which gives some indication:

Dear Robin,

I have been meaning to write to you for such a long time to tell you what a wonderful job you and the team did with our staff on the Training Academy.

We have had a very turbulent season, sadly, being diverted at times by lack of money and visitors and bad publicity. However, the staff have consistently achieved high accolade in all the feedback we receive.

We had a number of redundancies earlier in the season and all the Site staff pulled together and reduced their hours to avoid any job losses. I have never worked anywhere else where the team spirit has been so strong—the cry of "we started together and we will finish together" was universally said. This I think is largely down to the wonderful job you did in the first two weeks of the Academy.

We are now doing end of season reviews with the staff and assisting them in finding work for the winter. One of the oft mentioned highlights is the team spirit and the role Findhorn had in developing that. They are still fired up to go on to do more and better things.

We have an end season party on the 12th of November at the Miners Welfare if you were able to come people would be very pleased to see you again. Let me know.

Best wishes
Katie Thorpe
Human Resources Manager.

ROBIN ALFRED

Sharing by E-mail

I always find it difficult to explain what "Sharing by email" is. It's a community of people around the world who know each other intimately, but have never met. It's a group of people who share the spirit of the Findhorn Foundation Communiy in their lives without ever coming into physical contact with one another. It's a vision that became a reality—or at least, a virtual reality.

After my first visit to the Findhorn Community in 1995 1 had an idea that it might be possible to maintain contact through the Internet with others who had been to the Community. I remembered our circle of people at Cluny Hill College on Experience Week, sitting, holding hands and sharing. I remembered the support, the nurturing and the openness and I imagined being able to do the same thing with a circle of people around the world, connected in spirit, and offering each other the same support.

As I wasn't even connected to the Internet at that point, this was some feat of imagination! But, to cut a long story short, we made it happen and now dozens of us every so often check our incoming email every day for messages from Australia, the USA, the UK, Holland, Sweden, Germany or Canada, the Gambia, Hawaii, Korea, Israel and Brazil, so it's always day and night, summer and winter somewhere in the group! The fascinating thing is that, as we share very different life experiences from such contrasting parts of the world, we also realise how many similar experiences we also share in the way we live our lives.

We've shared joys and sadness, worries and curiosities. We've helped each other through troubled marriages, through illness and through house renovations. We've shared experiences of flower remedies, of books and of visits to Findhorn. In a way none of us quite understands, we have become not just a community, but a family.

In his new book, *A Pilgrim in Aquarius*, David Spangler mentions the Internet as a metaphor for the new age—a place of imagination that is real to those involved in it. I think it is more than just a metaphor; it is a vehicle to help us extend our awareness and thinking, as he puts it, "outside the box of materialistic thinking".

Without physical presence, or the memory of previous physical relationships, we have had to focus much more clearly on spirit to build our group. But the relationships we have developed have an emotional depth that frequently surprises us, generating feelings every bit as real as those sparked by more conventional relationships. I'd like to think of it as co-creativity in action—our step outside the box towards the new age.

DAVID GORDON

Breaking Through

January 1988. I'm driving back from a 6-month stay in the Findhorn Community, blasting down the A74, wondering what on earth I'm going to do next, when I fall asleep. Bouncing off the central reservation barrier helped wake me up! And the shock had a similar wake-up effect on my addled brain. By the time I'd limped back to London, I was clear what to do.

A good idea often takes the wrong form initially. I had been convinced I should create a centre in Scotland, linking up with Findhorn, and worked towards this for two years. But the trail went distinctly cold. So then I started gathering a group of people for a collaborative venture in London and again found that all the interest disappeared as soon as money was mentioned!

The feedback seemed to be "Do it yourself. Do it in London". But it took a car-crash to wake me up to the realisation. The answers that had refused to come for nearly three years, while I resisted releasing my dependency and fear of going it alone, arrived in just five days.

London, I realised, needed a centre, a congregation point for the growing band of "people taking charge of their lives through selfemployment and other personal growth routes". My self-employment courses would give us a launch pad and we could take it from there. Findhorn in London. An oasis of peace and light in a busy city.

I walked into some freehold premises I'd seen twelve months before, which were still available (the first unlikely coincidence), and put down a deposit. "I'll be back in eight weeks with the balance," I said optimistically. One way and another I needed to find £140,000. I had £14,000 and access—I believed—to another £40,000. So all I needed was £86,000. "Easy!" a fund-raising specialist assured me—but six weeks later he'd got nowhere.

I took the problem into meditation and asked why when it felt so right the money wasn't forthcoming. "You're gonna need more clients." So I drew up a list of potential collaborators and in some desperation, called my bank in rural Essex. "I need £86,000 and I need it by Tuesday." I was not a little surprised when after a couple of questions the manager said "Well, this sounds like the sort of proposition we ought to be backing. Can you come and see me on Monday?" At the end of our meeting he said, "Look, I can't get you the money by Tuesday. Would Friday be OK?!" I could live with that, but I still had to get my sticky fingers on the other £40,000, which just would not come.

I was deep into listening to messages from the universe (still am) and landing the money from the bank felt like a big message, so why the hold-up on the rest? Back to the meditation stool. "What's up guys?" "You gonna need more clients, *dumbo*." I realised that while I'd drawn up the list of prospects, I hadn't done anything with it! So off went a letter inviting them aboard, and along came the next £10,000. Deciding to do something is not commitment. Booking the ticket is. Only then does the Universe know you're serious and sends you the funds.

What I learn from this is that when money is apparently not working for me that's when it's working hardest! My job is to spot the lesson. Usually there is something I need to do differently or something I need to let go.

Even when 'The Breakthrough Centre' opened, with builders hammering away during the launch party, we were £10,000 short, but this only served to 'concentrate the mind wonderfully' during our first year. The universe supplied what we needed, not what we wanted, and applied sound financial criteria—not to incur debt unnecessarily.

The learning has continued over the twelve years since then, especially during what at the time seemed a total disaster. I had called the Government's Training Agency to find out where we stood with our crucial contracts for the next year. "Oh that's all been scrapped," I was casually informed. 15 years development and a £250,000 commitment to property and marketing down the drain, without so much as a consultative document! I had made the classic blunder of putting my trust in princes.

We performed miracles over the next year, but by June 1995 it became clear Breakthrough had to shed its original skin and I set about reinventing it. It took two nail-biting years, letting go of everything I'd built up. But the result is that I enjoy it more, and this quality overflows into the work I do facilitating connections and dreaming up solutions with clients. I actually get paid for my time too! I have more time to write, develop my skills and do counselling sessions with many more people, and life has become tremendously rewarding all round. When you've done 'O' level trust, you move on to 'A' level!

The nightmare of wondering where on earth next month's £7,500 will come from is gone. I had created a centre of peace and light ... and a staggeringly stressful workload which totally frazzled me!

There is a time to commit, to fight, to take those brave, risky initiatives everyone else benefits from, and be visible. And there is a time to let go. The problem is staying committed too long!

ANDREW FERGUSON

ℱ

Planting Findhorn Seeds in Bolivia

Here I am writing my story in Findhorn...Visiting for the first time years after I was connected to it on inner levels.

Born and grown up in Germany I moved to Bolivia in January 1987, together with my Bolivian husband Carlos and our two sons Joaginn and Rafael. There it was that Carlos 'fulfilled his mission' in bringing me to Bolivia. My life turned into a totally different shape. In the same year we went through a deep crisis which resulted in the ending of our marriage. At this time, in my spiritual study group we were taught about the angelic realm and the nature spirits. So, this was something real and not only 'stories for kids' and I remembered that I had heard, years ago, about a group of people somewhere in the north of Europe running a garden working together with nature spirits—and I had thought 'might be some crazy hippies'. Remembering that, I thought to myself—going now to Germany, I will try to find out something about this group.

I met this wonderful, vital old lady, who in former times had organised talks about healthy nutrition and vital food—and had just come back from Findhorn! Her eyes were bright and she was sprinkling joy, telling me about her experience. She gave me the book 'The Magic of Findhorn' by Paul Hawkins. I was really thrilled about the way this came to me. And as I read

183

this book about Findhorn it drew me deep into it. I lived it, I felt it, I laughed and I cried. I was deeply shaken and was touched in the innermost core of my heart about this divine guidance, preparation and working out a new vision for humanity. I felt myself connected to a high-volt energy cable.

One morning, while reading the book, there happened something like an energy-shift. It was like opening a curtain and a bright light was shining in and I saw a piece of land with mountains, virgin forests, little rivers running through, black and fertile soil, a great beauty and harmony. I knew it was 20 hectares in size. And then it was like a voice telling me: "It is not your job to go to Findhorn to live and work there, but to take its seed and to plant it into this soil in this part of the world, Bolivia". The 'curtain' closed and I just sat there, not being able to move or to think.

Getting back into 'normality' I thought, how could this work out? How should I start? What should I do? Where should I go? With whom should I do it? There was this mixture of getting active on one side and deep doubts on the other. This was only the beginning of my transformation process, a testing, triggering and preparation to do God's will and to trust the guidance, that things are going away from what my linear mind was thinking about. God's paths meander and circle like rivers with joy and playfulness. My constant lessons were about the well-known three Findhorn 'P's—patience, persistence, and perseverance. Let go, don't be attached, flow!

Of course, my German mind was calling for action. Where is this land of my vision? I started to seek for it, but felt helpless. One morning in my meditation I heard the words, "you don't need to search for the land—if this is your mission, it will come to you!" How could that happen? My doubting mind asked. But then I went on with my 'normal' life. Lots of details happened in this divine guidance, putting the puzzle together.

January 1993, with a group of friends, and my sons—who were spending their holidays with me—we planned an excursion to a place I felt drawn to. It was a very special and mystical mountain which I had never found the time to visit coinciding with a guide who could take me. We planned to camp for a few days. We drove through a beautiful landscape and finally entered into a valley where I could see this mystical mountain in its total beauty. On the other side of the valley appeared another mystical mountain with the exact shape of a great pyramid. Arriving down by the river I felt certain the land of my vision was somewhere here!

Three months later, I was offered a piece of land there, 20 hectares! It was overwhelming; it was exactly as I had seen it. I could feel the strong energy and was moved by the purity of nature. My new partner, Angelino and I went into the virgin forest and meditated. I attuned to the nature spirits, giving my deep thanks and telling them that I felt very honoured to be allowed to enter this pure place. I felt it was an incredible gift. I told them about the mission and asked not only for their permission to build a centre in this place but that I also wanted their collaboration in this work. I would deeply respect their answer and would withdraw if they would not agree. The answer was—how could I describe it? Like very loving hug energy. It was like being cuddled. The acceptance was clear. Angelino received the same answer. Then began the long bureaucratic haul to get all the papers in order for the purchase.

I had recently received a letter from Charles Peterson from the Findhorn Foundation telling me that he and Joshua Kippurt had an invitation from Argentina to give an introduction to Findhorn together with some activities. He asked if there was any interest in Bolivia. I wrote back, that nothing similar was known in Bolivia, but offered to organise for them to give Findhorn presentations in the three main cities of Bolivia. I could not guarantee that costs would be covered because there was no experience of how it might work out, but it was worth a try. And we did it! Slide shows, which were well attended, some sacred dances and games with fewer people and experience weekends with even fewer people who were courageous enough to try something totally new and unknown—and were thrilled with their experience. Me too! Charles fell in love with Bolivia and now returns here every year.

One day I read a small note in the newspaper telling about the forthcoming Earth Summit in Rio de Janeiro (May '92). I got the strong feeling that I needed to go, without knowing what I would do there. I was overwhelmed seeing so many people coming from all over the world, exploring the work they do for the betterment of humanity and protecting nature. I found a stand from Findhorn, wow, I couldn't believe I was meeting 'true Findhorn people' and seeing a lot of photos about this magical place. I talked to them about my vision and asked if there were people in Findhorn who help to raise similar centres in other parts of the world. The answer was "No, this is not done" but they offered to write down my address and see what could be done.

I was then connected to another group of active spiritual servants that I still work actively with today. It was the Institute for Planetary Synthesis, a global organisation, weaving a global network of pioneers, people forming new groups in ten fundamental fields of human activity, called the ten seed groups. They are helping to prepare the coming world civilisation with planetary awareness, leading to planetary citizenship. Practising in daily life the spiritual values such as love of truth, personal responsibility, sense of justice, constructive cooperation, and selfless service to the great whole.

On 17th June 1993 all the papers were ready and I became the owner of the land. For the solstice in June I organised the inauguration, starting the ceremony, together with a small group, with a bonfire in the evening of the 20th. The celebration lasted for seven days with meditation, ceremonies, prayers, and enjoying being in nature.

In meditation I was shown the design of the house, octagonal and on three levels: The lower part for activities, hall and kitchen in an open shape, three sleeping rooms, and a bathroom with divided units. Second floor with an all- round balcony, being our private space, my working room and sleeping/living room. Third floor, under the roof, a meditation room. Angelino organised a group of workers, and together with an architect friend who contributed his services, we designed and started to create the centre.

We started building in October, clearing the place, making adobe bricks from the earth, preparing the place for the house and running water from a natural spring to the building site. We came to build for a few days every week. We slept in tents and had to bring food and everything we needed with us. One day when the walls had just begun to grow, a very special blessing was given: Just over the house a rainbow circle appeared! A complete circle, round and in horizontal position with bright colours in the sky, no rain, almost no clouds, the sun shining brightly. I have never seen anything similar! Fortunately I took a photograph.

Two other remarkable incidents happened with nature. One week it was raining very hard and we all sat in our tents and could not build. So I directed myself to the spirits of the rain, giving thanks for the service it is always doing in providing water for the plants, animals and human beings, consciously sending my love to them. Then I told them that we were going to build a divinely ordered light centre and that we had to get on with the building, and could they be so kind as to stop raining on the building site so that our work could continue. It was Tuesday and I had to return home where I had other things to do. On Saturday our master builder arrived to get the money to pay the workers. He told me "Senora, something very strange has happened. For the whole week it was raining all around but not at the building site and we could go on working!" In silence I gave thanks for the water spirits.

The other experience was with the fire spirits. We had just moved to live in our new house one year later, September '94, and were still finishing the building details. It is usual at that time of year for the farmers to burn their fields to prepare them for sowing. One day I arrived home from Santa Cruz and I could see that the whole back of the Pyramid Mountain was burning. Of course I got scared and started to pray immediately. Angelino and I tuned into the fire spirit, giving thanks to its transformation and purification service, and asking it to please not destroy the beautiful fern forest, or our centre. Four days later the fire was stopped by rain. We saw that the fire had totally respected our borderline, the land was black and all burnt on one side and green and untouched forest on the other side. Not one centimetre was burnt! If I had not seen it with my own eyes I would not have believed it! Nature spirits respect human beings, when human beings respect them and are grateful for their service! And they are great teachers! I have learnt a lot from nature since living in this place and there is a notable co-working between us.

I feel that Findhorn was started on hostile ground to show that it could be transformed into beauty, just as the world, although hostile in many places, can be transformed through human understanding of the whole and respectful commitment. My place was in a natural paradise formed only by nature without any human influence; it is now about showing how to co-create paradise together with people who are aware of the laws and purpose of nature, putting together the inherent potentials, co-creating more beauty and opportunities to grow.

MARION REMUS

F

Casting the Net

As I recall, the history of our Net connection began like this: our computer whiz (Stephan Wik) proposed to our powers-that-be, that there are some serious benefits to be had from having a connection. They agreed. So, he and I wrote to the administrators of JANET, the Joint Academic Network, with a proposal for the Findhorn Foundation to become a JANET site. (By the way, JANET is the Net that UK universities and other academic bodies use.) Our application was accepted, but it had strings attached that made us decide that we were not able to join JANET.

Our perfect opportunity came when we were offered a grant by Gaia Villages Trust of Denmark, to try out a Net connection for six months (thank you for the help!). So a number of us, me included, have had a connection to try out for free for the last six months. We went for Soft Arc's 'FirstClass' E-mail and conferencing software. It is an easy and friendly system (no having to learn weird machine codes) that goes well with Macintosh computers (the Findhorn Community is completely Mac-ed); lots of things that Mac users are very familiar with.

I took the opportunity during those six months to roam the Net whenever I got the chance (and whenever the boss wasn't looking because I also had to hold down a regular job within the Human Relations Department) and just about made the shift from newbie to net nerd.

Then my partner Marijke and I got to talking about the purpose of the Internet in the greater scheme of things. This developed into a charged and inspired conversation.

We found that we needed to draw on the idea that, with technology, we have been recreating a lost part of ourselves. For example, transport systems as substitutes for astral or mental travel; telecommunications as substitutes for telepathy, and so on. An important feature of the Net, related to this, is that it is a network. So, unlike phones or faxes that are mainly used to connect two individuals, the Net is frequently used in a way that reflects an aspect of the way the mind works: waves spreading out from a source (for example, the spreading activation models of how humans understand language). Messages on the Net often spread out in waves, sometimes very rapidly and extensively if they captivate a lot of people.

Another vital feature is that the Net is not controlled or censored by powerful vested interests, unlike the conventional media of press, radio or television. The downside of this includes the 'flame wars' that occasionally erupt, when insults are traded back and forth. However, the vital thing is that large numbers of people are actively taking part in (and not just passively watching) discussions about all kinds of radical things, such as spirituality, mysticism, paranormal phenomena, etc. These discussions are not shaped by programme makers, slanted in safe directions or made to fit comfortable existing models of the world.

What I think is happening is that more and more people are absorbing really new ideas very quickly and they are then capable of being effective processors of the evolutionary energies that are flowing through creation. If people were not being exposed to the ideas flowing around on the Net (while at the time feeling part of a true globality, thus creating anchor points) these energies would effectively "go in one ear and out the other". In other words, I see the development of the Net as being a very helpful part of the incarnation of universal energies. I experience it as a guided process. There are, if you like, 'Internet Devas' overseeing its development.

For example, I have a couple of Internet friends with whom I exchange about such things as the *Celestine Prophesy*, out-of-body experiences and the like. I think that it is in conversations such as these that we re-make or re-order ourselves in more universal ways. I also see this as an example of what author Brian Swimme (*The Universe as a Green Dragon*) describes as the Earth awakening through the human mind. It is part of the process of moving from the scientific-technological era to the Age of the Earth. Here is a quote from his book:

"The creative fire within the human venture now focuses on bringing forth something entirely new, a form of human life that envisions itself within the interconnected dynamics of the unfolding Earth reality. The tribe will not be the center of the human world, nor will the civilization, the culture, nor the nation-state. It will be the Earth community as a whole that will be understood as our home, our womb of creativity and life."

I think this is a useful context in which to see the development of the Net. I believe that, through the Internet, some of us are recovering the experience of being part of a global community. We are re-imagining ourselves as universal beings.

MICHAEL FORSTER

Update: Written in the late 1990s this was truly visionary!

ℱ

Miracles in the Aegean

The story of how the Findhorn Foundation was created, from its early years in the caravan park, was the main inspiration for myself, my husband Stefan Preuss and two others—my sister Tina Agiorgiti and her ex-husband Harald Jordan—to found an intentional community on the Greek island of Evia.

In 1994, after several coincidences, Stefan and I chose a site on a spectacular seacliff overlooking the Aegean Sea. It was breathtaking but the fact that the road to it was only accessible by jeep, and that there was neither electricity nor telephone, presented us with a huge challenge and a great test to our faith. We thank God for the existence of natural springs, providing us at least with our own water supply.

For the first few years we lived in big Sahara-style canvas tents, furnished with beds, tables, closets and carpets. It was just the four of us with occasional guests from abroad to help. Our first visitor was actually a lady from Findhorn called Voula. Coincidentally she was the daughter of one of my father's best friends whom he had met in a hard labour camp during World War II. And neither of our fathers could for the life of them comprehend why their daughters (for whom they had worked so hard to provide with the opportunity of a University education) should wish to live in such a bizarre manner. Voula lived in a caravan in the north of Scotland, and Tina and I in our isolated place on Evia. And hard labour we did every day—just like our fathers in their labour camp!

There was a difference though. We had chosen this way of life. We were building, carrying rocks, shovelling out vegetable gardens— even shovelling our own manure! So I would often ask myself why I was doing this. I mean, sure, the four of us had had a vision to create a "place of healing power", but when we worked from morning (4.45 am was the wake-up gong followed by meditation) until sundown, I sometimes felt like I was in a hard labour camp too! And what was even more crazy was the fact that I had chosen this over a 'comfy' life.

There were snakes here and scorpions, and I wasn't used to it at all. Sometimes I'd lie awake at night and have thoughts about the vipers. And I would think, I could die out here because of a crazy dream—is it really worth dying for? The wind would howl through the tent walls and on Spring nights there was thunder and lightning so we couldn't even sleep in our tents because the metal poles were perfect lightning conductors; we would rush to some old stone ruins to shelter from the elements. These were the not-so-nice sides of Mother Nature.

Oftentimes I would hear this cynical little voice inside me asking, what on earth are you out here for? What does it matter anyway? Do you think you are going to change the world? And then I would think of Eileen in her caravan, in the middle of nowhere in the north of Scotland. Her patience and perseverance were a true inspiration to me. Her book, *Opening Doors Within*, was my only lifeline. I read it every single morning and sometimes re-read it later in the day. It was the thing that kept me going, and reminded me that miracles were possible. And do you know what? Something amazing happened one day during a thunderstorm. Stefan and I left the stone house and went outside to see if the storm had ended and...ZAP! We were struck by lightning! Stefan was struck on his heart, making him fall to his knees, and I was hit on my forehead (at the Third Eye). Several people witnessed this in disbelief. We were fine—except for a slightly dizzy sensation, and even felt a pleasant 'high' from this Cosmic Electrocution. And what is more, after the storm was completely over, a glorious double rainbow appeared over the sea, and we spotted dolphins...miracle after miracle!

For me, there are more everyday miracles, like the fact that each year now many people from all over the world appear on our doorstep to stay awhile and help. Some, like Lisa, a Finnish woman who has just renovated one of the old houses, would even like to live here.

We now have solar electricity, computers and a mobile phone— more miracles! And the local government clears the road more regularly so that ordinary cars can get here. But most thrilling of all is the fact that I finally live in a beautiful little house, after having lived in a tent for so long.

So my gratitude to Findhorn is for the inspiration to Expect A Miracle, and to live by Faith.

ALKESTIS AGIORGITI

The Quest

What if...there could be a course you could follow that complemented the familiar emphasis on outer knowledge, skills and understanding with inner reflection on meaning, vision and purpose? What if...such a course was based on Open Learning, so you could follow it wherever you live? What if...this course offered you the choice of informal learning, and additional options for telephone coaching support, an experiential residential week, and possibly accreditation?

There is an idea—and more than an idea, a project—to create just such a course of Open Learning material for spiritual and personal development currently underway. It is an innovative project combining a number of elements. Firstly, it requires the writing of course materials suitable for people to pursue their spiritual and personal development within their own setting and possibly working alone. Secondly, the project looks to adapt the idea of a residential 'summer school' by offering an optional, short experiential component, initially at the Findhorn Foundation but later offered by other organisations and residential centres with parallel interests. Thirdly, whilst recognising that many people would take up the course and follow it alone the course creators dreamt from the beginning of building two different ways for students to find support. One means of support is a long-term aim to establish learning networks [Quest Centres], putting course students in touch with each other so they can work together. A completely new form of support was also conceived which would combine the best and relevant elements of mentoring, supervision and spiritual direction and which in a group setting would form a peer group of 'spiritual companions'.

The possibility of such a course was dreamed of by Janice Dolley and Joycelin Dawes, and soon joined by Ike Isaksen. Janice had been a lecturer at the Open University since it was formed and is a longterm activist in many networks to integrate spirituality with daily, mainstream life. Joycelin has been a teacher and involved in community activities and was working at the Findhorn Foundation as a member of a year-long project to re-imagine and revivify the Foundation. Ike was working full-time as the Co-Focaliser of the Education Area at the Findhorn Foundation and had experience in the theatre and a particular interest in the metaphor of 'the Hero's Journey' in individual lives. The three of them came together in 1997 and into early 1998 and brought together a larger team of people committed to bringing the idea to fruition.

The essence of the project is to write original material that forms a course in spiritual and personal development of individuals, embracing their private, work, social and spiritual lives, and to do so by drawing upon the world-leading expertise of staff at the Open University in Milton Keynes in England and the extensive experience built up at the Findhorn Foundation Community of people finding a transformational and heart-opening opportunity to integrate their inner daily practice with their outer daily activities.

The advantage of Open Learning as the medium for a course of personal study, reflection and review is that all you need obtain is the course material, either in traditional printed form as a book or folder with complementary audio tapes and reading supplements or alternatively accessed through a site on the World Wide Web. Many thousands of people follow courses in Open Learning every year and find it a flexible way of marrying their individual development with the demands of their lifestyle. The rate of change in Information Technology means that there will be a huge increase in Open Learning opportunities over the next few years, even to the point where some kinds of traditional educational institutions change out of all recognition. We intend to take full advantage of the opportunities offered by access to the Web to create a virtual student community for Quest students.

Janice, Joycelin and Ike took the idea to colleagues at the Findhorn Foundation and at the Open University and readily found interest and enthusiasm for the idea. During 1998 and early 1999, the project began to grow slowly. Firstly, Ike and his Co- Focaliser of Education at the Findhorn Foundation, Clive Kitson, felt that it would be a good idea if some of the Foundation co-workers gained experience of Open Learning in personal development. They offered three bursaries for people to take the Open University [OU] course in Personal and Career Development [PCD]. Three women were interested and although only one completed the course, the experience gained was useful. They also appointed Joycelin to work part-time to support the PCD students and champion the project for a course in spiritual and personal development. We all became more aware of the need to design such course materials to be appealing to people whose interests and experience were inclined more towards active experience and review than reading and intellectual study. And the one student who completed the course found it enormously rewarding.

At this point, the course on Personal and Career Development [PCD] was due to be revised and re-written. All Open University courses have a 'shelf-life' after which they are suspended or updated and revised or substantially re-written. Joycelin and Ike were invited to join the team of OU staff and consultants that had been brought together for this task. Their strengths and experience offered the OU team the chance to extend the revised PCD further in the direction of embracing an inner dimension in learning, which the team was keen to include. It also meant that Joycelin and Ike gained some experience in the creation and writing of Open Learning material. Over many years, the Open University has developed a collaborative team ethos in course writing that meets their need to maintain a high standard and a broad approach to the subject in hand that is widely respected in their products.

The project began to acquire a momentum of its own. It came to the attention of the Trustees of the Findhorn Foundation who responded favourably to the ideas and at the same time, in late 1998, invited Janice to become a Foundation Trustee on account of her extensive knowledge in adult and community education. Janice, Joycelin and Ike began to look at how the project could be supported and financed and actually written. It was agreed between them, and in conjunction with the Education Area of the Foundation, that Joycelin would act as Course Team Leader, [later widened to also include the role of Project Manager] taking overall responsibility for the writing and production of the course.

Together they planned a seminar over a long weekend to bring together a creative group of people to generate material to form the basis of the course. They had an ideal venue at the Coach House, a beautiful retreat house on the Black Isle, overlooking the Moray Firth in north-east Scotland, which offered quiet, comfortable accommodation with space for a group to work together in an idyllic setting. This was important. Janice, Joycelin and Ike were planning to bring together a group of people, all of whom were extremely busy in their own lives; it was asking a lot that they all got together in north-east Scotland for four days. If the seminar were held in a beautiful and nourishing environment, then each person who came would gain some benefit from the long weekend as in return they gave of their creativity and inspiration. The invited group was made up of twelve people, seven women and five men, largely though not entirely British, and six of whom had close current working ties with the Findhorn Foundation and six with links with the Open University. All were invited and came in their personal capacity and because they were interested in the project. Between them, this group brought a wealth of experience in: education, mentoring, psychotherapy and counselling, open learning, course tutoring, music, theatre, parenting, spiritual directing, practical service work, management, organisational behaviour, medicine, psychology and much more.

This group met over a warm, sunny late April weekend in 1999 and over four days, mixing large-group work and sharing, small group investigation and reflection, meditation together, walks and meals, they created the essential materials that later formed the core conceptualisation and framework of the course. The weekend was remarkable in that they also experimented on themselves to develop a form of peer spiritual mentoring through sharing the story of their journeys in groups of three. The people in each group took it in turns to be the storyteller, the mentor and the observer and from this the group gained much useful insight and learning about the needs and provision of spiritual companioning. They also created a map of life-long spiritual journeying, an exploration of what they identified as common and fundamental life issues and which they pursued through key questions to identify the issues, move through the transitions, chaos and stuck-ness to a heart and mind and spirit-opening attitude to moving on. They developed a conceptual framework through which eventual students would be able to integrate their personal experience and situation with the wider setting in which they live and work—Self and Context Awareness—and began to tease out the questions and answers given to the perennial questions by the major world faith traditions. A major set of outcomes!

Joycelin left the weekend with the daunting task of writing all this down, turning very exciting and creative brainstorming and ideas into words that captured the essence and quality of alive-ness of the work just done. This proved to be a challenge. For about three months, each time she tried to get into the writing in depth, the words and phrases dried up. Eventually, after much reflection and reading, she realised that she would only be able to write up the work after she had created a conceptual framework for the whole course. Once it became clear that this needed to be done, it happened amazingly quickly. The conceptual framework was written in two to three hours in one sitting one Monday morning and has remained virtually in that same form since. The only alterations that have been made in consultations with a growing range of people is to tidy up some of the sequencing and clarify the language. At the point of writing this story, there are further consultations on the framework that are to be concluded and then the next task is to actually begin to write detailed material and exercises. En route, the project was named 'The Quest: fulfillment, joy, meaning and purpose in life'. It is also closely linked to other enterprising initiatives under active consideration at the Foundation, principally the possibility of launching a service for telephone coaching, aimed initially at people wanting support as they complete a course or workshop at the Foundation and attempt to integrate what they have learnt in an environment that may not support them and the changes they are making in themselves and their lives. The telephone coaching could well be extended to cover the first stage of student support for the Quest.

At this point, the project becomes significantly more labour intensive and financial resources are required. This has, so far, proved to be the trickier task. At this stage, there are many people highly committed to the project in a personal capacity and who bring with them a wealth of relevant professional experience. The Findhorn Foundation is acting as a champion and key stakeholder for the project, drawing in other institutions and organisations in a consortium of potential users. The intention is that the Foundation takes responsibility supporting the writing of a first full draft of the course, and engaging a wide range of perspectives in the testing and critical review process. Whilst this is being done, we can look at the best way to actually publish the material and the possibility of its use by other partners. The eventual hope is that the Open University will formally become a partner, at an institutional level, and offer the Quest as one of their courses. Janice herself is due to retire from the Open University in September 2000 and, fortunately, her successor is also a keen supporter of the Quest. It will be some time before it is clear whether or not the OU will be formally interested in the partnership and, meantime, it seems the best step to get a first developmental draft written so everyone can see what the Quest has to offer.

The Findhorn Foundation, however, which had mothered the project so supportively hitherto, is introducing for the first time its own

Development Fund to support enterprising projects that cannot be financed within existing departmental budgets. So Janice, Joycelin and Ike drew up a development plan for the Quest project that delineated a clear first phase, taking one year, during which the first developmental draft could be written. At the time of writing, a full business plan for Phase 1 of the Quest project, due for completion by October 2000, has been submitted to the Foundation's Development Fund group and the Trustees and the outcome of their decision is awaited. The target date of completion by September 2000 is an important date as in October 2000 the Findhorn Foundation will host a major international conference 'The Spirit of Learning' which seems a highly appropriate time and place for the international launch of the first phase development of the Quest.

There are other developmental plans for twin-track education of the outer and inner dimension and many of these will travel in the same direction as the Quest. The Wrekin Trust is resourcing the compilation of a Resource Directory of learning that incorporates a spiritual dimension. Many universities and colleges have established courses, programmes, units that recognise the need for an inner core dimension in learning, including work done at the OU, John Moores University Liverpool, Sussex and Bath Universities. There are groups that have challenged mainstream thinking and are establishing themselves as independent units, such as the Centre for Human Ecology, the Human Potential Research Group and School of Independent Studies in North East London. There are new colleges, based on ecological and spiritual principles including Schumacher College as well as the accreditation that the Findhorn Foundation is considering extending for some of its courses. There are growth points within the established churches, some small and some well-known such as the Alternatives Programme at St James in Piccadilly in London. There is a network of Open Centres up and down the UK with a bi-annual newsletter through which many opportunities for diverse holistic learning are offered. Many networks connect their members through newsletters and initiatives that are relevant to outer and inner development. Amongst these networks we could point out examples such as the Wrekin Trust, the Medical and Scientific Network, World Youth Service and Enterprise [WYSE] and the Brahma Kumaris World Spiritual University. There are other channels of interest emerging, such as the recently established section for Transpersonal Psychology within the British Psychological Society. The Quest is not an isolated initiative but one that is richly embedded within a much wider impulse in education that is fast becoming part of the mainstream. In fact, in order to bring all these kinds of initiatives together in one forum, there are consultations taking place to set up a University of Spirit. This is to parallel the University of Industry spearheaded by the UK government which is itself a response to rapid social and economic change which is affecting both work and learning. The intention of a University for Spirit is to create a container for a holistic and integrated education and learning for the next millennium. The Findhorn Foundation, with its wealth of experience garnered over many years has an important role to play in the 'virtual' University and the Quest is a project that will make that experience more fully available to the wider world of education and learning.

JOYCELIN DAWES

Update: The Quest is very firmly established and fulfilling all hopes and expectations. www.thequest.org.uk

F

Tibet—A Pilgrim's Diary

Insight into one of the Sacred Journeys organised from Findhorn

Mountains...Mountains in every direction as far as the eyes can reach. Countless shades of brown against the crystal clear, blue background of the sky. And nothing more: no city lights, no farmlands, no people. At times a small river or a little lake appears, decorating the landscape like a piece of turquoise. I can almost breathe the silence of this emptiness while flying over this land called Tibet.

A little later we land at Lhasa airport. To keep the Chinese immigration officer happy we all line up neatly one by one in the exact order of the names on our group visa. Everything is being checked carefully. He finally decides to let us through. Our group of eleven people is in Tibet at last. We meet the friendly Tibetan who will be our guide for the next eight days and then drive to the hotel.

The first and the lowest point of our journey is Lhasa, Tibet's ancient capital now dominated by Chinese settlers, 3700 m. above sea level. In this altitude it's quite common to experience mild symptoms of what is known as Acute Mountain Sickness (AMS), such as headache, tiredness and shortness of breath. Luckily most of us had already spent four weeks in Nepal where we had sufficient acclimatization while trekking in the Himalayas. "Drink at least four liters of water every day; make sure you eat regularly; don't talk about politics; prepare your psyche (and your bottom) for the bumpy roads; use high protection sun block every day; don't drink alcohol or shower on the first day..." are some of the suggestions given to the group.

Equipped with plenty of water bottles and warm clothes we set off the next morning to visit the legendary Potala Palace. Slowly, slowly we take our steps through the endless halls and corridors of this magnificent building which used to be the winter residence of His Holiness the Dalai Lama, but is now degraded to a museum. As every Wednesday, the Palace is packed with pilgrims—incredibly devoted, simple and poor-looking Tibetans from all around Asia, who had at last made it to this holy place. Wearing long, stiff, dark woolen skirts, the Nomad women are decorated with big, robust pieces of turquoise and mountain coral around their necks and in their black hair. Often I catch myself being stunned by the beauty of their spirit as they mumble their prayers, paying homage to the buddhas and deities.

Traditional vegetable noodle soup for lunch, and then off we go to our next destination, the holy Jokang Temple. This is one of the few places left in Tibet where the monks are still allowed to perform their daily prayer rituals, called pujas. After paying for the tickets we are led inside through long, dark corridors into large meditation halls, all richly decorated with ancient thangka paintings and colorful golden statues of Buddhas and deities, some more than 2000 years old.

Although some of us are still being affected by fatigue and lack of oxygen, we all drag ourselves out of bed the next morning for yet another day of walking and exploring in and around Lhasa. We visit two of the largest monasteries in Tibet—Sera and Drepung—followed by a visit to His Holiness' summer residence, the beautiful Norbulingka. Here we are, in the Dalai Lama's home, looking at his precious personal belongings. A strange feeling comes over me. How is it possible that I can visit the residence, even the bedroom, of His Holiness, yet he himself cannot?

We are all feeling much better and acclimatized when we start the next part of our pilgrimage which is taking us through the most magnificent Tibetan landscapes towards the ancient monasteries of Gyantse and Shigatse and then back to Nepal. Travelling in three land cruisers we are accompanied by our cheerful Tibetan guide, a former monk, whose knowledge about Buddhist sites is vast and detailed. We are all happy to finally get out of 'Chinatown' and see the 'real' Tibet. There is much to see indeed—prayer flags fluttering in the wind on top of the high passes, little Tibetan villages still carrying on a life which seems to take us back in time for a thousand years, some yaks grazing on the rocky mountains. And the silence...

Each time we stop for a break on one of the passes, I climb up right to the top and sit there as if I am alone in the world, seeing nothing but mountains and hearing nothing but my own breathing. This experience alone would have been worth coming for, so I don't mind that the land cruisers break down occasionally, that the temperature in my hotel room is just above freezing, that I have diarrhea from time to time, and that every day our lunch consists of the same noodle soup.

I'm happy, I'm sad, I'm full and I'm empty as if there is a part of my heart that I left behind when crossing the 'frontier'. And I'm coming back next year for another dose.

MARIS WARRIOR

ℱ

Tom
A Gift in Disguise

I've so enjoyed the whole process of writing a book. It was not something I had ever planned to do. The house isn't littered with my first chapters. In fact, my mild dyslexia makes me a slow reader and poor speller and caused me to steer clear of books, book shops and libraries for years.

So how, you may ask, did my first book get written? Shortly after stopping work as a Probation Officer, I attended a talk at the Cheltenham Literary Festival. I was given a feedback Questionnaire asking for my occupation and I resisted writing 'housewife' and instead put writer and traveller. We were just leaving to trek in the mountains of Ethiopia so the latter felt true but I hadn't written anything but court reports since University. So, being an honest type, I hurried home and wrote an article about travelling to Egypt with Tom, our nineteen year old son who has mental disabilities. A magazine published it and people read it and said they would like to hear more. I then realised that I wanted to explain all we had learnt and gained from parenting Tom.

Writing the book meant delving back into my memories and also reading again the stacks of reports on Tom, from teachers, doctors and psychologists that we had collected over the years. I was surprised at the tears and anger that surfaced yet found the viewing and releasing of these feelings very healing. The whole process was also enlightening. Parenting Tom was a lonely struggle for us and achieved on 'automatic,' with little help from any experts. Not having a clear diagnosis of his problems meant that we were not linked into support groups for his particular condition or offered textbooks to read up on the subject.

The first half of the book details the journey of Tom's birth, education etc., and our search for answers and healing, while the second half evaluates the experiences we went through as a family. It was while writing and hoping for better understanding that I sought out other parents in similar situations and was surprised to discover how much we had in common.

After completing the manuscript and sending it off to the publisher, there is a long wait before the printed book is in your hands. I felt quite numb during this period but anxiety rapidly increased in the time between the book being published and the first reader's feedback. I had read another autobiography, which had scared me. It had pointed out that, once published, other people you meet know all about you, while you may know nothing about them. What would this mean?

In fact, for me it has only been a pleasure. I knew from the start that some people would not like the book. It is impossible to write a book that pleases everybody. However, it seems that, by telling our story, I have created an opening for others to share their feelings and experiences. My next door neighbour, an 80 year old lady, near to tears after reading the book, leant over the wall and asked if she could come round and talk about her grandchildren. This has been one of many such incidents.

The book has also been a vehicle for healing relationships in my life. I visit the Foundation fairly regularly and always greet Eileen Caddy if I happen to see her but have never known how to knock on her door. We were not close when I lived in the Community, probably because she represented to me a spiritual part of myself with which I was not yet in touch. Having read my book, she was one of the first to write to me and asked me to visit her the next time I was up, as she looked forward to becoming good friends with me. I was thrilled and did just that, and now know the way through her front door!

I have been completely surprised and delighted by the number of letters I have received from people, particularly parents. It was not something that I had anticipated. The second one was from a mother who had faced problems with her sons and had been given a new and helpful perspective through reading the book. The act of writing the book had been healing and worthwhile for me and I justified publishing it by saying to myself, if one person benefits from reading it, then it was worth publishing. Letter number two fulfilled that ambition so, in my mind, I changed it to ten thousand people!

Many people have asked how Tom feels about the book. He loves it. I read the manuscript to him and he accepted, stoically, the good and the less good about him. In fact he surprised us with breakfast in bed the next day! I think he found it helpful to review his life from outside himself. But, more importantly, Tom claims the book as his. He enjoys signing copies. At the end of the book I describe a guided meditation in which we each climbed a mountain and asked a wise being about the purpose of our lives. Tom came down and told us clearly, "I am here to show the world that I am lovable the way I am."

Through the book he is able to send this message out, on behalf of all those with disabilities, to far more people than his immediate friends and family.

HENRIETTA ROSE

'Tom, a gift in disguise' is published by Findhorn Press www.findhornpress.com

Restoration

In 1987 I launched the Trees for Life project to restore the Caledonian Forest. I felt called by the last few surviving trees in the desolate, deforested glens of the Highlands to help them—to do something to heal the land here. I began to unfold a vision to restore an area of about 600 square miles in the north-central Highlands to a wild, natural forest, and eventually to reintroduce all the missing wildlife species which originally lived there.

Practical work began on a small scale in 1989, and moved forward significantly when we entered into partnership with the Forestry Commission to work on their land in Glen Affric—one of the best fragments of the 1% of the original Caledonian Forest which still survives. The project attracted the involvement of well-known environmentalist David Bellamy and led to Trees for Life being declared the UK Conservation Project of the Year in 1991.

During the early 1990s, the project grew steadily. We launched a programme of volunteer work weeks, in which participants spend a week in Glen Affric, planting trees and carrying out other essential conservation activities. These weeks provide hands-on experience of the Findhorn principles of attunement to spirit, cooperation with nature, and 'work is love in action' in a beautiful remote location—a combination which has a powerful effect on many people.

In 1993, Trees for Life was established as an independent charity specifically dedicated to forest restoration in Scotland. I'm in awe at how much the project has grown since then. Now we have a committed and inspired staff of seven, and an asset base of over £200,000. For me, that's the power of Spirit, and in many ways I feel that we at Trees for Life, and those involved in other independent projects around the Foundation, are learning for ourselves the same lessons of manifestation etc. which Peter, Eileen and Dorothy put into practice all those years ago.

We've now planted over 410,000 native trees and fenced more than 300 hectares (750 acres) of land for forest regeneration. We've established working partnerships with major organisations such as the National Trust for Scotland and the Royal Society for the Protection of Birds (RSPB) and we've articulated a set of Principles of Ecological Restoration which guide our work. Perhaps most importantly though, we've acted as a catalyst for native forest restoration to become broadly accepted in Scotland, to the extent that our long-term vision, including the return of missing species such as the wolf, is now widely discussed and is gathering increasing support.

Now, it appears that the time is ripe for a larger goal to be put into practice. I had a dream in which ecological restoration—healing the

Earth—will become a primary and uniting focus for humanity in the next century.

The morning after this dream, I opened the mail and found that one envelope contained a special issue of Time magazine entitled 'Our Precious Planet: Why saving the environment will be this century's biggest challenge'! Synchronicity such as this is a clear sign for me that Spirit is at work, and that I'm being given a sign for what I need to be doing.

My vision is to see the United Nations declare the 21st century the Century of Restoring the Earth. This has the potential to act as a pivotal point around which people, resources and energy can be focused into creating a new co-creative relationship with the rest of Nature and repairing much of the havoc we've wrought upon our planet in the last 150 years or so.

We live on a wounded world. Gaia, the living planet of which we are a part, is ailing. Parts of her are sick, as a result of pollution of the air, rivers and oceans, and parts of her are dying, through the destruction of ecosystems and habitats, and the extinction of species, which is now estimated at up to 150 per day.

We are all perhaps aware of some small part of this situation—a local forest cleared for a new road, or the fact that there aren't as many butterflies around as when we were younger—but how many of us can grasp the cumulative impact, the totality of the effect which humanity and our industrial consumer culture is having on the planet just now?

Such a global perspective can be obtained by considering the following: natural forests all over the world have been reduced to less than 5% of their original area, and 8,753 species of trees are threatened with extinction. Breast milk in British women has been shown to contain up to 150 toxic pollutants; 18,000 lakes in Sweden are dying or dead from acid rain; 18,000 square kilometres of the Gulf of Mexico are a 'dead zone' with no fish, clams or shrimps, due to eutrophication from fertiliser and animal manure runoff in the Mississippi River; the Black Sea marine ecosystem has totally collapsed, because of sewage and fertiliser runoff, over fishing, and toxic pollution; and 11 million hectares of arable land are lost each year through erosion, desertification, toxification etc. Many other examples highlight the same trend—the relentless destruction of ecosystems and the impoverishment of our planet's ability to support life, both human and non-human alike.

To put it bluntly, our culture is in the process of killing off much of the other life on our planet, and many of our current resources are directed towards this destruction either directly or indirectly. For example, according to figures for 1997 (the most recent year for which they are available) every day the world spends US$1.97 billion on weapons and the military—an annual expenditure amounting to US$721 billion, or $120 for every man, woman and child alive today.

Meanwhile, 28 years after the publication of the 'Limits to Growth' by the Club of Rome, every government in the world, and every major international institution (eg the World Bank, International Monetary Fund, World Trade Organisation etc), is still committed to the philosophy of unlimited economic growth. Our culture is heading myopically towards an unarticulated but nonetheless clearly visible goal—the enslavement of the planet, the harnessing of all available 'resources' for human material gain.

At the beginning of the 21st century, I believe that we need to prevent further environmental destruction and make major efforts to help reverse the damage which has already taken place.

Although our planet is wounded, Gaia, like other living organisms, has the ability to heal herself. In scientific terms, this has been documented through examples such as the reestablishment of tropical rainforest on the island of Krakatau in Indonesia, following the catastrophic volcanic eruption there in 1883, and more recently in the USA through the recovery of devastated forest ecosystems following the eruption of Mt. St. Helens in 1980 and the massive fires in Yellowstone National Park in 1988. This process of Earth healing—ecological restoration—is a natural one, but it is being prevented in most situations throughout the world today by the scale and intensity of human activities. What we need to do now is stop interfering with that process, and instead help it to take place.

Around the world, concerned individuals and groups are beginning to do this, by practical action to help restore their local ecosystems. Example of projects under way include initiatives to restore salmon runs to rivers in the Pacific Northwest of North America, to restore the highly-threatened tropical dry forests of Costa Rica, to restore the Caledonian Forest in Scotland, the reintroduction of Arabian oryx into the wild in Oman and the restoration of mangroves to areas of Viet Nam's Mekong Delta which were defoliated and destroyed during the war there.

These and the growing number of other similar projects are a good beginning for the essential work which lies ahead of us— restoration, on a co-ordinated, global scale, of our world's fragmented and degraded ecosystems. The healing of the Earth, combined with a cessation of our nature-destroying activities, has to become the centrepiece of all human endeavours, the cornerstone of all policies and practical actions, in the decades ahead if we wish to avoid the most calamitous event in our planet's biological history since the extinction of the dinosaurs 65million years ago.

I propose that we establish the goal of Restoring the Earth as the first shared task for all people and every nation, to provide a visionary and positive beginning to the new millennium, to lift human spirits beyond the depressing news about the state of the planet, and as a declaration of our intention, as a species, to transform and heal our relationship with the rest of Nature. This goal transcends all national boundaries and racial and other divisions between peoples, and provides a realistic but positive vision of hope for the future. Because restoration involves nurturing the life-giving and healing capacities of the Earth, it also provides a powerful contrast with our mainstream culture's current suicidal direction of 'the enslavement of the planet'.

So, how might this come to pass? In meditating and thinking about this for some time, I've been inspired to initiate a concerted campaign to get the United Nations to declare the 21st Century as the Century of Restoring the Earth. The UN embodies the necessary global perspective to truly represent the shared aspirations of people everywhere for a healthy planet.

This declaration would be accompanied by a call to the people and nations of the world to unite in cooperative, practical action to help with the healing of the planet. To help catalyse the action which is required, I propose the establishment of two new organisations— the Earth Restoration Service and the Global Restoration Network. The Earth Restoration Service will be an international programme for volunteers of all ages, but especially young people, to come together on specific Earth-healing projects, whether it be tree planting to help restore a forest, cleaning up polluted beaches and rivers, or helping to remove unnecessary roads from wild landscapes. The Global Restoration Network will link up existing restoration programmes, so that they can share their experiences, skills and expertise, and will act as an information and skills resource for anyone wishing to initiate a new Restoration project in their local area.

Funding for these schemes and a myriad of practical projects would come from a special fund into which every nation is required to contribute, as a global tithing, 10% of its existing military budget, either in cash or in kind, through the use of military resources and personnel. This will represent a recognition of the fact that true security has nothing to do with weapons, but instead depends upon having a healthy planet to live on, and will also provide a new sense of value and purpose to the military. In the following years, this percentage would be steadily increased as larger scale, more ambitious restoration projects are implemented. Examples of these could include a scheme to restore forests to the Sahel region of Africa, a 10-year programme for the complete clean-up of all toxic and chemical waste sites, an international initiative to green all the world's largest cities, and plans to reintroduce endangered large mammals and other threatened species to their former ranges. Other projects will involve the cleaning up of all the world's major rivers and the removal of large dams to allow them to flow freely, the conversion of all the world's farming to organic agriculture and a massive solar energy conversion campaign. Small-scale local restoration projects should be introduced as part of the curriculum in Schools everywhere, while major universities would be encouraged to set up whole new departments to provide the research and scientific basis for the larger ecosystem-scale projects which will be initiated on every continent.

Does this sound like an impossible dream? I don't think so—I believe that many if not most of us carry similar aspirations and hopes in our thoughts and hearts. We have the knowledge and the ability to put it all into practice. The only thing we need is the motivation and commitment to make it happen. Just as President Kennedy's declaration in 1961 that the USA would put a man on the moon before the end of that decade galvanised the resources of his nation to achieve that goal, so too can the declaration of the 21st century as the Century of Restoring the Earth help to liberate the creative abilities, aspirations, skills and commitment of people everywhere to make the healing of the Earth a reality.

With ideas, energy, enthusiasm and inspiration from members of this Community this project is moving forward significantly and we are receiving impassioned support from a wide range of well-known people. We have circulated a proposal about this project to leading people in environmental and scientific circles, to spiritual and religious leaders and to influential individuals and organisations concerned about the fate of Nature and the world. I believe that if we can gain enough support and endorsement from such individuals and organisations, and publicise the initiative widely through the media, then the proposal can be put before the General Assembly of the United Nations with a reasonable chance of being adopted. A resolution supporting the proposal was unanimously adopted at the 6th World Wilderness Congress, held in India in October 1998.

My own experience has shown me that ecological restoration is not just about helping to reconnect the strands in the web of life. It also helps to reconnect the people carrying out restoration work with some of the most important things in our lives. It helps to reconnect us with our power as individuals to make a difference in the world, with the quality of healing, with the presence of spirit in nature and, perhaps most importantly, with a sense of hope for the future. The practice of restoring degraded lands also connects the practitioners with the place where they work, and for me this represents a 'coming home' in the deepest meaning of that phrase. Out of that connection arises a communion with Nature, and in working consciously with that, guided by the love and care of my heart, I've seen the land and the forest around me respond in seemingly miraculous ways. In large part, that is where the success and inspiration of Trees for Life stems from—by acting in alignment with our inner connection with Nature, the Caledonian Forest is regenerating quickly, in some cases quite spectacularly and in a way which touches all those who come to take part in or see our work.

The challenge which awaits us now with regard to the state of the world's ecosystems is to take the founding principles of this community's work of co-creation with Nature—that all life is interconnected and linked, in both spirit and physical reality alike, and that conscious human love nurtures the life force of all plants and everything it is directed to—and apply them all over the world to assist with and accelerate the healing of the

Earth. Restoring the Earth offers perhaps the best opportunity to forge a new human culture, based on the recognition of the sacredness of all life, which will allow humans to live in balance and harmony again with all other species, while at the same time drawing forth the highest qualities from within each of us.

What I do know is that by following my heart, by putting spirit and my inspiration into my life and work, I can make my dreams and visions real and thereby make a positive difference in the world. I see that many of us here at Findhorn today are engaged in this process in our different areas of focus, and I think it's one of the purposes for which this Centre exists—to demonstrate what ordinary individual human beings are capable of doing.

ALAN WATSON FEATHERSTONE

Alan's project, Trees for Life, continues to grow and flourish as do the trees that the organisation plants. The millionth tree to restore the Caledonian Forest was planted on 20th May 2012! The work on regenerating the Caledonian Forest has had a global impact by inspiring so many people around the world to re-evaluate their approach to forests and to recognise the essential role that they play in the survival and maintenance of life on Earth.
www.treesforlife.org.uk

There and Back Again

It was time to leave! In spring 1996, the lease on the house that I rented in Findhorn village came to a traumatic and abrupt end. This brought up my old, deep rooted fear of being homeless. I have discovered that the most effective way to overcome fear is to feel it, and face it. So, instead of rushing to find another house to rent, I decided to feel what it was like to live in the world without a home.

I also wanted to experiment with the principle of freely offering my skills and experience to people who asked for them, while trusting that my needs would be met. I sold or gave away most of my possessions, and, packing only what I could carry, I set out to explore a new way of being.

Firstly to Costa Rica, where I had been invited to help facilitate the World Summit of Children. I was encouraged and inspired by the qualities of these young people—the potential politicians of tomorrow. After this conference I was invited to stay with a Costa Rican family to support them through a difficult situation. They introduced me to a group of people forming a community in the cloud forest. I moved up there and together we formulated a vision for the Community and developed programmes and projects to provide for its sustainability. After a few months I was invited to stay in a Guest Lodge on the Caribbean Coast and help to create programmes for Eco-Tourism. By this time I was learning to be open to possibilities, and to allow each opportunity to lead naturally to the next. It was in this manner that I lived in Costa Rica for six months.

After that I traveled through many countries and lived in 92 places. These included a tin shack in a tropical forest and a ski lodge in the Alps; a seminar centre in the desert and an apartment in Manhattan; a straw hut on a palm-fringed beach in Asia and a house in London.

Although I had been occupied in a variety of ways, I most enjoyed the times spent in coaching people. I find coaching to be an effective way to be of service. I use coaching methods to support people in coping with life changes, and creating their strategies for achieving their goals. In this way I have been involved in a variety of projects: Ecological tourism; computer manufacturing; refugee support; television production; complimentary therapy; hotel management; peace negotiations, and dance theatre.

My coaching style is now one to which I bring my whole self. My experience in psychology, business, group dynamics, communications, and motherhood, all help in my work. But chiefly, my role is simply to create a safe atmosphere and ask the appropriate questions. People are quite capable of working out their own solutions when they feel loved, listened to and respected.

If travel broadens the mind, what have I learned?

I have discovered the old saying, "Home is where the heart is", to be true. When I feel at home in myself, it doesn't matter what kind of building surrounds me.

I have learned that positive intention creates magic!

To be clear about what I need—I discovered how little I need to live a full and rich life!

I have learned that values are relative. Offering my skills and time to a person in need of them has value. Whether this is restructuring an organisation or caring for a cat. Being welcomed into someone's home when I need shelter has value. I learned to stop comparing values. Does sitting with a dying person have more or less value than helping a company remain in business? I no longer make that kind of judgment; I now simply do what inspires me.

I learned to let go of my attachment to being right...Mostly! I have discovered that my way of doing things is not the only way, or even—shock horror—the best way! I have learned there are at least 92 ways to wash dishes, make beds, run organisations, and bring up children.

I have learned to travel light. Having to carry everything I own has concentrated my mind on what is essential. A great antidote to consumerism!

I have learned that people are even more remarkable than I could have imagined! Total strangers have shared their lives, their homes, their fears, their hopes and dreams with me. They have been open to new ideas, and been creative around values and exchange. They have taught me so much!

I have learned to trust that whatever I need will turn up—somehow! I found out that I limit the possibilities if I put restrictions on how those needs will be met. Take travel for instance. My mind used to think only in terms of having money to buy tickets. No longer! I have discovered that tickets sometimes turn up out of the blue; that people love company on long journeys; that there are many ways to get from A to B. I have traveled on everything from a camel to a Presidential Jet!

And now I have returned to live again in Findhorn. Why? Good question! I thought that I was merely making a stopover on my way to somewhere else. But no! Apparently it is time to put roots down into the soil here and to make my contribution to the evolution of this Community, particularly to its development as an Eco-village. So, I am building a house here on the Field of Dreams (a miracle story in itself!). It would seem that in discovering that I no longer need a home of my own, I can now have one, and it is to be in Findhorn. That's okay with me. For, although I have learned that one place is as good as another, Findhorn is...well... Findhorn.

KAY KAY

CHAPTER ELEVEN

EVER EVOLVING

This community has been evolving since Eileen, Peter and Dorothy parked their caravan on these sand dunes all those years ago. It is a place of experiment. A place to try out new ways of doing things, both personally and collectively.

There have been attempts at many forms of community structure, management styles, and decision-making systems—some more effective than others. All them courageous and with the best of intentions for the good of the whole. Even so, there seem to have been opportunities for feelings of separation, misunderstanding, mistrust and disempowerment to emerge. How these have been, and will be, dealt with is a measure of the conscious awareness of those involved.

There have been a few rough edges over the years between the folks in the Foundation and the people who live in community around it. This also applies to the relationship with the people in the near-by village of Findhorn. The current evolutionary steps in the Community's development may create greater harmony and cooperation.

Over the Years

Memories of Living in Community

When we came in 1981 there were perhaps a couple of dozen people closely linked to the Foundation who were not members. We decided to join the new category of Associate Membership. We were asked to pay around £50 a month each and half that for the two older children (10 and 8) for the privilege of being allowed to connect, maybe work for the Foundation, and make use of facilities such as the sanctuary etc. I gasped,

"You must be joking! That's what it costs us to live" After a while we talked to some friends about it. "Just decide what you want to pay and tell them," they advised. So we did just that—and we were thanked and it was accepted.

1981:'Orientation' was then a 7 week programme of introduction to the Foundation as associate members. We were asked to do this but it was not compulsory. We were happy to do so, but with three children of 10, 8, and 2 we obviously couldn't do it together. I don't know how it happened but I was the one who did it first. This was a major decision—Richard was usually the one who led the way and did things first—and it was an interesting situation! My wonderful Orientation group warmly welcomed him and the family to join us at suitable social times. It came as a big shock when he did his orientation and it was made very clear to me that I was not welcome to join—I was not part of the group. Different groups— fascinating lessons...

I hadn't been here long then, and I had pretty definite ideas of how I wanted my children to be treated. At that time Liza was in charge of the children's area of the community and something she did didn't please me, so I let her know. One day she turned up on my doorstep and said she'd like to talk it through! This amazed me— what courage—not the way I was used to things being done. My respect for her was huge and I was so thankful for the opportunity to talk, and to begin to learn another way of dealing with conflict.

1982 and later: For a year I worked in the Publications Dept one day a week; mostly folding book pages in company with guests and dear Elfreda. She had been here many years, was a healer, hard worker, and a wonderful gossip with a delicious sense of humour. I learnt a lot about the community from her—both her stories and her very special being. We had a lot of fun. She remained a special friend and was always good for a laugh as she graduated to helping out with welcoming guests in the Community Centre. She eventually became confused and ill and needed to go to hospital. Dear Elfreda. She was still so pleased to have visitors—but I was glad she chose not to stay there very long. She had finished her work here and left with dignity.

1983: A few of us met daily at 5.30 pm in the caravan of an elder of the community, to meditate for the well-being of the community. A man named Charles and I tended to rub each other up the wrong way. One day I thought "I've heard of the idea of silently sending love to somebody and that it can work wonders—I'll try it". So I did. At the end of the meditation Charles turned to me, beamed, and said something loving. I was amazed and thrilled. From that point on our relationship was considerably improved.

Oh dear—remembering names! I have got quite good now at saying "remind me of your name" or "when was it we met?" When people visit

209

here I might well touch a life as a result of a chat over supper, a dance in a dance week, by leading a meditation in the Healing Sanctuary, or one of many other ways by which I might be remembered where I don't myself remember. The most embarrassing situation I had was a week after I had participated in a two-week healing workshop. I had no idea who the lady who greeted me was. She had been in the workshop with me, but as I knew she had left Findhorn I had lost her from my memory—but she came back!

A major excitement in my life was when Patch Adams first came to visit. Both doctor and clown by profession, he is a large man with a huge heart. I attended the workshop he ran and was inspired— perhaps re-inspired—to bring my clown out into the open. He challenged us to go into supper wearing underwear on our heads. For me that was huge fun: to wear crazy clothes, to dance and sing in the street,to interact more with people on a fun level—to wear face paints. Yet for me, Patch stands for much more. His huge underlying compassion for people and our need for fun and laughter, love and sharing. I continue to be inspired. "How are things here?" he asked me on another visit. I gave a "Sort of ok" reply. He said vehemently that the Findhorn community is a very inspiring place and is giving so much. He was insistent that it is important that we who live here should remember this.

DIANA BROCKBANK

Findhorn Village

Findhorn village. The name evokes images of lovely old white-painted cottages, of little pebbled lanes that weave in and around the pretty and well-kept gardens.

A long stretch of houses, built of stones from a local quarry and situated so that they face across Findhorn Bay to Culbin Sands, leads you into Findhorn. On the left side of the road are grassy banks where you can sit and watch the tide as it moves in and out and high up in the sky is an osprey, which was until recently very near to extinction in Scotland. Today it is nesting in the Culbin Forest and it likes to hover over the bay. The only thing destroying the idyllic scenery are the big and noisy Nimrods that come charging full blast through the air as they take off and land at the RAF airbase next door.

Behind the village are the dunes and the marshland and the North Sea. But in the village you are well protected from exposure to the harsh winds and salt water. There you are in the middle of a community as old as the village itself, 300 years or so. The village has been lost twice in its history.

Once washed away in a great flood and once covered by sand. So the village that we know today is actually Findhorn village in its third incarnation and it's still going strong.

Having painted the picture postcard image, let's look deeper into lives here and see who are the people born and bred here whose parents, grandparents and great grandparents lived here before them? What kind of lifestyle do they have in today's Findhorn, and why has there been a notorious lack of warmth between the village and the Foundation, going right back to the very beginnings of our Community?

In the October '96 I felt a pull to join PR, although I had no previous background in PR or marketing. As soon as I said "yes" to that impulse, I felt another pull; this time to start attending church in Findhorn village. In the ten years I lived here I have never felt attracted to the church and yet there I was, on a warm and sunny August Sunday, bicycling down to the village and nervously entering into the heart of Scottish Calvinist Christianity. Sitting on the hard wooden bench, not knowing quite what to do with myself, I was greeted by one woman who said how she wished that more of "us" would come and share their sacred space sometimes.

I attended every Sunday service and after six months the ice finally broke and the old Scot who gives out song books also gave out a little smile. Since then more smiles and little chats and signs of recognition have followed. After a holiday, when I went back to the church again, I was greeted like an old friend. The warmth in people's eyes was so heartening. I felt quite at home in the conventional church setting! I just loved to sit there amongst friends and fellow travellers on our journey home to God.

The one woman who greeted me has become a good friend and, being a native Scot, is immensely helpful when it comes to getting to know and understanding the nature of a traditional Scottish village. We spend a lot of time talking and sharing our different cultures and gradually she is introducing me to others in the village. It feels sometimes like we're walking where angels fear to tread as the ground is very tender and a lot of tact and diplomacy is required. I often don't have a clue what to do or say next. God is silently called on and asked to take over and conduct the process, and the grace with which things are unfolding strongly suggests that God is very much present with us in this bridge-building and peace-making venture.

The most frequent criticism I hear has to do with the Foundation's perceived 'closed doors policy', ie why aren't our meetings about the future development of The Park and Eco- Village open to the villagers? We can attend Findhorn village's Council meetings, so why can't they attend ours? Another complaint is that we use the village, its name and its resources-the pubs, the shops, the beach, etc-and that we don't appreciate/reciprocate, at least not in ways that the village can understand.

I've been doing a little research into what kind of appreciation or reciprocation the village would be able to understand and take in. An interesting picture is beginning to emerge. Findhorn, a traditional fishing village, has its roots in the old close-knit, hardworking and cooperative society where everyone depended on everyone else for survival. Families intermingled and everyone belonged. Those trends are still alive, though slowly fading, in the village today. If you have a couple of spare leeks in your garden, you drop by your neighbour and leave them on the kitchen table. If you go to visit someone, you bring a little something: biscuits, flowers-anything! The idea is not to spend money but to share and make the energy go round. Much like in the Foundation Community.

In the village that 'give and take' culture is slowly disappearing, and the Foundation is a contributing factor without even knowing it. The fact that many people associated with the Foundation live in the village, but spend most of their time at The Park takes away from the village life in Findhorn village itself. Houses are frequently being bought and lived in by people who seem to take little interest in the culture and traditions of Findhorn. A fear of being taken over has crept into some people's minds.

There are other reasons too why the old lifestyle is dying out in Findhorn, and the villagers are the first to admit it. Their young people go away to the cities and only a few return to live. The old cottage industries are long since gone and most people today go by car to Forres and shop in the supermarkets where prices are competitive.

So there are only a few shops and businesses left in Findhorn now, but they are the heart of the village and they are where you meet everyone, have a little chat and keep up with local news. There is the Royal Yacht Club, the chandler's shop to equip you with everything in the nautical sphere, and there are a couple of cafes. There is the boat building workshop. And there is the small Heritage Centre showing what it was like in the 'good old days'. I'm reliably told they were hard! The two pubs, the Crown & Anchor and the Kimberley, are both equally frequented by the villagers, the RAF and by the Foundation. It's hard to disagree deeply over a cool pint! The Church is the spiritual heart of the village of course, and Sunday services are sacred times.

In summertime the older men sit on benches along the shore and watch life, and there's plenty to watch. Wind surfers and boats are out on the water, and sometimes water skiers. A family of swans live in the bay and swim close to the shore; children play near the water and throw bread to the swans and birds, and lots of people are out walking or sitting on the banks. If Findhorn village is not heaven, it's not far away. Wouldn't it be great if the Foundation could expand its feelings and gestures of community to include more of the village whose name it so proudly uses? We, the Foundation Community, are actually part of Findhorn village. The boundary line between Kinloss and Findhorn runs straight down the lane that also divides us from the RAF base. And so I feel we need to own up to being part of a bigger community than just our own. As Jonathon Porritt, former leader of the Green Party in Britain, once told us at a conference: "Turn your chairs to face outwards! You're already living in community. Don't opt out, opt in!"

So I constantly question how we can continue to reconcile the past and current alienation and paranoia between the village and ourselves. First, we officially adopt the attitude that we would like to do so and that we're committed to doing our part. Having said this, there are a small number of people in Findhorn village who are determined not to see anything good coming from the Foundation and they are probably forever beyond our reach. But I'd like to see us actively reach out to and befriend the great majority of people who are either neutral or mildly puzzled by who we are and what we're doing.

A visit by nine women from the nearby town of Lhanbryde, was recently arranged. They looked a bit nervous on arrival, introducing themselves as Mrs. McDonald, Mrs. Scott, etc, but three hours later we were hugging and saying goodbye to Peggy, Mary and the rest of the girls!

Despite our annual Open Days and Winter Gatherings, the Foundation has not yet managed to make itself and its ethos known to its immediate neighbours. There seems, however, to be a seachange and a softening of hearts and minds right now and I'm happy to report that both camps are making moves in the right direction.

The Findhorn Bay has now been designated a Local Nature Reserve. This aims to protect and further the great variety of rare plant and animal species which take their refuge in and around the bay. The area is an intricate system of water life, shore life, dunelands and human life and it takes quite a lot of awareness to keep a healthy balance of all these interconnecting life forms.

The Foundation had a representative elected onto the Nature Reserve Management Committee and guess who it was? I'm so excited by it, even when I'm having to plough my way through thick documents written in legal language and having to practice saying "Mr. Chairman", and "Members of the Committee", every time I want to say something!

I'll leave you with images of a sunset over the bay and of the mountains across the water merging with the sea and the sky, making it hard to see where one ends and the other begins. In Scotland the veil between the worlds is said to be thinner than in most places and watching the sun setting behind Findhorn village on a summer's eve, I can well believe it. Ah!

ELIZABETH TONSBERG
One Earth

F

Thoughts On The Way Home

As I was meditating about the relationship between the Findhorn Foundation and the community of people who are associates of the Foundation, I saw a stone thrown in the middle of a pond. I watched the ripples going out and out from the centre, but when the ripples reached the outer edge of the pond, those ripples returned to the place where the stone was thrown in the first place. As they did this, I realised that there is no separation between us and that we are all One.

We all need each other and it is important that there is no feeling of separation, no 'they' and 'us'. How easily we can slip into that way of thinking and we must watch out and be very careful that this does not happen.

The Foundation needs to embrace the associates and the associates need to embrace the Foundation. How can this be achieved? There can be more giving and receiving, more sensitivity to each other's needs. Everyone is so busy that we forget to look to the needs of each other. Let us change that and see what happens.

The Foundation is like a living, breathing being; it breathes in and out. If it spends all the time breathing in, or out, it will surely die. So there needs to be a balance, collectively, of a steady breathing in and out, of giving and receiving. When we are all doing that, the Foundation and the associates will find that the whole body will be healthy and whole.

I feel it comes down to caring, to loving one another, to seeing each other's needs when we are sensitive enough and aware of one another.

I see a very strong and powerful partnership between us, for unity is strength. Division and disunity creates weakness so let there be no weak link in this partnership. Let us find unity, unity in diversity, for we are all unique but we are all moving towards the same goal; our realisation of oneness with God, the Divinity Within. We are all finding our way 'home' to the Source. As we work towards that goal we will find unity, peace and harmony, and let us give thanks that this is taking place now.

EILEEN CADDY

Postscript: Eileen wrote this in 1990. Since then a number of structures have been tried in order to create unity, harmony, peace and a sense of togetherness within the whole Community. The development of the New Findhorn Association (NFA) is the latest and greatest step in this evolutionary process.

The Courage to Change

This Community's structure has been gradually evolving over the decades. In the beginning years of the 60s it was informal with no explicit organisational structure. In the 70s it grew to a scale where it needed some structure and, starting in 1972, that was provided by the newly-formed Findhorn Foundation. I think of the 70s as the 'manor house' era, during which the Foundation was the community and the community was the Foundation.

The overall community, however, kept growing and diversifying and proved to be too complex to contain in any one organisation. Part of this diversification came through spinning off activities that were once in the Foundation, beginning with New Findhorn Directions in 1979 as a 'for profit' arm of the Foundation. Another part came through the development of sister organisations, like Minton House, which were never part of the Foundation but were clearly part of the community. My image for this process is the gradual adding of various 'buildings' around the 'manor house' until, on the ground, a metaphorical village existed. In this 'village' the 'manor house' is still the largest single building but it is nevertheless just one building in the steadily growing 'village'.

In 1995 I spent four months living in the community while my late wife, Diane, worked on preparing the October conference on Eco- Villages and Sustainable Communities. That time gave me the chance to get to know the 'village', to see the ways in which it was happy with its informality and anarchy, and also to feel the places where that energy was starting to chafe.

When I returned, I got the clear message from many in the community, that the old anarchy was no longer serving the needs of the time. The community as a whole had grown to the point where the Foundation was only about a quarter of the overall population and less than a quarter of the annual financial turnover. And with the major land purchases by Eco-Village Ltd and Dunelands Ltd, much of the community's land was now owned outside of the Foundation. Yet because of its history, the overall community still often looked to the Foundation for a kind of leadership and for services which the Foundation could no longer provide. Energies were blocked, tensions grew, and opportunities were missed.

A number of attempts were underway to find a fresh start, but there was also a clear sense that more was needed. The Findhorn Bay Community Association had started in 1996 as an attempt to provide a structure for the overall community, but its membership was less than 20% of the full community, so it didn't have the critical mass it needed... The Foundation had spent two years in a 'reinvention' process which, while it had accomplished some change, had not done as much as had been hoped to relieve people's growing sense of frustration.

As I discussed all this with friends in the community it became clear that the Foundation could not take its next steps in isolation— the community of which it was a part also had to shift—and the community could not take its next steps unless it dealt with all of its parts. Out of these conversations a plan emerged for me to come in January (with financial support from the Foundation, the Findhorn Bay Community Association, Phoenix Stores, various friends of the community, and later also from Minton House, Eco- Village Ltd, New Findhorn Directions, and Big Sky Printing) and we would see what we all could do to enable those next steps.

The basic goal was to formalise the overall community, including creating a 'village council' or some such democratic forum through which it would be possible to deal consciously and openly with those issues that concerned the community as a whole. To develop this community-wide structure we adopted a process that used three parallel tracks:

1. An 'open forum' in which anyone was welcome to contribute their ideas, lead activities, or otherwise contribute their inspiration to the process. This track was analogous to the 'civil sector' or 'NGO sector in mainstream society.

2. A 'council of organisations' in which the leadership of the community's more than 30 organisations were invited to help shape the new community structure (analogous to the 'business sector').

3. An elected 'constitutional committee' whose task was to blend the input from the other two tracks with their own work and produce a proposed community constitution which would then go back to the community in the form of a referendum. This group would be analogous to the 'government sector'.

At the first community meeting on 7 January, we set ourselves the goal of electing the Constitutional Committee by the end of the month and then completing the constitution in six weeks in time for the referendum in the middle of March.

Electing the Constitutional Committee proved to be no simple task since there was, up to that time, no clear definition of who was part of the whole community, there had never been a communitywide election before, and there was no list of eligible voters. We found our way through this maze of "can't be dones" by saying that, for this one election, anyone who had resided in the Findhorn/Forres area for at least a year and who currently was or had been significantly involved with one of the community's organisations was eligible to vote. A voter list of almost 400 names was quickly assembled and by the time we had the 'candidates forum' in the Universal Hall on 22 January the ballots were all prepared with the names of the 21 candidates who were running for the 12 seats on the committee. The election ran until noon on 30 January, and that afternoon, Lambert Munro, a councillor with the Findhorn/Kinloss

Council, oversaw the counting of 231 valid ballot papers in our first election.

Meanwhile, on 29 January, we had our first meeting of the Council of Organisations at Minton House. This was the first of a series of meetings which brought the organisations into closer communications with each other and provided valuable input to the Constitutional Committee.

Those who were elected to the Constitutional Committee got down to work on 1 February and met three times a week for the next six weeks. It was intensive, but it was not as dry and formal as the name—Constitutional Committee—might suggest.

We began, in our first meeting, by asking, "What planetary purpose does the Angel of Findhorn want the community to serve over the next few years?" and we stayed attuned to the angelic kingdom throughout our process. The responses to this question were eventually synthesised into the constitution's statement of purpose: *"to be a diversity of people, showing by example, a way of living in the world in alignment with Spirit, in co-operation with each other, and in service to the Earth."*

We developed clear ground rules for our process which included using coloured cards for voting: green = I support; blue = I'm neutral; yellow = I have questions; and red = I oppose. We would often attune before using the cards, and if anyone held up a yellow or red card, we would encourage them to share either their unresolved questions or the reasons for their opposition. The ensuing discussion would often lead to modifications to the current proposal so that all could support it. In addition, on the back of the red cards were the words "off track" and everyone was empowered to hold up this sign whenever they felt the discussion had gone astray. This proved to be an effective tool for enabling the whole group to stay focused.

We also took time for ritual. One that I would like to mention was our yin/yang ceremony. Each member of the committee brought two objects: one that symbolised for them the positive aspects of yin and another that symbolised the positive aspects of yang; and each spoke movingly about their objects and the qualities they represented. At the meeting after this ritual we had a wonderful discussion about leadership which in turn powerfully influenced the structures that eventually went into the constitution.

And so it was that we gradually covered all the fundamental questions that needed to be addressed, such as: how is membership defined; what are the powers of members; what are the governing structures for the community; how are decisions to be made; how are elections to be held etc. A small group of us took the committee's decisions and drafted them into the formality of a constitution. The committee as a whole then refined this draft into the 'Constitution of the New Findhorn Association' to present to the community.

The new constitution calls for two categories of elected positions.

There is a 12-person council (a part-time voluntary position) and the more unusual role of the Listener-Conveners which I would like to describe in more detail. These two, elected, paid, full-time people —a man and a woman not in a primary relationship with each other—serve the community by listening to the members, sensing the pulse of the community, being spiritually attuned to its purpose, identifying key issues, and focusing appropriate community attention on these. They have the power to convene meetings, initiate games, catalyse new groups, and in other ways help the community take its next steps in areas as diverse as economic development and connection to Spirit. Their function is to accelerate the evolution of the community and its members towards their highest potential. They are also the non-voting co-chairs of the Council, focusing the Council's attention on the issues that truly concern the community.

The council also appoints groups with advisory or special roles that serve the community. Chief amongst these are Peacemakers who mediate disputes which are not completely within a single organisation; Neighbourly Relations, a group that includes local non-members and establishes and maintains good relationships with others nearby in the immediate Findhorn-Kinloss-Forres vicinity; and Global Elders, three to five individuals living further afield who are respected, willing and available to bring a global perspective to community affairs.

While the constitution was being finalised, people were stepping forward to stand for the elected positions. I was pleased that the first person to stand for the new Council was Eileen Caddy. She was eventually joined by sixteen other candidates for the Council plus we had six candidates for the two Listener-Convenor positions. All these threads came together on the evening of 15 March in a community meeting in the Hall that combined a presentation of the proposed constitution to the community, a candidates' forum and a distribution of ballot papers for the referendum on the constitution and election to the new positions. Over the following days more ballots were distributed (again about 400 in total) until the election closed on the Spring Equinox, 21March. When the 231 valid papers had been counted, the constitution had been approved by 95%, and Listener-Convenors and the new Councillors had all been duly elected.

The New Council got straight to work. The process we had been through had given them a good start but there will certainly be many challenges to be faced to integrate these changes into the life of this Community

ROBERT GILMAN

With a Listening Heart

I feel privileged to have been elected as the female Listener- Convener for two years. My co-Listener-Convener, Fabien Barouch held the post last year also, and he and my predecessor, Hannah Albrecht, worked extremely hard to successfully ground this initiative. We can now pay attention to identifying and strengthening areas of common ground, while highlighting aspects that could use some attention.

The NFA was designed to be a cauldron into which every part of this community can be put to make a rich concoction that will nourish and sustain us all. The structure is not one of managing, of hierarchy or of needing large amounts of money to sustain itself. The intention is for this to be a light but strong way of holding the process of community evolution. To offer another metaphor, I see it as a clear plastic bag (with apologies to environmentalists!). It is made from a tiny amount of material; it is economical; in itself it occupies very little space; yet it is very strong and it can hold a surprising amount. The fact that it is transparent means that everything in it can easily be seen.

There are many issues to be addressed and projects requiring focus. In the role of Listener-Conveners, Fabien and I intend to have an awareness of the overall and ever-changing picture and to support all community members to fulfill their individual potential and that of the community.

As we listen to people we are beginning to see the threads that are emerging to be woven into the tapestry of sustainable community. The member organisations are each working on a different aspect of this. Sustainability is most often thought of in terms of ecology and economy. These are being addressed in many ways.

Within the development of the Eco-village we are concerned with the built environment, the generation of renewable energy, recycling, and environmentally friendly waste disposal.

With Ekopia—our Community Resource Exchange—we are creating cooperative ownership and the management of financial resources for the benefit of everyone involved.

There is a vision for a Bureau to provide services such as a skills database, accommodation information, business services, project start-up advice, and car-pooling.

However, social sustainability is also a vital element in the life of acommunity. And that, I believe, starts with attitude. Our attitude to each other, to our neighbours and to the Planet we live upon. We are all familiar with this kind of statement but what does it really mean in our daily lives?

I think it requires us to ask ourselves some fundamental questions. How much do we care about and respect one another? Are we honest with each other? Are we compassionate? Do our differences separate us or do they add richness to our lives? Do we gossip and make judgements about people based on what we hear? What kind of welcome do we offer to people? How much responsibility do we each take for our words, choices, behaviour, and actions? Do we blame others when things are not as we would have them be? Do we expect someone else to make things better? Are we envious of people who have what we do not? What are we committed to? Are we reliable? Do we let our fears run our lives or can we encourage each other to be courageous?

It seems to me that the kind of community this will evolve into in the future is dependent upon our attitudes today. Within the container of the NFA we are creating a culture in which the Findhorn Foundation no longer expects—or is expected—to provide the support structures for the whole community. This is a cultural shift. This new culture of empowered, responsible organisations and task oriented, special interest groups is now the foundation upon which a new form of community is being built. Our personal and collective attitudes will determine how sustainable that community will become.

KAY KAY
Written in 2000 for the first issue of Eco-Village Voice

Update: The progress of the NFA and the huge shifts that have taken place in and around the Community over the twelve years since this was written are detailed in the following three chapters.

F

CHAPTER TWELVE

DEVELOPING AN ECOVILLAGE

The Global Ecovillage Network that was created following the Ecovillage Conference at the Findhorn Community in 1995 uses the following definition of an Ecovillage:

'Ecovillages are urban or rural communities of people, who strive to integrate a supportive social environment with a low impact way of life. To achieve this, they integrate various aspects of ecological design, permaculture, ecological building, green production, alternative energy, community building practices, and much more.'

The majority of the accounts in these final chapters, which cover the years 2000 to 2012, have been written from my perspective or my personal experience of being closely involved in these events and activities.

The development of The Field of Dreams has been pivotal in the creation of the Ecovillage in the Park and has done much to change the appearance and the sustainability of this Community. The Park Planning Group monitors the progress of this development and holds the house owners, designers and builders to required guidelines. The Field Residents Group was a place where all those who were in the process of constructing their homes on the Field could get to know one another, find mutual support and share useful information. In writing about these and describing the building of my house shows how all of this was experienced from a personal perspective. The acquisition of the land for the Duneland development as described in the piece by John Talbot has created further possibilities for the development of the Ecovillage.

The Field of Dreams

John Talbot, an engineer, Simon Richards, an architect, and a few other people formed Eco-Village Ltd. (EVL), through which to purchase six acres of farmland from the neighbouring Bichan family, who are very nice people of high integrity. This site was named the Field of Dreams.

The work was then to gain the necessary detailed planning permissions, prepare the land, put in the roads and the services, mark out the plots and manage their sale. EVL's intention was to close the company down when all this was accomplished. As a lot of interest had been expressed regarding the project, this was not anticipated to take more than a few years.

The land sloped north to south. Some parts of the southern strip were often waterlogged and could require a lot of drainage work. Because of this and to avoid The Field, as it became known, looking like an ordinary housing development, it was decided that houses would be built mostly on the western and northern areas rather than over the whole of the site.

The overall plan was for a semicircle of houses to be built around the west and north edges of the land leaving the rest as an open space. This was envisaged to be either a village green or some form of communal garden. In some places the houses would be only one row deep, other places two and in one short area three rows deep. Stringing all the plots along either side of one road, with a short loop at the end where there were three rows of houses had a double advantage. One was leaving a large open space and the other was keeping to a minimum the cost of laying the road, providing street lighting and installing the underground cabling and services to each property.

Most of the houses were to be one and a half stories high with the upper rooms in the roof space. The North end of the site was bordered by land that rose sharply by a few metres upon which there already existed a row of trees, which would provide some screening. This was the area in which taller, 2 1/2 story dwellings could be built. This was to prevent these from blocking the view of smaller buildings, from taking the light from them or casting a large shadow over them.

Provision had been made for parking for only one car per dwelling. Rather than in garages under or attached to each house or parked on land around each house, the parking spaces would be grouped in several car parks, masked by greenery, and in different locations along the road.

This meant that each plot could be quite small and therefore more houses could be built on the residential part of the Field. Placing houses close together on either side of the road could give the feeling of a village street and the careful positioning and the differential in height could provide most houses with some view of the open space.

Having presented the development plan to the community for approval EVL sought planning permission from the District Council. The Planners were persuaded that within the ethos of our community it was unlikely that many people would have two cars and quite a few people would have no vehicle at all. Also that home-owners would prefer all cars to be parked in specific car parking areas and would not mind the inconvenience of walking up to 100 metres to their cars.

It is still a mystery how the planning authority came to approve of this when planning regulations at the time clearly required each house to have space for the parking of two cars. Perhaps they thought that choosing to live in this Community meant that people would prefer to huddle close to one another and that these odd notions around cars and car parking fitted in with other strange behaviour such as meditation and vegetarianism!

Having agreed that two plots would be made available for buildings of Community benefit – which would eventually be the Moray Arts Centre - EVL received planning permission to proceed with the development of the land for the construction of 44 houses.

Because of the location of The Field the designs for these houses could be innovative. Findhorn Village is a conservation area requiring any new buildings within its boundaries to be designed to fit with the local vernacular (style of building) and blend in with the rectangular shape of the traditional fisherman's cottages of this coastal region. However, none of the houses to be built upon The Field could be seen in relation to existing houses in Findhorn Village or from any main thoroughfare. This meant that house designs would not be obliged to fit within the constraints of the local vernacular. The houses on the Field of Dreams could be built in any style, using any materials and construction methods that complied with building regulations. This created the prospect for possibly more barrel houses and other exciting structures.

Some of the people wishing to buy plots were living in or around the Community. Others were people who were familiar with the Community and a few people knew very little about what they were intending to become part of. Each applicant was required to write a letter about him or herself and be interviewed by EVL to discuss their reasons for wanting to become part of the Community through building their home on the Field of Dreams. The people who had very little knowledge of the Community were encouraged to learn about it and spend time in it before committing themselves.

(After EVL closed down following the initial sale of the plots, some of which then changed hands, this process was then handled by Listener Conveners, as it is now, when houses on the Field are being re-sold.)

The development took much longer to complete than anticipated, even though the first house was constructed relatively quickly. Gillian commissioned Simon Richards to design a pleasing, if fairly conventional two-bedroom house. Although Simon designed only some of the other houses, many of the design features of this first house were themes echoed by some of the other architects.

This might be one of the things that influenced the restrained approach to design on this development. Only a few people have taken advantage of the unique location of the Field to explore really innovative design. Perhaps this was also due to the conservatism of some architects or their clients, although, with some designs it was clearly a matter of economics. A simple, unadorned rectangle with a gable ended pitched roof is traditionally the cheapest form of construction. By adopting this style, people on a low budget could build a home on the Field of Dreams. Another economical approach was the construction of a row of small terraced houses. These Centini Studios, designed by Simon and developed by EVL, were intended to provide 14 low-cost dwellings.

In the end only 40 houses were built as four people chose to each purchase one and a half plots upon which to build larger houses or have bigger gardens. The final house was completed in 2011. By which time most people were well settled in, most gardens, although small were well-established, the green was regularly played on by children and gathered upon by residents and others for parties and celebrations throughout the summer.

There is a range of opinions on the success or otherwise of the Field of Dreams. Some people in the Community wish there had been fewer houses built on the site; others are uncomfortable that having large and small houses juxtaposed shows there is financial disparity between people living in this Community; others would have preferred more cohesiveness in the designs, and some think that in order to create a sense of equality within community, all the houses ought to look the same.

These last two preferences have influence the ongoing development of the Ecovillage as the houses built so far on Duneland have been constructed in one design style.

On the other hand, there are Community members who enjoy the interesting variety created by the different designs, shapes, sizes and colours of the houses on The Field and who appreciate the innovation and the use of the variety of eco materials being demonstrated. There are those who, while understanding and agreeing with the desire for as much cohesion in community as possible, believe it is also important to respect individuality.

From my experience in Findhorn, and other places around the world, I have observed that some people reject living in community because of a fear of becoming homogenized in some way and losing their individuality and autonomy. These are often the very people whose skills, experience, passion and enthusiasm might guarantee a community's sustainability. It seems that it is often from a position of autonomy that some individuals – and organizations for that matter – can contribute most effectively to an holistic, vibrant and robust community. The Field of Dreams seems to be an attractive and practical demonstration of individuality being expressed within a collective.

Most of the courageous people who have been willing to invest money, time, effort, determination, and fortitude into building their home on The Field have made a significant commitment to the sustainability of this Community and thoroughly enjoy living there.

Even so, there have been a few challenges for them to rise above, such as lack of privacy and other difficulties arising from living in close proximity to neighbours. Most of these have been overcome through cooperative neighbourliness.

One challenge has been parking – or lack of it. The expectation of one car per household has proven to be over optimistic, as families of several generations and people needing cars to do their work outside the Community have become residents. People working from their homes on the Field such as therapists, artists, life coaches and consultants of various kinds have clients who might also need parking facilities. Several of the houses on the Field offer bed-and-breakfast and many of their guests arrive in cars.

This challenge has been partly addressed through neighbourly cooperation of various kinds. Some people needing two parking spaces have made arrangements with people who do not need the one allocated to them. Car sharing has been a community activity for many years and this is now being enhanced by a more structured carpooling system.

There was no provision made for parking for the two plots allocated for the buildings of Community benefit. Together these became the site of the Moray Arts Centre that is in need of some parking for staff, students, visiting artists, workshop leaders and participants and visitors to exhibitions and other events.

Even so, he Field of Dreams feels safer, less cluttered and more pleasing to look at than perhaps it would if cars were littering people's gardens or parked along the narrow roadway.

A great deal has been learned through the development of the Field of Dreams and this knowledge now informs the decisions being made regarding further development of the Ecovillage.

Park Planning Group

The Park Planning Group (PPG) was initiated by John Talbot to guide and monitor the development of the Ecovillage. The group consists of people representing various stakeholder groups within the Community. Some of these were the landowners - The Foundation, Dunelands and, for a time, EVL – later replaced by a Field of Dreams resident representing those Titleholders.

Fortuitously, the skills among these representatives include engineering, architecture and other skills in design or construction. As Listener Convener – elected to be the 'ears' of the Community - I represented the Community membership. In this capacity I attended and eventually chaired PPG during several of the busiest and most exciting years of the development of the Field of Dreams. My previous experience as secretary to a small architectural practice came in useful.

PPG's role was to approve plans on behalf of the Community before they were presented to the Moray Council Planning Dept for approval. However, our responsibility was to find a balance between holding strongly to the principles of Ecovillage development while supporting individuals through the new experience and the minefield of eco-construction.

We developed a strict code of building practice (far more Draconian than those of the Local Authority) and guidelines for the use of building materials. Based upon research and the experience of John Talbot and others, we listed all the materials used in construction - from foundations to chimney - under four main headings: Recommended materials; Approved materials; Materials requiring some research, explanation and justification; and Prohibited materials, (locally referred to as OJDB - over John's (Talbot) dead body!)

Most of these guidelines were to ensure ecological and environmental protection. Many were for the avoidance of toxic materials, whether a material itself or toxins that had been used in its manufacture.

One recommended material was of course eco-paint. Although we expected that many of the larch or cedar timber-clad houses would be left to weather naturally, it was anticipated that some would be painted. It seemed to me that the colour chosen to paint a house was likely to have as a great an impact on the eye as its size, style or the method of its construction. I suggested that under the guidelines for eco-paint we could include a recommended colour chart of complementary colours so that whichever one was chosen for painting the exterior of a house would blend in with or complement neighbouring houses painted in any other colour on that chart.

As eco-paints are made from natural pigments, ranging from charcoal to soft white, with many beautiful natural colours in between, there could be plenty of choice. Some people in PPG thought this would be a restriction of self-expression, however, and so the suggestion was rejected. There were later to be expressions of regret around that decision.

The process for receiving approval from PPG required applicants to prepare detailed plans showing the floor layout, north, south, east and west elevations of the building, its position on the plot and calculations for shadow cast at both Winter and Summer Solstice. A list of the building materials specified would also be included. These were presented at a PPG meeting where the group would make initial comments of concern and suggestions for improvements if necessary. Sometimes proposers were required to make some essential changes or to research some of the materials.

The plans and information on materials would then be pinned up on a large board in the Community Centre for several weeks. On the sheets of paper provided, people were encouraged to express their views about this proposal or raise questions concerning it. These comments were then reviewed by PPG and taken into account when considering final approval.

The more we learned about the complexities of this process the more efficient and supportive we could be towards prospective house builders. From experience we soon recognised that the Moray Council Planning Dept would most likely approve any plans already approved by PPG. So it was with some confidence and pleasure that we congratulated each proposer who secured PPG's approval. The plot owner would then lead all those present at the meeting to his or her plot. The land and building venture would be blessed and the plot owner appreciated for his or her commitment to the creation of the Ecovillage.

As plots were sold and plans drawn up the work of PPG increased. We were presented with plans for large houses and small houses, simple designs and complex structures. Although most were to be built in timber, there were also some stonemasonry and stuccoed straw bale constructions. Many people were courageously experimenting with new materials for roofing, cladding or insulation or with new types of space and water heating.

Some people were working with experienced eco-architects and designers and others were not. Some people kept well within the construction and material guidelines and others either misunderstood or chose to ignore them. Skills of diplomacy and clear communication were sometimes needed in the PPG meetings!

One of the challenges of living in community is that the wide range of skills, interests and activities of some individuals can create occasional conflicts of interest. This was something we were extremely vigilant about in PPG. Sometimes a member of the group might be the architect or engineer on a design up for approval. Sometimes members of the group presented plans for their own houses. On one occasion, the architect and engineer partners in Eco-Village Ltd, both PPG members, presented their plans for a cluster of houses that Eco-Village Ltd was proposing to construct. How many interests were potentially conflicting there?

Even though the other members of the group would have little doubt that any of these proposals would be to the highest eco-standard, on all of these occasions the people presenting their plans would 'step out' of their PPG role and present their plans as anybody else would have to do. The remaining PPG members would then give those plans the same due diligence as those from anyone else.

The wealth of knowledge and experience within the Park Planning Group continues to be immensely beneficial to those engaged in the ongoing development of the Findhorn Ecovillage.

Building a Home - A Mystery

Whilst I was in support of developing The Park as an Ecovillage I had no interest or desire to contribute to its evolution by building an eco-house there, to say nothing of being without any money to buy land and build. So it was with great surprise that I began to have the urge to consider the possibility.

I know better than to ignore this kind of urge. I don't know whether its guidance, intuition, information from the collective unconscious or some idea that's been percolating away in the deep recesses of my mind. I only know, from my experience, that to ignore such promptings is unwise. Either because they will get louder and more insistent until I take notice of them or because circumstances will arrange themselves and become increasingly uncomfortable until there is little choice left except for taking the prompted action. How the intended outcomes will come about is often unknown. It's a mystery! However, I do know that it is vital to hold to a clear intention and that commitment has magic in it!

As I began to seriously consider this idea, the money I would need to build such a house began to turn up. Firstly, I was notified that a small insurance policy that I had forgotten about was about to mature. Then, sadly, my dear old Dad died. I had no idea he had the money that he left me and I wish he had used it to make the last years of his life more comfortable.

I still had nowhere near enough to buy a plot and build anything on it and so the mystery continued. Then a couple of friends told me of a design one of them - a boat builder - had for a small, inexpensive, single person dwelling - about the size of a caravan and designed along the lines of an upturned boat. These structures were to be produced as prefabricated modules that could be brought to site and fitted together in whatever formation was required. Very interesting and exciting!

In further discussion it emerged that we each had enough money to buy a third of a plot and build one of these little units.

We selected a suitable plot on the Field of Dreams. As my friends did not have immediate access to their funds, I paid the deposit. A few days later I received a letter from EVL explaining that, as there was planning permission for only 44 houses on the Field, our building three dwellings on one plot meant that EVL would be unable to sell two of the other plots for building purposes. Therefore they were increasing the price of our plot to offset this loss.

Although this came as a shock I could understand EVL's situation. The cost of purchasing the land, levelling the site, constructing the road and putting in all the services must have cost a lot of money. The plots were taking much longer to sell than had been anticipated and most of those allocated still had only the deposit paid upon them. Being unable to sell two of the remaining plots could cause them problems.

My building partners immediately pulled out of the project. This left me with a deposit on a plot that I could just afford to buy on my own yet without enough funds to build even one of the little boat designs.

Obviously, the simplest course of action would be to drop the whole idea. However, I did not feel that it was the right thing to do. Perhaps it was because of some sense that I was supposed to be part of the Ecovillage? Maybe it was because I had become excited by the prospect of building my own home? I think it was more likely to be plain stubbornness that led me to continue.

And then, a family flat in London was put on the market. I had a share in this, although no title, and I had not expected it to be sold for many years, if ever! Due to the ridiculousness of the London property market, I received enough money from my share of the sale to build a two, possibly three-bedroom house! Mystery solved? Perhaps!

I chose Bernard Planterose to design my house. He is, among other things, an artist and environmentalist. I could have given Bernard instructions on how I wanted the house to look. However, having had experience of design I do not believe in hiring designers and then restricting their creativity. Instead, I told him that I wanted the house to be of modern and stylish design; to offer flexibility of use and for there to be a sense of light and space in as many rooms as possible.

Knowing how long the creative process of architecture can take I was surprised when only a week later Bernard asked if he could bring his initial ideas to show me. Not only did he present me with sketches, elevations and floor plans for a beautiful and elegant building, he had also made a delightful scale model. It seems that the whole concept of the building had arrived in his mind almost intact. I hardly changed a thing!

Most people on the Park Planning Group seemed pleased to see this innovative design. Their only concern was the choice of roofing material. The design was for a number of connected mono-pitch modules. In height restricted buildings – this was a one-and-a-half story building with some of the rooms in the roof space – more height can be achieved over a larger room area through having single sloping roofs rather than the usual inverted V pitched variety. However, that means that the pitch is gentle and therefore tiles and slates cannot be hung upon it.

The options for materials available to us were: zinc, which was very expensive; steel sheeting, which was lightweight and inexpensive; grass or some form of living roof, which required a sturdy construction to bear the weight and would give the design a rustic look rather than the intended elegant, Zen-like appearance.

We had chosen steel. In the building materials guideline this fitted under the heading of 'Requires explaining, researching or justifying'. We did all three. We discovered a steel roofing manufacturer in Sweden who produced their product in great colours, recycled their steel and had a good track record for supportive employment, environmental and social responsibility. Our kind of heroes!

The only disadvantage was the miles of travel. As the sheets were light in weight and occupied relatively little space it was decided that this was acceptable. Steel roofing was then moved to the Approved material list. This was to be of benefit to a number of others on the Field who were looking for an inexpensive, good-looking roofing material.

We were a little surprised when this out of the ordinary design progressed so quickly through the District Planning Office. Some of the planners expressed their enthusiasm for the potential of what might be built in the Ecovillage.

I had wanted to have Build One build my house. This was a construction cooperative that had recently been started up in the community. It was made up of a group of skilled people specialising in eco-building. It was led by Mark, who, as a master builder and teacher, had overseen the work of the Findhorn Foundation's Building School that had built the half dozen houses on Pine Ridge. Unfortunately Build One was already committed to other work at the estimated time of my build and so another builder was contracted.

He had quoted a reasonable price and a relatively short time scale for the job. This was due to the fact that much of the construction would be prefabricated in his small factory and so would not be subject to being delayed by bad weather. It seemed to me that timber construction did not need to take place entirely outside in inclement weather in which construction workers were soaked or frozen, building materials might be damaged and timelines and schedules could lose all meaning. Module construction in dry surroundings would seem to offer some solutions to many of the challenges of construction.

After some time it became apparent that this builder had underestimated the cost of the build and, as a result of other events beyond his control, he would be unable to complete the job. This is the worst situation for any potential homebuilders to find themselves in and usually results in litigation. Being contracted to one builder who has already purchased materials or has started building makes it extremely difficult to find another willing to take over and complete the construction. Even if the contract can be dissolved, amicably or otherwise, there may be disputes over who owns materials already purchased.

Quite a lot of money had already been spent on design, engineering, planning permission and timber for this house and so it was debatable whether it would be more sensible to find a way to continue with it or to cut our losses and go back to the drawing board to design a smaller or cheaper house. More mystery!

With all of our fingers and toes crossed, Bernard and I approached Build One. To their credit and our immense relief they agreed to take on the job when they had completed the house they were currently building. They estimated what could be realistically achieved with the design within my finite budget. The design was stripped to its bare minimum in order to be built within these new parameters.

With the intention of finding mutually beneficial outcomes, discussions were held with the two building companies and agreements were made that suited everyone concerned. Win-win!

Working together throughout the construction, Mark and Mary, who was his partner and the Build One business manager, Bernard and I monitored the financial progress. There was a need for constant adjustment as the price of raw materials fluctuated, new or better suppliers were discovered and money saved and shaved in some areas could be spent on others.

Over the months I grew very fond of the Build One team. I respected them for their integrity and the quality of their work. They were honest, fair and generous, sometimes to their own detriment. There were occasions when they had underestimated the time needed to complete something, such as some complex joints, and were willing to absorb the extra cost as part of their learning curve. I would sometimes query this when it seemed too unfair on them.

Visiting the building site was an enjoyable experience. There was no coarse humour, no bad language, no arguments with the architect, no sloppy workmanship and no attempt to try to con the client. All was harmonious, industrious and good-natured. Perhaps, one day, all construction sites will be like this!

Some features had disappeared during the design stripping down process. However, through some very careful purchasing I was able to replace at a fraction of the price the hand-built spiral staircase, designer kitchen and state of the art bathroom with simple, functional and yet elegant alternatives. Designer taps could wait!

One feature that could not be replaced was the mezzanine floor intended for halfway across the high, self-contained guest room and planned as a sleeping platform to provide extra accommodation. As this was an expensive and non-essential item it had been one of the first things to go.

Towards the end of construction Mark asked me to take a look at something in the guest room. Opening the door I was greeted by the smiling faces of the Build One team. Looking past them I saw that they had built a smaller, yet perfectly adequate version of the mezzanine floor. It was explained that most of the timber used had been left over from other parts of the construction. There were vague replies of 'savings here and shavings there' to my question regarding where the money to pay for working time had been found. This led me to think that most had been shaved from their profit! I was touched and grateful.

A timber alternate step staircase designed and built by Philip Stewart - jazz pianist and harpsichord builder, would later reach this floor. This design is a way of putting the proper number of steps on a staircase in half the space normally required by having alternate left-foot, right-foot treads at half the height of standard steps. It works brilliantly and is much safer to use than a ladder.

Even with all of our careful planning and cost cutting we found that we were just that little bit short of money to fully finish the job. It was decided that the piece to be left uncompleted was the painting of the interior of the house. We had already bought the paint for both inside and out and had enough in the budget to pay people to paint the exterior. I had painted the interiors of most of the homes I had lived in and so by tackling one room at a time I knew that I could do the same with this one. That was okay with me.

I had reckoned without my friend Marg and the generosity of many people in my Community.

On the weekend I was to make a start on the painting, Marg turned up accompanied by half a dozen other Community members carrying brushes and rollers. Two of these people were Mark and Mary, who were volunteering their Saturday to teach people how to prepare for painting by masking the door and window frames, how to correctly apply eco-paint and then clean the brushes and rollers afterwards. The whole house being painted in the same soft white, chosen to reflect light and accentuate the sculptured shape of the rooms made the job easier.

More people turned up during the day. Some came to paint and others to bring food – homemade cakes and biscuits, and loaves and fillings for sandwiches. The directors of the Phoenix Community Store generously donated soft drinks and the makings for teas and coffee. I have no idea where the mugs, plates, knives and spoons came from!

Several people turned up with music players and their favourite tracks, so we had a variety of music around the house. Opera and classical in one area, jazz in another and 1970s and '80s disco in another. New people arriving would gravitate to the area of their preferred music.

Word got around and other people turned up on Sunday, including a friend from Findhorn village. By the end of Sunday evening the whole house interior had been given two coats of carefully applied paint. All brushes, rollers and paint trays had been cleaned. All dust sheets, masking tape and empty paint cans had been removed. Job done! Mystery complete!

This remains one of the most memorable weekends of my life.

The Field Residents Group

As the first house was being completed on the Field of Dreams and long before a spade had been dug into either of our building plots, Joan Wilmot and I started the Field Residents Group. This was initiated as a way for everyone intending to build on the Field to be supportive of one another. At that stage some people had bought their plots, others had only put down a deposit and a few were ready to commence building.

We met on the same Sunday afternoon each month in one or another of our homes. At the beginning it was in Gillian Price's house, which was the first to be built on the Field. For a long time this was the only house on the expanse of flat, cleared land and so it became sympathetically known in the Community as the 'Little house on the Prairie'. To us aspiring homebuilders this house was a place of inspiration.

Through these meetings we became well acquainted with one another. We shared our hopes and our dreams and viewed each other's proposed plans with interest and enthusiasm. As future neighbours we offered empathetic listening and support to one another as we each went through the highs and lows, the joys and challenges, the successes and disappointments and dramas associated with house building.

As we each went through the building process we added information to the useful files that Gillian had started. These files contained information about such things as sources of eco materials, the comparative performances of everything from boilers to eco-friendly light bulbs, reliable trades people and any useful tips and wrinkles that we had discovered through our experiences.

These were enjoyable gatherings, which offered a warm welcome to people who would be newly joining the Community when their homes were constructed. As these people were sometimes unfamiliar with the Community they received a great deal of help from their future neighbours in all aspects of Community life. We were also able to offer information and our experience of things in the local area such as schools, health practitioners and other professionals.

By the time each house was completed the new residents were already on very friendly terms with their neighbours and had joined in with car sharing arrangements and other cooperative activities.

During the first few years the expanse of the Field that was prepared for building looked like a wasteland. The Residents Group bought quantities of wildflower seeds and worked with an artist and garden designer to create a spectacular pattern of planting that was a joy to behold. Enough of the first year's flowers reseeded themselves over the next year or so to provide a pleasant showing until houses took their place.

Not everyone who bought or put a deposit on a plot actually built a house on it. Some people were unable to get their finances together. Others realised that living in an Ecovillage required a greater commitment to living with environmental awareness than they were willing to give. A few people with an unrealistic expectation of community life changed their mind about living here. We bid them farewell with best wishes for their future and prepared to offer a welcome to the new owners of these plots.

As the years went by, the people who had already built their homes continued to attend these meetings, to get to know and be supportive to newcomers and to those still to build. One or two of the first houses to be built were sold long before the final house was completed. The new owners – almost all of who were newcomers to the community – received a warm welcome into the Field Residents Group.

After EVL closed down following the sale of the last plot, the responsibility for discussions and negotiations regarding the ongoing maintenance of the infrastructure of the Field was taken on by this Field Residents Group, which then became properly incorporated into the Title Holders Association.

An Ecovillage is much more than a collection of eco-friendly buildings and environmentally sustainable utilities and services. Such a village is more likely to be an enjoyable place to live if all those involved take time to get to know one another and consciously develop strategies for creating harmony and cooperation.

The Findhorn Ecovillage is being developed within an existing community, in which, through the creation of the NFA, a clear identity and structure has evolved. Even so, the opportunity for those people building their homes on the Field to share the experience and gain support from one another has been immensely valuable.

Those of us benefiting from this experience share in the recommendation that any group coming together with the intention of creating an Ecovillage pay as much attention to the social and cooperative structures as they would to its physical construction.

KAY KAY

Dunelands

Completing the Eco-Village Puzzle

Since its birth, the community has been based in a little caravan park comprising 22 acres. It is made up of Pineridge, the main caravan park and the area around the Universal Hall. Initially, the Foundation owned only this latter area. In the 1970s there had been a small expansion with the purchase of Cullerne, about 8 acres, just a few hundred yards away, and we finally bought The Park in 1983. It was our birthplace, our spiritual homeland, and the site of our future eco-village.

I have been the "chief planner" for the Eco-Village Project since about the mid-80s when we began to seriously study what we had to work with and what an eco-village might actually look like. What I found interesting was that all of the land we owned was physically disconnected. Pineridge, the caravan park, the Hall, and Cullerne were all separated by land owned by the Wilkie family, making it very difficult to plan a village with many of the key pieces missing! But the land wasn't for sale and there were plenty of other things to do with the land we already had. So we just got on with it and waited.

In 1995, we bought 6 acres from our neighbours, the Bichan family, and the pieces began to come together. This land is the site we've called the Field of Dreams and it made the link between Pineridge and the caravan park. We've been given planning consent for 44 houses there and building is well underway.

It was the Wilkie Estate though, that would really bring things together from the eco-village point of view, giving us all the land connections; little bits of roads, woodland to manage, land for more windmills, and most crucially, the area between Cullerne, Pineridge and the Hall which we dubbed the "Magic Triangle"; owning this land would give us some room for future expansion. In addition, there was the wide open dunes area, a very important ecological site and one of the last areas of acid heathland in Britain left unspoiled.

Encouragingly, a few years ago, the owners hinted that they might want to sell the estate. It was jointly owned by two retired couples. The wives, who had been cousins of the late Winifred Wilkie, inherited the land when she died. They lived in the south of England and it was not easy for them to come up and look after things, so they suggested we make them an offer!

We discussed a purchase price with which we both felt comfortable, and agreed terms. They felt they would like us to have the land, and it would save them a great deal of trouble if they could sell it to us privately, without having to go through estate agents, advertising and the like. They wanted the sale completed in about 6 months, and it was important to them and to us to keep this as quiet as possible to avoid controversy which the purchase of a large area of land by anyone related to the Foundation would almost certainly create and which might interfere with the completion of the sale.

So I and others set about raising the funds. The Foundation itself, given its limited resources, couldn't help so we concentrated on private individuals, needing to raise £180,000. After a few months we had around £70,000 but it seemed to level off there and we had exhausted possible sources of finance. Needing to keep things under wraps meant we had to rely on the "quiet" word and trusted the power of manifestation. There was no great panic when the pledges tapered off but I was aware of the clock ticking and the deadline approaching. Inwardly, I resigned myself to the possibility of not making it; perhaps it wasn't meant to be after all.

And then, with little more than a month to go, I met someone who had expressed an interest in investing. It was the day before I was due to fly out to Australia on a visit and I should have known something was going to happen! After we had talked for a while and I had given him a sense of our vision for the land, he simply said, "I like the idea and I'd like to see it happen. How much do you need?" Not banking on anything, I told him the six-figure sum, expecting to hear the normal five or ten thousand that others had pledged, but the reply was, "Yes, I think I can manage that all right." And there it was. We had the money and the sale could go ahead!!!

I have had the privilege over the years, of hearing Peter Caddy tell many of his manifestation stories, and indeed have one or two of my own, but this was truly a miracle and I have to admit that it took a little while to absorb what had happened. I had to ask the person a few times and check back with him over the next couple of weeks, and the answer was affirmative. Previously we had released the land, trusting that if it was meant to come to us it would come in God's timing, not ours, and suddenly without warning, the right person came along with what we needed. It WAS a miracle and it felt wonderful!

The race was on. I called a solicitor who set up a limited company for us. I then asked friends to be the initial directors, and let a few people know that things were moving so that when I returned from Australia after a couple of weeks, we would be able to get to work putting everything in place and collect the pledges (we had 20 investors). The new company was named 'Duneland' – no connection to the sci-fi books! It was incredibly tight timing but we managed to meet the deadline, making the final deposit at about 4.30pm on the last day, just before the bank closed. Phew!

We now owned this land and had been given the responsibility of being good custodians. So we gave away a large part of the estate! The dune area, about 250 acres, was put into a separate trust, and made part of the Findhorn Bay Nature Reserve. The 'Findhorn Dunes Trust', is jointly run by members from our community in partnership with residents of Findhorn Village. We have had a series of meetings with the village, with which there has previously been much tension, to see how we can use this opportunity to build better communication and to do the right thing for the land. Much healing has already taken place between our two communities through these meetings, and we hope it will continue.

JOHN TALBOT

Update: Over the years since John wrote this piece the relationship between the folks in the Community and most people in Findhorn Village has improved greatly due to the collaboration around the Findhorn Duneland's Trust and other co-operative initiatives.

The Community has been immersed in years of lengthy deliberations on how best to develop the Magic Triangle. There were a number of people who preferred that the land be left undeveloped in order to protect the high-energy Power Point located in that area. On the other hand there is an urgent need for the further provision of affordable housing in the Community.

Duneland Ltd. commissioned Gaia Architects to prepare a master plan for the whole of the Magic Triangle. This was prepared through a number of workshops with the Community including a version of the 'Planning For Real' process and followed a 'Listening to the Land' process led by Margaret Colquhoun of the Life Science Trust, and Camphill Architects. It identified the current site as Phase 1 for higher density residential development.

This master plan was submitted to Moray Council for Outline Planning Approval. It gained consent in 2008 for 40 residential units (across phase 1A and 1B) plus ancillary facilities. Within the 40 units, eight were to be for 'affordable housing' and a Cohousing Cluster of 20 households.

There is also a large plot suitable for a conference facility/ community hotel with pub/ restaurant and 3 additional plots suitable for offices, artisan workshops, community businesses or educational facilities. Progress can be viewed at: www.duneland.co.uk

More than Buildings

The Ecovillage network's description of an Ecovillage at the beginning of this chapter makes it clear that an Ecovillage is made up of much more than eco-friendly buildings. It is a whole package that includes methods of energy production and energy saving, environmental approaches to waste management, wholesome and sustainable methods of food production and sustainable approaches to economic, social and community development.

www.gen.ecovillage.org

A great deal of information about all these is available at:

www.ecovillagefindhorn.org

This site gives details of the Findhorn Wind Park, the living machine—natural sewage and wastewater management system, Earth-Share, this community's food production and community food share scheme, Ekopia, our Development Trust and Community Resource Centre, which is responsible for our community currency.

At the time of writing, the Findhorn Ecovillage has the lowest recorded ecological footprint for any community in the industrialized world, just half the UK national average.

The most comprehensive education curriculum on design and education can be downloaded for free at:

www.gaiaeducation.org/index.php/en/download-the-curriculum.html

This Ecovillage Design Curriculum is an official contribution to the United Nations Decade of Education for Sustainable Development

The social and community aspects of Ecovillage development in this Community are detailed in the following chapter.

KAY KAY

CHAPTER THIRTEEN

CHANGES

By its very nature this Community is a place of change. Based on the commitment to conscious awareness, many of the changes over the years have been gracefully and smoothly implemented. Even so, as in most societies, cultural change can be challenging to some people and in consequence might take time.

The many changes that have taken place within and around the Community, especially since the end of the last century that are described in this chapter, are through my experiences before, during and after my time as Listener Convener. Carrying out the duties of this role provided opportunities to gain insight into the thoughts, ideas and concerns of individuals while developing awareness of the complexity of the bigger picture. Having the complexity identified provided the Community with opportunities to recognize where simplicity lay or to the changes that were required to create simplicity.

Becoming One

The following is a description of the role of Listener Convener that was formulated during the creation of the New Findhorn Association.

The role of Listener Convener is to be the ears of the Community. To be the person who:

- Takes the pulse of the community.

- Listens to the concerns, ideas and suggestions of Community members.
- Listens for conflicts between individuals or within organisations.
- Listens to hear of innovative ideas.
- Listens to spot trends and to observe the Community mood.
- Welcomes new members.
- Supports organisations and businesses.
- Empower grassroots members to take new initiatives.
- Facilitates communication across the Community.

After bringing what has been heard and observed to the attention of the Community Council for discussion and decision, a Listener Convener is to implement the decisions made by Council. He or she is to convene whatever meeting seems appropriate to share that information, address those concerns and support the ideas and suggestions that could help move the Community forward in its aims. These meetings might be brief discussions of a few interested people or gatherings of the whole Community to address issues that affect them all. They might be to raise awareness, to resolve conflict or to contribute towards the development of the Community. The Listener Convener also initiates or supports the development of Community projects and activities.

The Community Members elect the Listener Convener to the post and pay his or her salary from their membership subscription. The Listener Convener is to be available to; accountable to, and in support of the individual Community Members while keeping in mind the needs and aims of the Community as a whole and to hold an awareness of the way in which the Community is perceived.

When I was elected as Listener Convener (LC) I had returned from about a year of quite arduous travels and had just completed compiling and editing the first edition of this book. I looked forward to holding what I believed would be a gentle and comparatively simple role. Bless!

It had been imagined that all the efforts of the Council and the LCs during the first year of the NFA's existence would now bear fruit in the second year with people registering as members and making their subscription contribution towards its functioning.

However, only about one third of the potential members did so. What had happened? Everyone had seemed so keen on the idea and the Listener Conveners and NFA Council had been elected with a great deal of enthusiasm. Was this low number a result of the gap between interest and commitment often experienced in project startup? Or was something else going on?

My co-LC, Fabien, and I carefully listened to people to hear their reasons for holding back on their commitment to this new, inclusive Community structure.

Clearly, some people still did not fully understand how the NFA would work. Others were happy with the way things had been or they could not see what benefit the NFA would have for them. These were often people who, although involved with an organisation, did not engage much with the rest of the Community.

There were some people who were concerned about what they perceived as the devolution of power from the Foundation to the wider Community.

Some people were deeply engrossed in their own life's process and had little time or energy for anything else and others were so financially stretched that even the lowest end of the wide sliding scale of subscription seemed more than they could afford.

Quite a few people were waiting to see the NFA succeed before they made their commitment to it. As the NFA could only succeed if people made their commitment to it this was pure Catch-22!

There seemed to be something going on regarding processes. There had always been many processes in the Community: for running meetings, for exploring difficult issues and for making decisions. New processes were being initiated all the time. I had already noticed a tendency for people to get excited about new processes that were then dropped in favour of newer ones that seemed more interesting or productive. It became apparent that some people considered the current restructuring of the Community to be just one more process. With this in mind they apparently believed that if they didn't jump on board this new structure, then, like buses, there would be another one along soon.

We heard that some individuals, looking for an alternative lifestyle, who were turning up in places like this Community often preferred living on the fringes of society. Therefore, the lack of structure that had existed before the creation of the NFA had been more to their liking. One person summed this up when he described the NFA as being like the railroad, the Sherriff and the Town Council coming to a frontier town.

There was also some discomfort around leadership. The word leader is not used in this Community. This dates from 1979 when Peter Caddy left the Foundation and the decision made by people there at the time had seemed to be to never again have anyone in a strong leadership role. Anyone responsible for a department in the Foundation or a project within the Community is usually called a Focaliser and managers of meetings or discussions, etc. are Facilitators.

Some people were uncomfortable with the idea of Councilors and LCs assuming any leadership roles, while others had specifically elected people they hoped would do so! However, the relationship between the NFA Council and the LCs had been carefully devised to be one of checks and balances to fit with the Community's culture around leadership. The Council employed the LCs who were accountable to it and who implemented Council decisions, while at the same time, the LCs informed and advised the Council and chaired all of their meetings.

Many of these attitudes seemed to be demonstrations of the 'Moving Towards' and 'Moving Away' attitudes and patterns of behaviour that I had learned from my studies of psychology and Life Coaching. I had learned that, while it is dangerous to generalise, much of human behaviour can be placed under two broad headings: Moving Towards - what is desired, or Moving Away - from what is uncomfortable. Neither of these are good or bad types of behaviour, nor are they appropriate or inappropriate behaviour. They are simply the two ends of the spectrum of ways for dealing with life. Whilst most of us engage in both types of behaviour from time to time, it seems that one of these tendencies is usually more dominant in us than the other.

People who move strongly towards their dreams and goals often create what it is they wish for. These people usually achieve their objectives and get things done. They are the pioneers, the entrepreneur's, the instigators of ideas and the initiators of projects.

The lateral and out-of-the-box thinking of these people can be radical and is sometimes uncomfortable for those around them. There is also a tendency for Movers Towards to become engaged in other exciting new ideas before fully grounding the previous ones.

Extreme Moving Towards behaviour can railroad over other people's concerns and objections to achieve the personal desires of an individual or a group, regardless of the damaging consequences to others.

People with the tendencies for Moving Away from what they don't want often seek the places or projects that offer ready-made solutions to their needs or difficulties. There seems to be a tendency amongst Movers Away to only move as far as they need to in order to feel comfortable again. Moving Away types of people often become loyal supporters of or hard workers in the causes and projects that offer the solutions they seek.

Moving Away behaviour can be resistant to any changes to the comfort or the security that has been found. Some people with Moving Away tendencies may feel the need to be guardians of pre-existing circumstances and/or might choose to engage in new or unfamiliar situations in order to influence outcomes. In defense of the status quo, Moving Away behaviour can undermine efforts to bring improvement, no matter how well intentioned those efforts might be or how potentially beneficial the improvements.

Those with Extreme Moving Away tendencies might consciously or unconsciously sabotage anything perceived as a threat to the existing security.

I had learned that significant change often triggers these attitudes and behaviours and the greater the number of people engaged in any change the longer it is likely to take for those at both ends of the spectrum to become aligned with some purpose. (This is one explanation for consensus decision making taking a long time).

Using this model as one way of assessing what was happening, it seemed possible that many of the people in Moving Towards mode were already engaged in the creation and development of the NFA, as this was obviously the way for them to create the kind of inclusive Community they wanted. The more cautious Moving Towards sorts of people were likely to join in as soon as they could see that they were needed for the NFA to achieve its purpose.

A few Moving Away types of people could already have become engaged in the process to ensure moderation of the more extreme ideas and to slow progress to a manageable speed. Seeing the benefits of the NFA being regularly demonstrated, more people with these tendencies would probably join and could become staunch and reliable supporters of this holistic and inclusive Community format.

However, some people with Moving Away tendencies might hesitate for some time before becoming a member of the NFA and may only do so when not joining would leave them uncomfortably outside of the Community structure as it became more widely accepted. There could be an extreme minority of people who might attempt to overtly or covertly undermine this cultural change.

After considering all of this it was apparent that encouraging everyone toward creating one inclusive and fully cooperative Community was going to be a delicate task that would require constant attention, compassion and openhearted listening. It became obvious that a large part of the work of the NFA would be to encourage people to feel sufficiently comfortable with the changes afoot to want to be included, while, at the same time, achieving enough of the changes and projects promised to keep the already enthusiastically committed people still engaged.

It was clear that some people would need time to align themselves with the purpose of the NFA and would benefit from having opportunity's to express their thoughts and feelings about it. The brilliant concept of the Listener Convener roles now became fully apparent to us and that the beneficial power of listening ought not be underestimated during times of major change.

So, we continued to listen to individuals, to groups and to organisations. We heard people's concerns and frustrations. Some of these we could help with immediately as we brought people together to deal with issues or to support new ideas and projects. Others needed to be taken to the weekly Council meetings or to the monthly Community Meetings that we had initiated. Some people apparently only needed to feel the relief of having their thoughts and feelings heard and understood.

One of the benefits of the NFA was that it gave the whole Community an ear and a voice in all Community projects through their LCs attendance in, and sometimes chairing of, significant groups. These included: The Park Planning Group, where decisions were made regarding the structural development of the Ecovillage; EDGE, where The Park landowners—the Foundation, Eco-Village Ltd., and Duneland discussed matters affecting their various responsibilities for infrastructure of the Park. Also included was a place on the Board of Directors of Ekopia, our Community Resource Exchange Centre. Through this project, as an Industrial and Provident Society, money was raised for many Community projects such as a Wind Park of six wind turbines and the community buy-out of the Phoenix shop from the Foundation and its development as the cooperatively owned Phoenix Community Stores Ltd., which included two cafes and bakery.

Over that year an increasing number of people made their commitment to the NFA as the benefits of the structure became apparent. It was exciting to observe the separate parts of the Community finally coming together as one.

ℱ

Finding Common Ground

A benefit of creating an inclusive Community structure was the opportunity it provided for establishing and agreeing common ground regarding principles, ethics and values.

The Common Ground document is a statement of these and of intended behaviour and actions that are commonly agreed to by Community members. The majority of people seem happy to commit to this agreement when joining the NFA, although, because we work with free will in this Community, a few people feel able only to aspire to these principles.

This statement of Common Ground is a living thing that has been evolving over years and is regularly reviewed for relevance and improvement of language. Although the Common Ground Group holds the focus for creating these statements the whole Community can be involved in the review process. The following statement is the version being worked with at the time of writing this book in 2012.

STATEMENT OF COMMON GROUND

1. Spiritual Practice I have an active spiritual practice to align with spirit and support me to work for the greatest good.

2. Service I bring an attitude of service to others and to our planet, recognising I must also consider my own needs.

3. Personal Growth I endeavor to recognise and change personal attitudes or behaviour patterns that are limiting. I am committed to the expansion of human consciousness including my own personal growth.

4. Integrity I aim to embody congruence of thought, word and action. I take responsibility for the spiritual, environmental and human effects of my activities.

5. Respecting Others I wholeheartedly respect other people: their differences, views, origins, backgrounds and issues. I respect all forms of life and other people's and the community's property.

6. Direct Communication I use clear and honest communication with open-listening, heart-felt responses, loving acceptance and straightforwardness. In public and in private I will not malign or demean others. I will talk to people rather than about them. I may seek helpful advice but will not seek to collude.

7. Reflection I recognise that anything I see outside myself — any criticisms, irritations or appreciations — may also be reflections of what is inside me, and I commit to looking at these before addressing others.

8. Feedback I am willing to listen to constructive criticism and work with it. I offer constructive feedback to others in a caring and appropriate way to challenge and support each other to grow.

9. Nonviolence I do not inflict my attitudes or desires on others. I step in and stop — or at least say that I would like it to stop — violence, manipulation or intimidation of others or myself.

10. Perspective I put aside my personal issues for the benefit of the whole community. I acknowledge that there may be wider perspectives than my own and deeper issues than those that I am immediately aware of.

11. Cooperation I clearly communicate my decisions to others who may be affected by them, and consider their views respectfully. I recognise that others may make decisions that affect me and I respect the care and integrity they have put into their decision-making process.

12. Peacekeeping I make every effort to resolve disputes. I may call for an advocate, friend, independent observer or mediator to be present and will use and follow the community's Grievance Procedure as necessary.

13. Agreements I keep agreements I have made and do not break or try to evade any laws, rules, or community guidelines.

14. Commitment I bring the spirit of this statement of Common Ground in all my dealings.

Knowing that our fellow Community members are working with the same agreed principles helps to alleviate any tyranny of niceness that might limit honesty. It encourages openness in communication especially with regard to risk-taking in expressing opinions and concerns. It is also of great help to each of us in our own spiritual and personal development and offers a mechanism for being supportive to one another. Caring and courageous Community members who know we each have an aspiration to better behaviour can gently point out to an individual any of their behaviour that is not congruent with their stated intentions and agreements.

F

A Change of Focus

At the end of his two years Fabien stepped down after being a wonderful LC and Rory O'Connell a gentle soul and accomplished musician was elected to the role. By then there were enough subscriptions for me to work full-time, although Rory would be part-time and continue his other part-time employment in the Foundation's Visitor Centre.

As the NFA rented an office from the Foundation in the back of the Visitor Centre, Rory and I were able to communicate with and support one another almost full time. This worked really well for almost a year until another use was found for those offices. The Visitor Centre was moved to another building and the NFA office was relocated to an office off the beautiful foyer of the Universal Hall.

Membership numbers were slowly increasing and most individuals and organisations seemed happy with the way things were going. This enabled Rory and I to concentrate less on encouraging participation and devote more time to developing the major projects to which the NFA was committed.

Project 1. The Youth Project
By then the Foundation had ceased to hold the Youth Project as a department due to the fact that there were very few young people around the place of whom hardly any were children of Foundation Co-workers.

With the widening out of Community membership, the numbers of children and young people in the Community were growing again. It felt a priority project for the NFA to initiate and manage a Community Youth Project. In order to get the project started a year's salary for a youth leader was scraped together from shavings off all sorts of budgets around the Community. Our young people were once more happily occupied in the Youth Building. There they were, and still are, being supported to expand their experience of the world around them beyond that of their immediate families and to learn the skills that will help them to develop as the remarkable people they undoubtedly are.

These youngsters have been engaged in a number of interesting activities since then. One of the most significant was to invite several dozen young people from an inner London Borough to stay in the Community for a couple of weeks. The lifestyles and experiences of these two groups were vastly different and they learned a great deal from one another. Our youngsters began to realise how fortunate they were to live in this place and the Londoners recognised that there were different ways of being in the world than ones with which they were most familiar.

Project 2. Skills Asset Mapping

Recognising that the greatest wealth in the Community (as in any organisation) resides in the skills and experience of its people, a major project was for the creation of a mechanism through which the skills within the Community could be identified. Through the processes undergone to establish the NFA we had identified who we were as a Community although not what we each had to offer. One of the obvious first projects was the Asset Mapping of all of our skills.

On registering with the NFA people were given the opportunity of listing their profession, trade and other skills. However, as less than half of the Community had so far signed up, the challenge was to identify the skills of those remaining. The task for discovering the abilities of several hundred people seemed daunting.

The solution proved to be quite a simple one - a telephone directory! It occurred to me that if we created a Community Telephone Directory with one section listing people's home numbers and another listing professions, trades and other skills, most people would recognise it as a simple way for them to make their skills known.

The skills were listed under a variety of headings such as professions, trades, services, the arts, food etc. Although a lot of work was involved in categorising the various headings and entering the information, there was very little of the anticipated need to chase people for their information. By the time the second updated issue was being produced almost everyone in the Community was listed in the directory.

Such was the variety of skills within the Community that most people were listed several times. The multiplicity of the skills on offer, and seeing who could do what, made fascinating reading. Many individuals had wonderfully unexpected combinations of skills. We discovered that people skilled in the building trades also offered such things as Tai Chi, crystal bowl meditation and a variety of healing techniques; gardeners had IT skills; voluntary cooks were therapists; accountants and office workers were also skilled artists and craftspeople. There were some rare combinations such as the dear woman who taught pottery also professionally taught people to be opera singers! (Supported by her skilled tuition a number of our young people have developed exquisite voices and have become professional performers).

It was revealed that around 20% of Community members were skilled in the healing arts, which included therapists and teachers of all disciplines, a variety of body workers and healers as well as counselors, life coaches and spiritual mentors.

As well as the professions and skills within the Community many useful telephone numbers of people and organisations in the surrounding area were included. Doctors, dentists, post offices, cinemas, schools, restaurants etc were listed, as were numbers for many leisure activities, social welfare, transport, and other services. We also listed some local trades people who Community members had found to be reliable. The Directory now runs to twenty tightly packed A4 pages!

This Community Telephone Directory has given newcomers easy access to the services in the area and has made it simple for people to deal for much of what they need with others within the Community. Not only has this been mutually supportive, it encouraged and underpinned the development of The Eko, our local currency, which we initiated in 2003.

Anyone thoroughly enjoying his or her job, who believes they are in the right place at the right time and remains excited about what could be achieved will know that this gives wings to the feet, joy to the heart, perspicacity to the mind and all the energy that is likely to be required. It was with this attitude that I agreed to stand as LC candidate once more and was elected for a second term of two years.

Getting There

For the Listener Conveners the constant pulse taking of this Community of approaching 500 people at a time of major cultural change and reconstruction required a lot of attention and compassionate understanding, especially when it was apparent that some people still did not see the value of our role.

Fortunately it was clear that the people who had been actively involved in the NFA since its inception comprehended and supported the purpose, the nature and the value of the Listener Convener roles. They also understood that much of the LC work was like an iceberg, with only a portion being visible.

Although the NFA Council was aware of all of our activities, the NFA members, who paid our salaries after all, were perhaps not. We realised that we had been so busy with our multifaceted work that we had not taken the time to report on it. We had also imagined, that, knowing the kind of people we were, folks would trust us to just get on with the work. We began to produce a weekly report of our activities.

Whilst the convening part of the LC role could be made visible, as could the results of many discussions and other activities, the listening part, by its very nature, often could not.

Many of the opportunities for being listened to that the LCs offered to people would need to be held in some confidence. These were such things as hearing of difficulties between individuals or organisations and setting up any Community Conflict Resolution procedures that became necessary or facilitating conversations between people in discord with one another who did not need or want to go through that complex form of conflict resolution. It also included the interviewing and welcoming of newcomers to the Community.

There were subtle elements to the listening role that required us to notice trends, to pick up the mood of the Community and to get a sense of what was going on. It was mostly this subtle listening that was not being valued. It was disconcerting that in this Community of all places the importance of listening to improve conscious awareness seemed not to be fully appreciated by some people.

It took a little patience and perseverance to eventually uncover that a number of those who had been voicing concerns were uncomfortable with the whole idea of paying the LCs a salary. Although these were mostly people on low incomes, a few were not.

When the LC role had been devised, it had been clear to those involved that it was a role vital to the development of an integrated Community, (it was supposed to be 2 full-time jobs) and that the skills, attention, awareness and commitment required ought to be remunerated. As the Listener Conveners were in service to the whole Community, it seemed appropriate for the whole Community to contribute to their salary.

During the first trial year, in which no NFA membership subscription had been required, the LCs, Fabien and Hannah, had worked hard putting on events to raise funds to pay their salaries.

It now seemed that using the bulk of the membership subscription to pay two people's salaries – even though, at £10.000 for full time work and £5.000 part time per annum, these were low relative to the amount of work and responsibility involved – went against the grain for some people in what was largely a community culture of voluntary activity.

This was understandable. Since the early days, being of service to one another and to the planet has been fundamental to the ethos of this place. Most people spend a great deal of their time volunteering in the Foundation or with other charities and worthwhile projects within the Community and were doing so increasingly in some aspect of the NFA.

A place on the NFA Council was a voluntary position, and a lot was expected of those Councilors through the way that the NFA had been set up. One or two of them worked almost as many hours on behalf of the Community as did the part time Listener Convener. So it was understandable that some people needed reassuring that the LCs were earning their money. Things settled down once people became more at ease about this and felt that their concerns had been heard and understood.

We also recognised that somewhere along the way the NFA had begun to take itself a bit too seriously and had forgotten one of the first rules in community engagement – to have fun! So, Rory and I worked with people to put on events such as quiz nights and barbecues, and, together with a talented team, we created a fabulous New Year's Eve party. This party had something for everyone. The blue Angel Cafe was turned into a bar. The seats were removed from the Universal Hall and replaced with little tables to create an intimate club effect for a cabaret. The tables were then cleared for a Ceilidh, (Scottish music and dancing, called by Jonathan Caddy), followed by a 1970/80s disco until seeing the new year in with champagne. World music was then danced to until almost dawn. What a night!

Rory decided to not continue for the second year of his term of office. Although this made the NFA technically unconstitutional my commitment to working until a replacement male Listener Convener was appointed a year later kept the cart on the wheels.

An even bigger threat to the survival of the NFA came from an unexpected quarter. From the NFA Council – or the lack of it. For the upcoming election too few people were willing to step forward as candidates for Council to constitute a quorum. This would definitely make the NFA unconstitutional.

The Councilors we had had so far were extraordinary people dedicated to creating an inclusive Community. Many of them had served the maximum number of years allowed by the Constitution and others were very busy people who felt that they had made as great a contribution as they were able.

Was this it? After all the excellent work that so many people had done over the last few years, was the NFA to come to an end this way?

However, it seemed that the NFA had reached the stage that many projects or businesses do when the real strengths and weaknesses become apparent and the persistence and perseverance of those involved is truly tested. I believed, as did others, that if we could hold the NFA through this next year then it would be unshakably established.

Current Council members and I talked to everyone who we believed would make good Councilors. These included some of the people who had already served for a year or two and who had been very effective. They all said the same things: They were busy with their jobs or running their businesses; they were already active in other ways within the Community; they had families or partners with whom they wanted to spend quality time and the level of commitment expected of an NFA Councilor would not allow for that. Obviously it was a time for a rethink!

The group of us involved in this rethinking came to realise that the amount of commitment expected of Councilors was really unsustainable. Working within the wording of the Constitution it was possible to reduce Council meeting time by half and have Councilors hold the awareness for certain roles within the Community without having to do much of the necessary work. Most of that work could be handled by other volunteers, in keeping with the ethos of the Community, with some coordination and supervision by LCs.

Enough excellent candidates stepped forward and were duly elected to Council. What a relief!

F

Who Listens to the Listener?

Joan Wilmot, who trains people to become Supervisors within the caring professions, listened to me while I received valuable regular supervision from her during my time as LC.

This supervision helped me to keep an overall view, while noticing details. It assisted me to remain neutral in my listening when the needs of individuals and those of the Community were at odds. It helped me to think of innovative ways of engaging people and to encourage increased Community interaction. It was especially useful in helping me to understand and get to grips with what was my 'stuff' - my concerns and my responsibilities - and when these belonged to others.

Although I had, for much of my time in the role, the beneficial mutual support of a part-time male Listener Convener colleague, the size and scope of the role could sometimes feel overwhelming. Even though I was an experienced Life Coach and could mentor others in making sensible choices and successfully managing their work and their lives, my commitment to the Community and to its enormous potential often led me to overextending myself or to have unrealistic expectations of situations and people and especially of my time and energy.

Joan helped me to maintain my equilibrium, create and uphold boundaries and to manage my time effectively - mostly! She assisted me to recognise and understand behavioural patterns – mine and other people's – and to deal appropriately with tricky situations. Without her support I'm not sure how effective I would have been in the role or whether I would have coped well during some of the most challenging times.

Joan offered this regular supervision as her voluntary contribution to the Community and has continued to do so. This is a notable example of how one hour of expertise offered every few weeks can have a significant benefit that can ripple out to touch many others way beyond the person being supervised.

I believe that anyone who offers personal care and support to people, leaders and those in roles in which trust is placed, can greatly benefit from having access to some supervision. This not only applies to employees, for whom receiving regular supervision is often part of an employment agreement, it also applies to volunteers in organisations whose work and activities can often be difficult and demanding. Supervision has become an important aspect of life and regular practice in many of the organisations within this Community.

Although some areas of supervision are similar to the principle and practices of coaching, the focus in supervision is to help people be more effective in their work.

In my experience some of the goals of supervision are:
- To ensure quality of work.
- To facilitate clear communication in working relationships.
- To manifest inspiration.
- To appropriately focus passion.
- To illuminate the flow of spirit in daily work and life.

Here are some more detailed goals as described on Page 59 of Supervision in the Helping Professions, 3rd Edition – 2006 by Peter Hawkins and Robin Shohet:
- To provide a regular opportunity for the supervisee to reflect upon the content and the process of their work.
- To develop understanding and skills.
- To receive information and another perspective concerning their work.
- To receive feedback on content and process.
- To receive validation and support both as a person and as a worker.
- To ensure that as a person and as a worker that person is not left to carry, unnecessarily or alone, any difficulties, problems and projections regarding their work.
- To provide space to explore and express personal distress brought up by work.
- To effectively utilise personal and professional resources.
- To be proactive rather than reactive.
- To support the development and achievement of personal and organisational goals.

More information on supervision by Joan and her colleagues from around the UK and at the Centre for Supervision and Team Development can be found at: www.cstd.co.uk

F

Change in Perception

As the Community had originally formed around three middle-aged people it was never the commune of sex, drugs and rock 'n' roll that some might imagine it to have been. However, from the earliest of days the lifestyle of those in the Community was sufficiently alternative to be markedly different to that of the local, traditionally minded Scots.

From listening to locals when I arrived in 1990, it became apparent that those living in the area in the 1960s had considered that the odd assortment of people of different nationalities, ethnic groups, social and financial status, choosing to live together in caravans and chalets on windswept dunes, seemed strange enough. When meditation, yoga, vegetarianism, alternative medicine, and gardening with something called 'co-creation with nature' was added to the mix then 'weird' became many local people's description of the Foundation. (Locals have always referred to every aspect of the Community as the Foundation.) Some of Peter Caddy's outspoken remarks about the Foundation's purpose and intentions also didn't endear it to many of the locals who perceived his statements to be arrogant.

Many of these local attitudes towards the Foundation have continued until the present day. Unfortunately, these attitudes have also been projected onto other organisations within the Community, and on to people who have never been members of the Foundation, many of whom have contributed and continue to contribute a great deal for the benefit of locals, other people in the region and beyond.

There is rarely an opportunity to make a second good first impression! Perceptions once formed tend to lead to assumptions that situations and people remain unchanged. And so it was perhaps inevitable that the sense of difference and division between the local people and those in the Community would take some time to be bridged - several generations in fact! However, bridged it has been to quite an extent. This has happened so gradually that some of the long-term residents on both sides seemed hardly to notice.

One role that was supposed to be held by an NFA Councilor was that of Local Liaison. However, when this was not held after the first NFA year it did not seem to matter too much as liaising, collaborating and co-operating had been taking place quite naturally over time and especially during the previous decade or so. (Much had changed since the late 90s when Elizabeth Tonsberg wrote her piece in Chapter 11.)

As increasing numbers of people turned up seeking a sense of community, they have built, bought or rented houses in and around the area. They have created or worked in local businesses and been regular customers in shops, restaurants, pubs, hairdressers, garages etc. and have used the services of trades people - plumbers, electricians, carpenters and so on. They have engaged in many local activities, groups and clubs. Their children have attended local schools in which some Community folk have also taught. Businesses within the Community have supplied goods or provided services to local people and employed some of them.

Locals buy food from the Phoenix shop and the bakery, eat in the cafes, attend classes on yoga, various forms of dance and take lessons in music, art and crafts. The universal Hall, which has always been a great venue for visiting theatre, dance and music companies is now being frequently used by local groups for performances and events.

A few of us have been supporting the development and activities of local community groups in the area for several years and because of this, and many other activities, strong friendships have been formed.

Having Listener Conveners as a point of contact through whom inquiries could be directed to the appropriate people and to represent the Community at local meetings and events has proved to be an easy and effective way for information to be exchanged.

As LC, I was invited to represent the Community in the group planning of events that were to take place on the Findhorn Peninsula to celebrate the Queen's Golden Jubilee in 2002. Representatives of the four communities in the area: Findhorn Village, Kinloss Village, the Findhorn Community and RAF Kinloss met several times over the months prior to the Jubilee weekend and thoroughly enjoyed these convivial and productive evenings.

We planned a children's party, a barbecue, a village fete, a craft fair and a dance. Although it was recognised that many of our Community members would be very involved in creating and supporting these activities, we were especially asked to hold a multi-faith service of celebration and thanksgiving in the Universal Hall.

This was an indication of a significant sea change in the attitude of many of our neighbours. The Community's commitment to raising consciousness on the planet and our acceptance of all faiths and spiritual disciplines had been a major cause of criticism and censure from some local people over the previous forty years.

The weekend was a great success. All had a great deal of fun and friendships were made or deepened. The service was wonderful! People within our Community represented various faiths and spiritual disciplines, and the chaplain from RAF Kinloss made a significant and delightful contribution. Sadly, the ministers of the local churches had declined to participate. Many local people stayed for coffee in the adjacent Blue Angel Cafe afterwards and chatted amicably with Community members. We knew that some of these people had expressed negative feelings towards the

Foundation and the Community in the past.

A small incident related to this event illustrates the need for ongoing awareness around public relations. The cafe is situated at the front of the Universal Hall and a few days before the event I checked that the manageress knew there was likely to be a flood of customers immediately after the service. Although, she had not realized this, she had time to arrange for ample staff coverage.

The cafe is the venue for Community artists to hang and sell their work and I noticed that the current exhibition was of very accomplished watercolours. When we arrived on Sunday morning to set up the Hall for the service we saw that that exhibition had been replaced by one of large, vivid paintings of the female form in exposing poses and with some areas graphically detailed. Yikes!

I think paintings of nudes can be very beautiful and that confrontational art has a role to play. Even so, surely people ought to have a choice in whether or not to be confronted? Some might not choose to be so along with their morning latte and croissant! It was surprising that permission had been granted for this artwork to be on display in the cafe where people brought children and especially on this of all weekends! Many of those at the service would be elderly and/or conservative people who might be tentatively putting their foot in the Community for the first time! Good grief!

The artist was nowhere to be found and neither was the cafe manageress. Anticipating some later fall out from both of them and with the agreement and support of an NFA Councilor, the paintings were removed and carefully placed in the NFA office nearby. After the service no one seemed to notice that the walls of the café were devoid of pictures. Awkwardness averted. Phew!

As expected, we were accused of censorship by the artist and of meddling in an independent business by the embarrassed manageress, who had apparently not viewed any of the artwork before giving permission for it to be hung. Ah, well!

F

Fly Past

The Findhorn villagers and those in neighbouring Kinloss village had already had to get used to outsiders since RAF Kinloss had been established in 1939. RAF personnel became regulars in the shops and pubs and those wishing to live with their families off base bought homes around the area. Some chose to retire into the area after leaving the service. Relocating from areas where property prices were higher enabled them to afford to pay more for properties than many of the locals. This had an effect upon property prices that was exacerbated from the 1970s onward when people coming to live around the Foundation also bought homes in the area.

This meant that properties around this area were considerably more expensive than in other northern Scottish rural villages, which resulted in few local first-time buyers being able to afford to purchase property in their home village. The resentment this generated amongst locals is understandable and that most of this resentment would be directed at the Foundation Community was almost inevitable. The latest wave of 'immigrants' into any society usually become the main focus for feelings of resentment, which takes attention away from ones arriving previously, who, by comparison, may seem to be more acceptable. The people in our community probably seemed to local people to be more alien than military personnel.

After the end of the Second World War, RAF Kinloss became primarily a base for training, surveillance, rescue and maritime support.

The caravan park in which the Community was first formed had originally been part of the base. The main thoroughfare through The Park was once part of an emergency runway that had diverted planes in trouble up an incline and onto the dunes around the area that is now the Magic Triangle on Duneland.

The drone of aircraft has always been a constant feature of life in The Park. As a training base, RAF Kinloss attracted personnel from all over the world and on most days, planes, usually the Nimrod surveillance aircraft, would be heard loudly practicing taking off, flying in a big circle out over the Moray Firth, around over the Bay and landing back on the base. Whilst such an everyday occurrence eventually became background noise, to which little attention was paid, there were times, such as during meditations, workshops and conferences when the noise became invasive.

Many years ago, Ram Das, suggested that we consider the few moments of the peak noise of a takeoff as an aid to mindfulness. He described to us, how, in monasteries, monks would periodically ring a little bell to bring people mindfully into the present moment. Turning this noisy annoyance into a benefit has helped many of us over the years. In recent years the people in the Kinloss public liaison office have informed us when there were to be a major training initiative or some unusual activities such as night flights. In turn, we informed that office of significant events such as conferences, so that these could be taken into consideration whenever possible.

RAF Kinloss ceased to be an operational base in 2011, resulting from stringent cuts to the military budget as an outcome of the 2008 Banking crisis. Although, for a while, some rescue and maritime support would still be available. Whilst silent skies will come as a great relief to many, the effect on the local economy is cause for concern. When fully operational, RAF

Kinloss engaged around 3000 people in some capacity, many of them locals. Personnel and their families have been involved in all aspects of life in the area and their absence will be noticeable. Kinloss primary school, for example, was denoted as a Community School offering breakfast clubs and after-school clubs to support the duty rosters of RAF parents. These also benefited the other children attending that school including some children from our Community.

The closing of the base is a big change in the area, the consequences of which will become apparent in time. For a brief history of RAF Kinloss go to: www.raf.mod.uk/rafkinloss/aboutus/history.cfm

F

Opening Times

The caravan park that the three Founders had pulled onto in 1962 had later been purchased by the Foundation and has always been one of its two campuses. The Park was solely the responsibility of the Foundation until the purchase of the Field of Dreams and Duneland in the 1990s.

There had for years been a small Visitor Centre to give information to visitors interested in the history and the work of the Foundation, to offer tours around the caravan park campus and to enroll visitors in the Foundation's short-term guest programme. However, apart from the occasional public events in the Universal Hall, (an annual Arts grant was received to support it as a venue for touring artistic companies), there was very little reason for local people to enter the Park.

For decades the Foundation had organised an Open Day during the summer to which local people were invited into The Park for afternoon tea, tours and talks with Foundation co-workers and volunteers.

In the plan to hand over to the NFA many of the Foundation's Community activities, Open Day was coordinated by Foundation and NFA together one year, and then the NFA took most of the responsibility for it the following one. However, after that, listening to people in The Park, Findhorn Village and the local area it was realised that having an Open Day was putting out a mixed message.

The situation in The Park had completely changed over recent years with the purchase of land by other organisations, the building of many private homes in the Ecovillage and the creation of dozens of businesses in The Park.

Although the Foundation's education centre in The Park was, as it had always been, closed to casual visitors, that did not apply to the rest of The Park. The Phoenix Community Stores, the Blue Angel Cafe, Big Sky Printing, Findhorn Press Publishing, the Moray Arts Centre, the Universal

Hall, the Pottery, several Charities, artists, trades people, consultants and therapists were all open 5 to 7 days a week. As were the dozen B&Bs, the Holiday Park and the Visitor Centre, the latter offering tours around the whole site most afternoons.

The general feeling was that an Open Day gave the suggestion that for the other 364 days of the year The Park was closed. With all this activity going on, and with 15 to 20,000 visitors to The Park each year, clearly it was not. Whilst we were all keen to ensure that important traditions were maintained in the shift to being an inclusive Community, it appeared that this tradition was perhaps not only no longer necessary, it might be being counter-productive. At the risk of disappointing a few local people who looked forward to their annual afternoon tea with us it seemed to be time to cease having an Open Day and instead to recognise that we had an Open Park and to more widely advertise the regular activities and public Park based events.

☞

Care in the Community

A neighbourhood care scheme was initiated by Dr. Cornelia Featherstone to prevent the care of people in the Community from being carried on the shoulders of a few generous hearted and sometimes overloaded people. Clearly the giving and receiving of help and support can become more evenly balanced and sustainable if it is carried lightly upon the shoulders of many people.

The structure of the scheme was beautifully simple and revolved around a mobile phone and a Filofax. Everyone in the Community knew the mobile was the number to ring for assistance from the scheme. Calls would be responded to between the hours of 8:00am and 8:00pm by a team of volunteers who each managed the phone for one day on a Rota system.

By coordinating calls from one central point – the filofax - where information was kept and regularly updated, it was possible to make sure that needs were met quickly and efficiently. Having each activity and every house visit logged and the recipients confirming that assistance had been received and feedback given on the experience made it easier for volunteers to be recognised and valued for the contribution they made.

Anyone in the Community could ask for assistance from the scheme or volunteer their time to it. The details of the volunteered skills and offers of support were written in the Filofax. These were recorded under the appropriate headings such as child care, elder care, pet care, lifts, shopping, cooking, domestic support, gardening and so on. The people offering these would be listed under each category - some were listed in several places.

People were encouraged to think creatively about what they could offer.

The volunteers also each had a page dedicated to them in the Filofax in alphabetical order. This page detailed their phone number/s and address, any limitations on their available time - only in school hours or not during weekends for example, and whether they had access to a vehicle. Everything they were offering was also listed on this page. The number of times their offers were taken up would be recorded on a follow-on page. This was to avoid the same willing people being called upon too often and to ensure that every volunteer had ample opportunity to be involved.

Although most people needed help only occasionally, there were a few, such as disabled people, the very elderly or those caring for ill family members, who required regular help. Their details were recorded in another section. Details to register there could be any special needs or conditions requiring awareness and contact details of relatives or professionals in times of emergency.

To overcome some people's reluctance to ask for help and to avoid any sense of helplessness, embarrassment or awkwardness in seeking support, everyone, including those who required regular assistance, were encouraged to also make offers into the system.

My experience is that almost everyone has something they can offer. Elderly people needing help with shopping or heavy gardening are quite capable of cat sitting or plant watering, preparing food for or visiting people who are feeling under the weather. A person who is housebound for some reason may be ideally placed to be a member of the coordinating team.

At the start of the project an event was held to raise awareness of the scheme and to raise funds to buy the Filofax and mobile phone and to create a fund for topping up the pay-as-you-go Sim card. This was also an opportunity for people to register their offers or needs and to volunteer for the coordinating team.

The telephone number of the phone was widely publicised and was prominently displayed in a number of obvious places, including the local shop and the Community newspaper.

The responsibility for coordinating the calls coming in was not intended to be onerous. The person responsible for the phone on the day would go about their normal daily activities while keeping the phone and the Filofax with them at all times. During the time of my involvement in the scheme there were twelve members of the coordinating team, which meant that each of us had the phone for one day in every twelve. Members of the team included several retired people, a full-time carer, a Listener Convener, a person housebound due to physical disability, a council member and the doctor whose idea the project had been.

The team would meet once a month to discuss any concerns or ideas; to arrange holiday cover for team members who would be away; to consider applicants or to welcome new members to the team. These meetings, which were relaxed and enjoyable events, took place in the homes of members and everyone involved would bring snacks or contributions to a potluck supper.

This project was not intended to replace essential medical care or to be used instead of calling for emergency assistance. The aim was to make it easy for people to offer and to benefit from a wide range of neighbourly help.

Some of the structure of this scheme was adopted into a project that was subsequently set up in a nearby town and similar schemes now operate in a number of places.

F

Money Matters

Over recent years there has been a major change within the economics of the Community. From the time when Peter, Eileen and Dorothy, pulled their caravan onto the dunes all those years ago, while awaiting a new work contract, the economic culture of the Foundation and of much of the growing Community around it has been predominantly one of low-income and simple living.

Since the beginning there have been people who have turned up with high spiritual principles and low funds. Traditionally, people becoming Foundation co-workers have lived in Foundation accommodation, worked in a department fulltime, and have had little spare time for other moneymaking activities.

Some could pursue their professions and trades within the Foundation, although others could not. Many people have chosen to make significant changes in their lives by no longer being identified by their work and so have replaced their old ways of making a living with new types of work to make the Foundation sustainable.

No one in the Foundation has grown rich through the work that they have done within the Foundation, on the contrary. Although Foundation workshops and other programmes are priced on a par with similar ones elsewhere, the income from them is not just required to cover the cost of a venue and the payment of facilitators, as it might be in many other situations. Each of the hundred or so Co-workers in the Foundation contributes in some way to every programme and they are sustained by income from those programmes.

The Foundation's work has always been supported by a huge amount of voluntary help from the community immediately around it. Some of this help has been professional expertise and much has been in everyday activities. These people have regularly volunteered with the teams in the kitchens, the gardens, maintenance and home care and also in the General Office, the Universal Hall, the Rainbow Bridge, the library and the Visitor Centre.

Most of both of these groups of people have chosen to live a relatively simple life while being of service to others. This has spurred the development of people's creativity and fuelled innovative thinking around economics. These include the sharing of available resources such as through the boutique, a place where still serviceable clothes, toys and other children's or household items could be deposited by people no longer needing them and then freely selected by those who would find them useful. Other methods for the exchange or sale of items supported meaningful recycling and so, although many people have come and gone over the years, much of their stuff has remained behind to be further used and enjoyed.

LETS (Local Exchange Trading System) has, since 1990, been an effective way for people to exchange with one another the skills or time they had for skills or time they did not. For information on LETS go to: www.gmlets.u-net.com and www.letslinkuk.net. Car sharing and later car-pooling has reduced the number of vehicles in the Community while giving many people access to cars when they required them.

A strong ethic of generosity and mutual support and encouragement for clear communication about wants and needs has ensured that no-one in the Community has suffered needlessly and people have been helped to improve themselves, their situation or that of others dear to them.

This has fitted well with the admirable intentions of living lightly on the planet and in voluntary simplicity. However, in some cases it has resulted in individuals living in substandard accommodation and in very reduced circumstances. In many ways this has not been supportive of long-term sustainability.

There have been people with financial security who have come to live in the Community over the years. Almost without exception they have been generous towards their fellow Community members and have been significant supporters of many activities and projects.

Over recent years there has been a steady shift towards greater individual and Community sustainability. Many more people coming to live in the Community do not feel the need to give up their usual way of making a living in order to 'find themselves' once more. They choose to continue with their professions or trades and some have created employment by developing businesses. The creation of the Ecovillage has required substantial investment and many of these people have the funds for the purchase or the building of a home and have also invested in major Community projects. This investment and other money being spent around the place has benefitted many people along the way.

When I arrived in 1990, The Park had an impermanent feel to it because most of the dwellings were either caravans or chalets. This was due to the need to comply with the regulations, when it was a caravan park, that all dwellings had to be easily removable. Since its purchase by the Foundation, very few buildings had by then been constructed in the Park. With the development of the Ecovillage, that sense of transience is disappearing. At the time of writing this book there are over 60 eco-dwellings in the Park with another 45 on the way, and several eco-guest lodges and other eco-friendly community buildings.

Some Foundation Co-workers now chose to receive salaries for their Foundation work and to live in their owned or rented homes. This has provided the basis for a sustainable family life, which is enhanced if a partner is self-employed or works outside the Foundation.

In the past, the approaches to life of this Community seems to have been considered too radical to attract financial support for projects from funders such the Enterprise Board. So we learned to be as financially self-sustaining within our Community as possible and with support from forward thinking individuals and organisations within our networks.

Locally, nationally and internationally, much of our radical thinking has become more commonplace and many people now share our attitude towards ecology and the environment.

This has resulted in an interest in the Community from a much wider range of people over recent years, including funders. Our contribution to tourism in the area has been recognised to some extent. The Foundation received a grant for the upgrading of their website, and Minton House received a grant to help with attracting a wider B & B market than people just seeking spiritual retreat. I also managed to secure a grant of £3000 for new signs at the entrance and around the Park as a result of the increasing tourist interest in the Ecovillage development. We were able to replace the old Findhorn Foundation sign at the entrance with one that invited people into a vibrant Community containing the Findhorn Foundation, an Ecovillage development and a variety of organisations and facilities of interests. We also erected a map of the Park to enable people to find their way around and locate the people and places they were seeking.

All of these have supported right livelihood and simple economical sustainability. However, we had realised that in order to achieve our aspirations for the Community we would need to evolve more sustainable economic approaches.

Working with the support and guidance of the Financial Services Authority, we created Ekopia, our Community Resource Centre. Formed as an Industrial and Provident Society and Social Enterprise this has provided the mechanism for local investment opportunities. Through Ekopia, finance has been raised for the construction of the Wind Park and the Community cooperative buyout of the Phoenix shop from the Foundation and its development into the Phoenix Community Stores – including 2 cafes and bakery, and many more Community projects. Through having this mechanism in place, and with Ekopia as a founding member of Development Trusts, some grants have been offered to the Community for such things as affordable housing. As the Listener Convener on the Ekopia Board of Directors during four of these years, it has been a joy to see how this improved level of economic sustainability has supporting the Community to flourish.

In 2003, with further assistance from the FSA, Ekopia established a local currency, the Eko. This has encouraged trading within the Community and with the other individuals and businesses in the local area that wished to participate. These include pubs, cafes, B&Bs, taxi services, trades and professional people. This means that money exchanged for Ekos - that can only be spent locally - remains in the area for the benefit of local people. For information on the varied work and achievements of Ekopia visit: www.ekopia-findhorn.org

F

Handing Over

Richard Brockbank, a maker of beautiful furniture and artifacts - heirlooms of the future, was elected as Co-Listener Convener at the beginning of my fourth year of office. Similar to his two predecessors, Richard had been in the Community for many years. (His family's arrival was described in chapter 11). It was such a relief for me to no longer have to carry the workload and responsibilities of both LC roles.

More projects and activities were initiated to further the Community's development and sustainability.

The success of the Telephone Directory was followed with a Community E-mail Address List. These lists helped us to connect easily with one another, and yet, there was still something missing.

With almost 500 people around the place it was not always easy to recognise who was who, and in what role, especially amidst all the guests and visitors. Even though, through the development of the Ecovillage and the creation of the NFA, the number of permanent members of the Community was growing, many people would still only be staying for a while to learn something, to experience community living Findhorn style, or to share their skills with us and then move on. All this coming and going made face recognition difficult. We needed help.

So we created the Photo board. A small photograph of everyone with a description of their role in the Community was pinned on a board covering one wall in the foyer of the Universal Hall. This made it easier for members, guests and visitors to put faces to names. Another one was later created in

Cluny Hill College.

A Bed-and-Breakfast List was created to show the accommodation available in Findhorn Village and the many B&B's that had opened up on the Field of Dreams and elsewhere in The Park. This has made it possible for greater numbers of participants to be accommodated for attending workshops, training programmes and conferences. It has also allowed people interested in this Community and the Ecovillage Development to more easily visit for holidays and short breaks. Many of these visitors return frequently, some to attend courses or conferences and many recommend this place to family, friends and colleagues. www.findhorn.org/visit/b-and-b/#.T6uHKu3o8UU

As the NFA became more established, many of the activities that hitherto had been managed by the Foundation were to be gradually handed over for the NFA to run. The conversations that would lead to this handover were begun. These included the Rainbow Bridge, the Park Library, the Park General Office and the Winter Gathering.

The Rainbow Bridge is our weekly Community newspaper produced in electronic and paper versions.

The Park Library holds a remarkable collection of books on esoteric subjects, spiritual and personal development.

The Park General Office has always been the hub of much of the communications within The Park. It houses a big photocopy machine that residents pay to use, and a public telephone. This has been the place where mail is delivered and sorted for visitors, Foundation co-workers and other residents. For half a century these people have called in to the General Office to pick up mail and use the notice board for leaving and receiving messages. Though the numbers of residents in the Park has increased with the development of the Ecovillage, mobile phones, the Internet and The Park being zoned for home mail delivery, now contribute to keeping the hustle and bustle of the General office to a manageable level.

The Winter Gathering is a wonderful concert that our many talented (often professional) Community members put on a few days before Christmas every year, for the benefit of our neighbours. A jolly gentleman in a red suit usually turns up to hand out present to the younger members of the audience.

As many people in the Community had always given voluntary assistance with these activities it was relatively simple for Foundation and NFA representatives to coordinate these activities together for a while and then for the NFA to take full responsibility for them.

When my 4th year as Listener Convener was coming to an end, I decided not to stand again for re-election. I was touched that so many people expressed their disappointment about this. However, even if I were to be successful, it seemed to me that I was no longer the most appropriate person for that role. My strengths are in getting ideas launched and projects to the point where they are established and stable, in seeing where potential lies, and supporting people to achieve their objectives. This ship called the NFA, had come safely through the breakers of doubt and uncertainty, and all hands had learned how to sail her. Membership was well above the critical mass needed for sustainability, and individual and organisational members seemed happy with progress. Many of the intended outcomes and projects had been successfully achieved or were well under way and everything was running smoothly.

In terms of 'forming, storming, norming and performing' the NFA had reached the stage of 'performing'. While there might be many adventures ahead it seemed to me that what the NFA needed now were efficient and conscientious LCs who would continue its development, maintain its sustainability and keep it steady. There were others better suited to doing that than me. Richard Brockbank was such a person and I was sure that so would be the others succeeding into the roles.

Even though those 4 years as Listener Convener were often challenging, they were also exciting and inspiring. I feel privileged to have been entrusted with that role during those formative years, during which many changes occurred and through which so many of us learned and grew.

KAY KAY

CHAPTER FOURTEEN

MAKING THE DIFFERENCE

This Community is committed to the raising of consciousness at a personal, Community and global level. Since 1962 the existence of this Community has been making a difference to the lives of many people. It has had a positive effect upon those who have lived and worked within it, on the lives of people living nearby, upon the many thousands of guests on educational programmes and participants in conferences, on casual visitors and the people who have read the publications that have touched the hearts and minds of millions of people around the world. People have been inspired to start or to deepen a meditation practice, to reconsider their attitudes towards one another and the planet, to form communities based upon this one or to model some of the ways of this Community in their own lives.

Making the Difference to Individuals

As a place for personal transformation this Community offers individuals the education, tools, opportunities and assistance that are supportive to them making that transformation. The stories shared throughout this book by so many people offer insights into the quality of the people who are attracted to this place and are testaments to their personal transformation and to their commitment to supporting the transformation of others.

The work of the Findhorn Foundation is to offer educational programmes in a supportive community environment that will help people to develop themselves and to work more with high human and spiritual values in their lives. Many people participating in these programmes continue with this education and some eventually become Foundation Co-workers, staff and faculty members.

As described in the previous chapter, many of the people who have chosen to live in the Community around the Foundation, have, since almost the beginning, volunteered their time in support of this valuable work. Some of these people have created or work in groups and organizations offering other programmes for personal and spiritual development, creativity and self-expression. Although these programmes often attract people from elsewhere, they are all available to Community members, providing them with opportunities for continuous education.

The Community's commitment to bringing spiritual values into everyday life includes a tolerance of all faiths, religions and spiritual observances, and the acceptance of each person's choice in this, providing it does no harm to others. Through these attitudes, Community members choose to be the change they wish to see in the world.

It is intended that work in the Community, whether it is growing food or building houses, be carried out with conscious care and the awareness of co-creating with nature. Although no one is obliged to meditate, the three sanctuaries – places of meditation and contemplation – in The Park and the one in Cluny Hill College are well used. There are open meditations in the morning, before lunch and before dinner each day, which are sometimes guided. At other times these venues are used by specific groups and otherwise are open to anyone.

The members of this Community are not angels. Nor are they superhuman. They have the same kinds of hopes and dreams as others do. They face the same kinds of challenges around money and health, family and work, as many others do. They have to deal with the same kind of choices and personality conflicts as many others do. And, because they are human, they don't always handle challenges well, work out the most suitable solutions, make the 'right' choices or deal appropriately with conflict.

It is the way in which most of these people face these challenges and the supportive and compassionate methods they employ to make their choices and deal with conflicts that, in my opinion, make them heroic. These methods include the taking of personal responsibility, attempts to find win-win solutions, and a commitment from each person to their own and other people's ongoing development. This is often difficult and uncomfortable and requires courage.

Recognizing, acknowledging and working to transform one's attitudes and patterns of behaviour that prevent us from being the conscious and caring human beings we choose to become, is best done with the support of people who understand. This understanding and support usually comes from people having gone through some similar transformation. This mutual support for continuous personal and spiritual development underpins life in this Community and makes the difference to everyone involved.

What is extraordinary about most people in this Community is that they are ordinary people who are aspiring to high ideals and attempting to live in an extraordinary way, and, to make that way become ordinary. By living sustainable lifestyles in balance with nature, in choosing to be part of the planet's solutions rather than part of its problems, through thinking globally and acting locally and personally, and in being supportive, compassionate and accepting of each other, the people in this Community make the difference to one another and add their contribution towards the conscious evolution of humanity.

F

Making the Difference Locally

Although it is not widely recognized, this Community has had a beneficial impact upon the region in which it is located. Ideas, projects and processes in the fields of personal development, education, health, business, economics and the environment that have been created or developed by innovative thinkers in this Community have had a positive influence over a wider area. Some of these are illustrated in the following stories.

Who is recycling?

This Community has been recycling for decades, long before it became an everyday activity for most people. The Community's recycling site has provided opportunities for the disposal of all of the usual items as well as many of the more tricky things such as batteries.

A large truck-sized container was provided by Moray Council for the collection of paper and cardboard. On one occasion several years ago a letter was received from them threatening to fine us for putting inappropriate items in this container. As this kind of container is normally used by businesses for recycling their paper waste, they have members of staff responsible for filling the container. The council did not seem to understand that we had, what was in essence, a public recycling site with hundreds of people leaving things. So there was no way we could monitor every item.

The NFA formed a group to be responsible for recycling who did an excellent job in keeping the area clean and tidy and being up-to-date on information regarding all aspects of recycling. They devised a system of stacking the cardboard and paper in a way for it to be easier to check what was going into the container. During this process they discovered several surprising items, including a corset!

At this time, a research student turned up in the Community who was looking for a project through which she could develop her skill in producing, conducting and analyzing consumer surveys. As Listener Convener, I suggested she conducted a survey on who was using our recycling area.

She did a brilliant job! For a week she hovered around the recycling area, in all weathers, interviewing the recyclers. Her findings were interesting and surprising. From the sample of people interviewed, it seemed that over 60% of the people using the recycling site were not members of our Community! They were locals who brought their recycling into The Park while they were engaged in other activities. These included: shopping in the Phoenix, visiting one of the Community's businesses, eating in the cafe, wandering around the Ecovillage development, going to an event in the Universal Hall and walking through The Park to the beach.

Without exception, these people were environmentally aware, irritated that there was no other convenient local site for the disposal of anything other than glass and very appreciative of the recycling facilities provided by our Community. Apparently some of these people had been using our recycling site for years.

The findings of this survey were sent to the Moray Council Department of Waste Management. They then recognized that we were more of a public site and stopped sending letters of complaint. Within a year they started a County wide curbside collection of recyclable items.

Local economic impact

I was invited to represent the Community at a public consultation event for the development of a strategic plan for the region. I had been placed in the Economic stakeholder group with people involved in various areas of private and public finance. So it was from an economical perspective that I was to give information regarding our Community's impact upon the region and its future.

The topics covered at the event were Tourism, Housing, Employment, Health, Education, Transport and the Environment. Each stakeholder group was to identify the services and projects that, viewed from their particular perspective, were likely to provide some significance for sustainability in the region that ought to be recognized in the plan. Coloured dots to represent those were to be placed on each group's map of the region.

Within my group I could show that this Community had been having a positive economic impact on many of those topics under review. An estimated £5 million was injected annually into the local economy directly from this Community. Around 25% of this was from the programmes and international conferences run by the Findhorn Foundation; a similar amount came from the Phoenix Community Stores shops, cafes, bakery and mail order business and the remaining amount from around 60 other organizations, businesses and sole traders in the Community. Much of this money came from outside the area and a lot came from outside the UK.

The many businesses within the Community offered employment opportunities, and, through providing everything from solar panels to gluten-free products, from environmentally responsible printing to complementary health care, they brought a lot of business into the area.

I described The Park as a well-established tourist site, which was estimated to have attracted around 15-20,000 people annually for several decades. These visitors came mostly because they were inspired or intrigued by the history and the work of the Community. Although more recently, people interested in Ecovillage development and in raising environmental awareness were also visiting.

Many people in the local area benefited from catering to the needs these people had for accommodation, cafes, pubs, gift shops, local crafts, produce and transportation. This resulted in a further un-estimated contribution to the region's coffers indirectly from the Community.

The total investment in the Ecovillage development of The Park was expected to be over £20 million. This would be mostly through individuals buying prepared land and building homes, although it also included the construction of the Wind Park and other initiatives. The Ecovillage construction, mostly from locally sourced materials, supported local industry and provided employment for local trades and crafts people and encouraged and supported small local businesses producing environmental products.

The cooperatively owned Phoenix Community Stores has won annual awards for years for being among the top health food stores in the UK. This attracts customers from within a radius of at least 50 miles and the thriving mail order business trades with customers all over the world. Sourcing as many supplies as possible from local growers and producers has helped many of these small businesses to remain viable until a wider demand for local and organic produce has become better established.

The Local Exchange Trading System (LETS), existing in the Community since 1990, has inspired the start-up of similar schemes in several towns along the Moray coast. These have enabled many of the people in this region of traditionally high unemployment to support one another in achieving a better quality of life than they might otherwise have enjoyed.

Working with the support and guidance of the Financial Services Authority, Ekopia, our Community Resource Centre, formed as an Industrial and Provident Society, has created a local currency, the Eko. This has encouraged trading within the Community and with the other individuals and businesses in the local area wishing to participate and to keep local resources local.

With further assistance from the FSA, Ekopia, which is a Development Trust, has provided local investment opportunities through raising the money for the construction of the Wind Park, which saves resources and to establish the Phoenix Stores, 2 cafes and bakery and to support many other initiatives that provide employment.

The many thousands of people from abroad, who travel to this Community each year to participate in events or just to see the place, make a contribution to the income of the two airports in northern Scotland and to the taxis and public transport that service these. While there may be some discomfort around the environmental impact of air travel, the sustainability of these airports is vital to the economy of Northern Scotland.

At the end of this process in the Strategic Planning event a lot of the dots on our map showing existing innovations and projects for economical sustainability were clustered around Findhorn.

Enrichment

Self-sufficiency is obviously an important element of sustainability and this Community has created many projects that, in demonstrating this, have also benefitted and enriched the lives of other people in the region. Through the Wind Park, the Community is almost entirely self-sufficient in energy and can sell spare capacity to the grid for the benefit of others.

By constructing the Living Machine, a natural sewage system, the eco-development in The Park no longer uses the already overworked local sewage treatment works.

A number of Community projects, through being independent of National or Local Government maintained systems, have also benefitted a wider area. The Moray Steiner School offers parents another choice of education for their children. Although started in the Community, this is now an independent school, educating other children from around the county. Unlike other nations, Steiner education does not attract funding from the Education Department in the UK and therefore parents and supporters raise the finances required for this school. This leaves public resources available for other local educational uses.

The complimentary health care practitioners, therapies and products available in the Community, have for years sustained people's wellbeing and offered some illness prevention to a wide clientele around the area. Some Healthcare resources in the region may have been conserved to some extent as a result of Community led projects that promote health, health education, wellbeing and independent living. Neighbourhood care schemes in some towns in the regions have been modeled upon or influenced by the one devised by the NFA.

The Community has made a contribution to the conservation of energy used locally in transport. A commitment to low car usage has encouraged car sharing and carpooling. Park and Cluny residents and guests are transported on the Foundation's small buses. Residents and visitors in the Park use the local bus service connecting Findhorn Village with the towns to the east and west, which will have helped this service to remain viable. The many cyclists in the Community may well have had an influence upon the successful local campaign for the creation of a cycle path to Findhorn Village as an extension of Scottish Cycle Route 1.

The raising of environmental awareness and the importance of ecological sustainability has been promoted through the development of The Findhorn Ecovillage and through Community organizations such as Big Sky Printing, which is among the very few print companies in the UK to offer commercial scale environmentally sustainable printing methods and materials. www.bigskyprint.com.

The charity, Trees for Life, has since 1989, been responsible for planting over 1million trees in Scotland and training many people in the benefits of reforestation and woodland conservation. www.treesforlife.org.uk

The Phoenix Community Stores revived the Findhorn Village Bakery that had been closed for many years. Organic, fair trade and locally sourced produce has been made available by them there and in their cafés in the Village and The Park. Having a couple of dozen different nationalities living in the Community at any one time has resulted in the Phoenix shop stocking an unusually wide range of ingredients so that local people have for years had the opportunity to produce wholesome dishes from Japanese to Mexican and Scandinavian to Indonesian. www.phoenixshop.co.uk.

From such a diverse group of people, locals have been able to learn everything from yoga to salsa dancing and international cookery to preparing natural skincare products. The universal Hall, the Moray Arts Centre and various craft studios, our Community choirs, music teachers, dance and theatre companies have enhanced music, drama, dance and arts and crafts in the region.

Local people experiencing physical, mental, emotional and spiritual challenges have received body care, counseling, therapy and support from a large number of professionals within the Community as have people attempting to recover from addiction or coping with the addictions of loved ones.

Searching for the future

Local groups and organizations have benefitted from the skills offered by some Community members through their involvement in environmental, social and community action and decision-making.

In 1996, a handful of Community members and local friends initiated a project – The Forres Forum – in the neighbouring town of that name. Responding to a difficult situation regarding the future for the youth of the town, this Future Search, three-day event, gave the Forres citizens the opportunity to envision and plan for the kind of future they wanted for their town and to galvanize themselves into action to create it.

Despite the attempts of a few powerful local individuals to derail the initiative, the citizens of Forres became enthusiastically engaged in the proceedings. Around 100 people: parents, teachers, young people, youth leaders, social workers, business leaders, police and Church leaders, gave their time to be representatives on the stakeholder groups that came up with ideas for projects and initiatives that would create that future and to make their individual commitments to seeing those to fruition.

All of this resulted in many community projects that have helped the people of Forres in a multitude of ways. The immediate benefits for the youngsters were the development of:

- A skateboard park.
- A youth café.
- A mentoring scheme for adults with skills and experience to support and guide youngsters.

Many other projects were created:

A significant initiative was the setting up of the Forres Community Resource Centre – referred to as The Hub. Run from an empty shop in the town centre this became the place where people went for advice and information on such things as fundraising and other financial issues, project startup and management, IT advice and training and networking, etc. Over the following years this helped with the establishing and the maintenance of many more community led initiatives:

- A LETS System - local Exchange Trading Systems. For a time this was the fastest growing system of its kind in Europe.
- A project for recycling, repairing and rebuilding computers and associated equipment to be made available to people requiring them.
- A project in which furniture and furnishings no longer needed were collected and stored and then redistributed to people who did need them. (This proved invaluable when, a few years later, the river overflowed its banks damaging the contents of many homes).

Over time, a more firmly established sense of community and cooperative working among people of many different backgrounds has led to the initiation of many more local projects. One was the High Street Regeneration Scheme. This was beneficial during the first years after a large national supermarket was built on the edge of town. Another project was to conserve several small pockets of natural beauty that surrounded the town and to protect them from development. Yet another was the creation of a trail - a footpath, bridleway and cycle-path out into the countryside. All this created fertile soil in which the seeds for Transition Town Forres have been planted.

Many of the people involved in the original event formed lasting friendships based upon this shared experience. Some of the local organizers learned much from this experience with which they have been able to improve their paid or volunteer work and some were later offered jobs in community organizations and local businesses. Others have been elected as representatives on local and regional councils.

The people we brought in to this event were professionals trained to facilitate the Future Search process. (I had first met their senior partner, Eddie Palmer, the previous year on the Trans-Siberian Express, of all places, while I was on route to participate in the International Women's Forum in Beijing.) Collectively they donated dozens of hours of facilitation and support time to this initiative and asked only that their expenses be covered. Through this event they achieved a reputation that has enabled them to facilitate this process in many other places around the UK and beyond.

The Future Search process would be useful to people in towns and local communities who are considering creating a cooperative citizen initiative such as becoming a Transition Town. It could be especially helpful in places where there are both well established, long-time residents and also some newcomers, who, because of background or ethnicity, might have very different perspectives to one another.

The town of Forres has since been considered by many people around the UK to be a shining example of successful community involvement and cooperation.

F

Making the Difference Globally

In the 50 years since its inception this Community has been a source of inspiration, and has made a difference to millions of people around the world. Through programmes, conference and publications it has inspired them to further develop and improve themselves, to explore or deepen their spirituality, to respect and care for their fellow man and the world around them and to bring high human values into all aspects of their lives.

Findhorn conferences on globally important issues have, for decades, drawn people from all over the world to explore these topics. These gatherings have attracted leading thinkers of the day who have inspired people newly alerted to these issues. People of great wisdom have shared this with others and have been re-energized by those people's enthusiasm and energy. The information, resolutions and outcomes of these conferences have often had a wide-ranging and positive, global effect.

The Transformation Game was created in the Community many decades ago as a beneficial tool for personal and community transformation. Played as an insightful and enjoyable board game for up to

4 people it can offer useful guidance on the steps a player could take in order to fully live the life that they choose. Trained, and accredited facilitators of the Transformation Game as a workshop are now located in many countries around the world. For more information on the Transformation Game and to find an accredited facilitator in your area, go to: www.innerlinks.com.

The half-century of experimentation in and demonstration of community living which has been so widely shared has been supportive and inspirational to many people starting and maintaining communities around the planet.

This growing interest is not restricted to intentional communities. Many citizens of local, urban and rural places around the planet are seeking more effective ways to live together in peace and stability, harmony and sustainability - the aspiration of most societies since human settlements began. This has proved to be difficult enough to achieve in places populated by people of a single race with the same beliefs. How much more challenging it now seems to be in the many places where widely differing cultural attitudes and experiences, normally separated by continents, confront one another in neighbourhoods, businesses and classrooms.

There are many people who are now realising that, for many of society's problems, community is the solution!

With the whole world facing the twin specters of environmental and financial crises, people in local communities are realising that now is the time to work cooperatively together towards a harmonious and sustainable future.

With 50 years of experience during which thousands of people of dozens of nationalities and a variety of religious and spiritual beliefs have found ways of living together cooperatively and enjoyably, the Findhorn Community has a great deal to offer to every type of local community.

Many of this Community's attitudes and activities have often been way ahead of their time. Meditation, yoga, collective decision-making, complimentary, alternative, holistic and sustainable approaches to health, food, education, economics and business methods, to recycling and other environmentally sustainable practices, were, for many years, considered by some observers of the Community to be odd, even laughable. Much of this radical thinking has now become mainstream. Although still on the cutting edge in some areas, the experimentation conducted in this Community 'Petri dish' and the demonstration of the results are now considered in many places around the planet as common sense and obvious solutions to local and global problems.

With the development of the Findhorn Ecovillage, the experimentation and demonstration has widened to include many more areas of environmental sustainability.

There are now exceptional education programmes such as the

Ecovillage Training and the Gaia Education Design for Sustainability, which incorporates Transition Towns Training. In these, participants learn the principles and skills and tools for developing sustainable Ecovillages, and benefit from a communitywide faculty of experienced people. These participants, especially those from developing countries, return home with the capacity to make the difference to how their societies plan for sustainability.

www.findhorn.org/aboutus/ecovillage/education/#.T64uHO3o8UV

It will be interesting to see how this Community continues to make the difference to individuals and to the Planet during the next 50 years.

KAY KAY

Postscript – Kay Kay

Kay Kay was based in the Findhorn Community for 18 years from 1990 until 2008. She remains an associate member of the community.

As a full-time writer, Kay now shares the information, knowledge and skills she has learned during her experience-packed lifetime. Her YOU MAKE THE DIFFERENCE series of books are intended to be of practical help and moral support to people who are endeavouring to make a positive difference in their lives, within their communities and to the planet.

MAKING THE DIFFERENCE BOOKS

YOU MAKE THE DIFFERENCE
through
ENJOYABLE & EFFECTIVE MEETINGS

Following the guidelines for constructive participation, for efficient chairing and supportive facilitation, adopting the suggested attitudes, implementing the methods, skills, tools, essential procedures and useful processes will guarantee improved effectiveness and enjoyment of any meeting.

YOU MAKE THE DIFFERENCE
through
EFFORTLESS FACILITATION

This book is packed with suggestions for planning and designing meetings and events, useful methods and tips for facilitation, empowering and productive processes and a variety of ready-made meeting designs to fit many situations. The implementation of these will guarantee inexperienced facilitators becoming skillful and experienced facilitators becoming even more accomplished – effortlessly!

YOU MAKE THE DIFFERENCE
through
ENJOYABLE & VALUABLE
VOLUNTEERING

This book contains simple and exciting methods for people to explore what skills and experience they could volunteer, where and how they can easily make their valuable contribution, how to look after themselves while effectively helping others and the many enjoyable ways in which volunteering will enrich their own lives.

YOU MAKE THE DIFFERENCE
through
EMPOWERING VOLUNTEER MANAGMENT

This book contains many suggestions for finding, recruiting, supporting, empowering, managing and keeping volunteers. Following these guidelines and using the insights into what volunteers need to be efficient, effective, valuable and fulfilled in their roles, will guarantee empowered volunteers.

YOU MAKE THE DIFFERENCE
through
SUCCESSFUL
GROUPS & PROJECTS

This book offers insights into how groups work and why they sometimes fail, successful start-up and maintenance of projects that achieve the purpose and objectives, methods for attracting and keeping appropriate members and volunteers. The adoption and implementation of the suggested attitudes, the strategies for obtaining resources, the efficient use of time, money, skills and effort, and the respectful, cooperative ways people can enjoy working together will guarantee success of any group or project.

YOU MAKE THE DIFFERENCE
through
INSPIRING COMMUNITY
SUSTAINABILITY

The answer to many of the difficulties facing society is creating a greater sense of community. This book is filled with information and insights, developed through decades of research and experience, on the elements essential for achieving sustainability in any form of community. Utilizing this information, adopting the suggested attitudes, and implementing the recommended systems and processes will guarantee greater sustainability in communities, whether they are rural or urban, traditional or intentional, Transition Towns or Ecovillages.

YOU MAKE THE DIFFERENCE
through
SMART TALKING

Each time we open our mouths to speak we will inevitably have an impact upon those to whom we are talking. This book aims to show the consequences of having a negative impact and offers insightful suggestions for creating a positive effect. Following these guidelines and the suggested attitudes, skills and tools that can relieve stress, enhance relationships and improve communication in so many areas of life will guarantee anyone becoming a Smart Talker.

YOU MAKE THE DIFFERENCE
through
SMART LISTENING

Each of us will inevitably have an impact upon the individuals to whom we listen that is either positive and beneficial or negative and potentially damaging to individuals and society. Implementing the attitudes, listening skills, tools and techniques suggested in this book will guarantee a positive effect that will greatly improve personal and working relationships, reduce conflict, enhance many areas of life and be supportive to people's confidence and self-esteem.

YOU MAKE THE DIFFERENCE
through
SMART TALKING
&
LISTENING TO CHILDREN

From the moment children are born they are learning to become the adults who will manage the future. What kind of future might adults be influencing through the way they talk and listen to children? This book is crammed with skills, tools, insights and suggestions on how adults can be supportive through their communication to the development of youngsters and contribute towards a safe, sustainable future in the hands of well adjusted, capable, empowered, responsible and caring people.

These books are available from Amazon and through Kay's website: www.youmakethedifference.net.

This website also offers useful guides on a variety of topics that are FREE to download.

Printed in Great Britain
by Amazon.co.uk, Ltd.,
Marston Gate.